VHDL Programming

with Advanced Topics

Louis Baker

John Wiley and Sons, Inc.
New York • Chichester • Brisbane • Toronto • Singapore

Baker, Louis.
    VHDL progrmming with advanced topics / Louis Baker.
        p.   cm.
    Includes bibliographical references and index.
    ISBN 0-471-57464-3 (pbk. : alk. paper)
    1. VHDL (Computer hardware description language) I. Title.
TK7885.7.B35 1993
621.39'2--dc20   92-30959
                                                CIP

Printed in the United States of America
10 9 8 7 6 5 4 3 2 1

Contents

PREFACE

VHDL is the VHSIC (Very High Speed Integrated Circuit) Hardware Description Language, supported by the U. S. Dept. of Defense and canonized by the Institute of Electrical and Electronic Engineers (IEEE) as their standard IEEE-STD-1076. In June, 1992, various enhancements were adopted as VHDL-92 (with the original version referred to as VHDL-87).

This book is about using the VHDL language for simulating complex digital systems. The intention is to go beyond elucidating the syntax and semantics of the language and examine how to use VHDL efficiently and effectively in all aspects of development, design, modeling, and so forth. To this end, you will find topics not often covered in books on VHDL, such as back-annotation, synthesis, discrete-event simulation, netlists, and fan-out.

The first section of this book is a tutorial on VHDL. An attempt has been made to present the overall structure in a natural way, so the novice can sort through the tangle of entities, architectures, components, and configurations. Modern computer languages are almost invariably composed of declarative and executable statements, and VHDL is particularly rich in the former. This leads, in my opinion, to some books overly concentrating on this aspect of the language and short changing the equally important aspect of writing the program statments that actually tell the simulator what the devices do. While the term "behavioral" has come to mean high-level specification (in contrast to "register transfer level" or "gate level" simulation), in fact all simulations at some level must specify the behavior of every component. (I prefer the terminology "functional" to describe high-level specifications of components without regard to their implementation.)

The changes to VHDL-87 resulting in VHDL-92 are discussed collectively in the final chapter of this section, Chapter 10, in order for readers already familiar with VHDL-87 to quickly update themselves. Throughout the preceding chapters, references to Chapter 10 are made as appropriate, so that the newcomer can learn VHDL-92 without first having to learn VHDL-87. The remainder of the book applies what the reader has learned about VHDL. Chapter 11 discusses basic data structures and mutual exclusion, with VHDL code examples.

VHDL simulations are a special case of discrete event simulations (DES). In order to understand VHDL, and use it effectively, you must understand DES. This is the subject of Chapter 12. Very often, such simulations are nondeterministic. Random external events, such as interrupts, and random sequences of instructions, are considered, and trade-offs such as optimal cache design are evaluated. The next section of the book discusses the details of such simulations, such as generating random numbers and random variates, and the design and interpretation of such simulations.

A key tool in simulating and synthesizing functional units is the Finite State Machine (FSM). A full discussion of this key concept is given in Chapter 13, with a variety of VHDL code approaches. This is one of the more important chapters of this book.

VHDL simulations are often for the purpose of developing a device that may not yet exist. The intent is to use VHDL for higher-level design, with a synthesis tool used to produce gate-level descriptions. Chapter 14 discusses the real-world considerations attending such a process, and gives hints for making VHDL most useful in such a process. Considerations are likewise given as how to write VHDL code that can be synthesized, how many logic levels to use in such simulations, and so forth. This process is not easy or straightforward, and generally involves iterating between high-level and lower-level tools as well as mixing levels of abtraction within a simulation. The process of back-annotation, or modifying the VHDL simulation to make it more accurately reflect the realities of the device as implemented, is of great interest. This important technique is discussed. Emerging standards such as IEEE-1164 for 9-level multi-valued logic, 1149 for Boundary Scan Testing, andEIA-567 Component Specifications, are covered, as well as the EDIF-2 standard for netlist exchange and the emerging WAVES standard for specifying simulation input and results. A number of matters of practical value are considered, including concurrent simulations, interfacing with other languages such as C, and real-world circuit considerations such as transmission-line effects and fan-out.

Chapter 15 discusses simulating microprocessors, and covers implementing typical components such as multi-phase clocks and pipelines, obtaining information about slack and critical paths, etc. Provided in this chapter is a rather large piece of code, a prototype test bench that was used as a proof-of-principle demonstration of a simulator for a real-time embedded system.

Chapter 16 finishes with a discussion of the simulation of the wide variety of bus protocols.

It is my hope that this book will be of value to those interested in digital simulation with VHDL, whatever their present level of experience.

About the Author

Louis Baker operates the consulting firm Dagonet Software in Albuquerque, N. M. Prior to this, he has held positions at Mission Research Corporation, Sandia National Laboratories and the Naval Research Laboratory. Dr. Baker has written four books and numerous journal articles on hydrodynamics and electromagnetic field propagation, computer interfacing, artificial intelligence, and computer simulation.

Section I

VHDL Tutorial

Chapter 1

Introduction to VHDL

MOTIVATION

VHDL is the VHSIC Hardware Description Language; VHSIC is an acronym for Very High Speed Integrated Circuit. It's development was sponsored by the U. S. Department of Defense and became IEEE Standard 1076-1987. In October 1992, the *Draft Standard VHDL Language Reference Manual* (LRM) for the 1992 revision was sent to the balloting group for approval, with ballots to be returned by Nov. 25, 1992. It is expected that VHDL-92 willbe approved.

VHDL is useful for specifying integrated circuits and then simulating them for the purposes of design and verification. VHDL specifications are accepted by a number of synthesis tools. A wide variety of VHDL tools work with a number of hardware accelerators, CAD/CAM/CAE systems, etc. Compass Design Automation, for example, provides an ASIC (Application Specific Integrated Circuit) toolkit, the ASIC Navigator, which produces a behavioral VHDL description of the device. Cypress Semiconductor produces the Warp 1 PLD Compiler, which uses a subset of VHDL to design PLD (Programmable Logic Device) implementations of finite-state machines.

Mil Std 454, Requirement 64, specified that Digital ASICs "designed after 30 September 1988 shall be documented by means of structural and behavioral VHDL descriptions . . . " This was broadened as of January 1, 1992 with Mil Std 454M, Notice 3, which changed ASICs to all "qualified devices." Also mandated was the use of VHDL's Waveform and Vector Exchange Specification (WAVES), IEEE 1029.1. The Air Force had announced in late 1991 the Software Intensive Hardware Risk Reduction Policy, which gives strong preference to contractors who use VHDL. This policy is discussed further under top-down design in this chapter. See " DoD Gets Serious About VHDL," *Military and Aerospace Electronics*, January/February 1991, p. 28. Actually, VHDL has often found more acceptance among commercial manufacturers than in the defense community. As this book goes to press, VHDL is neck-and-neck with Verilog in user base, and it is anticipated that it will have surpassed Verilog by the end of 1992, because its user-base growth rate is higher. Various other aspects of VHDL simulation are being standardized, such as the choice of logic levels (MVL-9, IEEE 1164) and proposals to develop a standard format for delay data for back-annotation purposes. LSI Logic, for example, has announced that source code for their ASIC library models will be made public once MVL-9 becomes a ratified standard (Egan, 1992). Standards such as IEEE 1164, IEEE 1149, WAVES, and others are discussed in Chapter 14. Familiarity with and adherence to these standards will bring dividends in code portability.

OUTLINE OF THIS BOOK

Section I of this book is a ten-chapter tutorial. Chapter 1 to 10 introduce the newcomer to VHDL. There is also a quick review of the changes inherent in VHDL-92 in Chapter 10 for those already familiar with VHDL-87.

Section II of the book is intended to provide examples of the application of VHDL, with appropriate background as needed. Chapter 11 discusses the uses of data structures and access types, along with mutual exclusion. Chapter 12 discusses discrete event simulation in general to provide the background for a better understanding of VHDL. Chapter 13 discusses implementing Finite-State Machines in VHDL. FSMs will often be a key tool in designing hardware as well as in simulating it with VHDL. The theoretical background is reviewed and a number of approaches to coding FSMs in VHDL are discussed. Chapter 15 discusses modeling microprocessors, with VHDL code for a test-bench proof-of-principle simulation included. Chapter 16 discusses some aspects of simulating busses.

PURPOSE OF TUTORIAL

The purpose of this section is to introduce VHDL to newcomers and to review the syntax and semantics of the language for those with some familiarity with it. You will not become fluent in VHDL by studying this chapter any more than you became fluent in FORTRAN, C, BASIC, or even English or some other natural language by reading a book. That will come only with practice- writing VHDL programs. At first, you will attempt repeating, almost verbatim, what you have observed. Compilers will be far less accommodating than your parents were in attempting to make sense of your attempts to speak VHDL. They will accept your programs, only to produce programs that when executed yield nonsensically wrong answers. But with perserverence, you will find your programs working more often than not.

This section is merely intended to start you along that road. It will provide the background you need to understand the examples of VHDL you will see later, in the rest of this book and in the real world. Therefore, do not stop at the end of this chapter and conclude that you understand VHDL. You may skip this chapter if you feel you have already mastered its syntax and semantics sufficiently. It will still be here if you choose to refer back to it for needed clarification or a refresher.

VHDL is IEEE standard 1076, adopted in 1987. It was consciously based on the Ada language, also a standard (currently in the process of revision). Much of the structure, such as the use of packages, basic syntax, and some of the terminology, such as elaboration and instantiation, are borrowed from Ada. Familiarity with Ada would be of some use in understanding VHDL. On the other hand, packages in Ada and VHDL are not identical in usage, so there is some potential for confusion induced by an assumption that VHDL usage slavishly follows Ada. Keep in mind that not all Ada implementors agree on interpretations of the standard. Code that works fine with one compiler may still produce syntax errors with others. This should be expected with VHDL as well. Ada has spawned efforts for standardizing programming environments and tools, such as CAIS (Common Ada Interface Support), APSE (Ada Programming Support Environment), and STARS (Software Technology for Adaptive, Reliable Systems). VHDL has sparked similar efforts, such as WAVES, which are unfinished and evolving. The reader should expect that VHDL will evolve as well, and should attempt to keep current with that evolution. The reader should not assume that anything is cast in stone and is immutable. Efforts such as WAVES, which will be discussed below, are potentially of great utility and it behooves the reader to stay apprised of such efforts.

VHDL-87 has 81 reserved words, more than most high-level languages, and VHDL-92 adds ninteen more. By contrast, Ada 83 has 63 (although the forthcoming Ada 9X effort adds a few), and C++ has approximately 45 (it is not standardized yet). This is, of course, due to the powerful functionality built into VHDL. This broad power should not be permitted to intimidate you. You will find that many features and reserved words are not necessary for most simulations. You will also find that many statements have alternative versions. This provides the user with a number of choices, enabling him to write more compact and simpler code. It makes life somewhat more difficult for the compiler writer, makes it difficult for the writer of books such as this to be comprehensive, and perhaps intimidates newcomers to the language. Feel free to ignore the alternatives you find uninteresting.

VHDL is insensitive to case. For example, the identifiers Bit-Field and BITFIELD are both treated as referring to the same object. It is a good practice to keep the reserved words of the language lowercase while identifiers should include uppercase for better read-ability. In general, we will follow the IEEE *Language Reference Manual* in notation. The reserved words will be boldfaced in this text. Various pre-defined attributes and packages will be uppercase, names of signals, variables, labels, and so forth, used in examples will be mixed; and lower-case terms such as sensitivity_list or boolean_expression will denote generic elements of the form de-scribed. Units, such as the time units ns and us as defined in the standard package, will be all lower-case by convention. Pseudocode (such as *declarations*) will be italicized. The not-equal symbol, as in Ada, is /=. Comments are preceded by the symbol -- and continue to the end of the line.

The IEEE *Language Reference Manual* is actually quite read-able. It is highly recommended that you have a copy nearby; this book will refer to appropriate sections of the LRM for those who are of a legal bent and wish to see the precise definition in particu-larly complex issues.

You may notice that some information is presented in more than one section. This is not due to senility on the author's part, but is an attempt to make these sections somewhat self-contained and therefore useful as a reference. The changes adopted as VHDL-92 are mentioned as appropriate and discussed in detail in Chapter 10.

LOGIC SYMBOLS

There are at least two sets of logic symbols one might encounter. The traditional symbols, given in MIL-STD 806B (26 February 1962) and elsewhere, are shown in Figure 1.1. The more modern symbols are ANSI/IEEE Std 91-1984 (and the International Electro-technical Commission publication IEC 617-12). An example is shown in Figure 1.2. The T-shaped block on top controls the group of logic blocks below. Here two signals, the lower one sensitive to transitions (as most clock signals), are shown controlling this block, and are ANDed as indicated by the ampersand (&). See Table 1.1 for the logic symbols. The AND gate has tri-state output. Both of the gates have active-low outputs, as indicated by the triangle on the output line. The ANSI set of symbols is much richer in expressive

power. On the other hand, the various types of logic gates all look
the same, and decoding a symbol with obscure notations could be

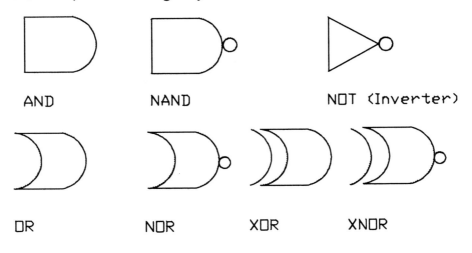

Figure 1.1 Logic symbols

somewhat tedious. In other words, these new symbols are overkill
for the purposes of this book, and we will use the more familiar
symbols. The *Signetics TTL Databook*, and many other similar

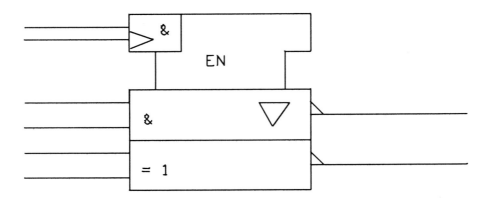

Figure 1.2 ANSI/IEC logic symbol

books, give both symbols for a wide variety of logic devices and
often have a summary of the IEC symbolism as an appendix.

Table 1.1 Logic symbols	
and	&
or	≥ 1
exclusive or	=1
not	(indicated on signal lines)

STRUCTURAL AND BEHAVIORAL DESCRIPTIONS

The terms "structural" and "behavioral" will be encountered frequently as forms of VHDL simulations. Structural simulations are modeled closely on the hardware description of a device. Simulations described as structural are therefore typically relatively low level. Such simulations are often classified further as gate level or register transfer level. Gate-level descriptions describe circuits down to the detail of logic gates, while register-transfer-level (RTL) simulation is written in terms of structural elements such as registers. In gate-level descriptions, the unit of data on the signals (as VHDL calls connections between devices) is the bit. At the register transfer level, the signals will take on values of bytes, words, and so forth.

High-level simulations are often referred to as behavioral, because the only the externally visible overall behavior of component devices is specified, rather than the precise structure of the components. There is no precise dividing line between what are called structural and what are called behavioral simulations. Some people would call RTL simulations behavioral simulations. I prefer the term "functional" for high-level simulations. The reason is that all VHDL components must ultimately be given behavioral descriptions. Even gate-level simulations will require a description of the behavior of the gate. Such behavioral code might be tucked away in some library and not be apparent, but it must be there for the simulation to proceed. Conventional usage will not likely be altered by one man's pet peeves, so expect behavioral, functional, and high-level to be used interchangeably in the literature describing VHDL.

Often simulations will be a mixture of these levels. As an example, an article (Dolin, 1992) discussed the development of an i486 motherboard by Arche Technology. A "bus functional" model of the i486, that is, a high-level or "behavioral" VHDL model of the i486's behavior insofar as it appears to the rest of the motherboard, was used. A number of Application-Specific Integrated Circuits (ASICs), such as the cache memory controller, were simulated in VHDL, which was then used with Viewlogic synthesis tools to produce the controller. Obviously, the ASIC description would have to be more or less gate-level (with perhaps some register-transfer-level component) to permit synthesis.

TOP-DOWN DESIGN

Top-down design is not a vacuous buzzword, at least not in this context. It corresponds to what Niklaus Wirth (1976) called "stepwise refinement" in the context of software development. VHDL is well-suited to top-down design. High-level simulations are done first, until the overall design is developed. Then the details are successively filled in.

The Air Force announced in late 1991 (Goering, 1991) a draft policy that would give preference to designs that used a three-milestone method, with simulation a part of each stage. "Not only does this policy say you have to use VHDL to do design, it also says you have to do a top-down design approach. You not only have to use simulation, you also have to use it before certain milestones." Stage I is called "concept," and corresponds to a high-level functional simulation. Stage II is called "prototype," and III is "limited production." Historically, people have use in-house design tools. The VHDL description was often produced as an afterthought. The result was a often a "flat" file, that is, a gate-level description or netlist with no hierarchical description of the circuit. Such a description of a circuit is nearly indecipherable by humans and of relatively little value for simulation. A high-level functional simulation would be impossible with such input. On the other hand, if VHDL simulations were developed for all three milestones, and these were made available, simulation at a variety of levels would be possible, presumably at levels corresponding at least roughly to behavioral, register-transfer-level, and gate-level.

BOTTOM-UP REUSE

The reuse of software components is easiest in a bottom-up manner. VHDL encourages such reuse through its support of libraries and packages. Through the use of the **generic** statement, parameters such as propagation delays can be set for a library component. Components can be developed and then saved in user libraries. Packages can be used to collect functions, subprograms, and so forth. The details will be discussed below when packages and libraries are discussed.

THE OBJECT-ORIENTED NATURE OF VHDL

Object-oriented programming refers to a programming paradigm in which data is paramount. Data items are collected together into related *objects*, and functions are viewed as *methods* that act upon these objects. VHDL is well-attuned to this approach, even if it does not employ the terminology. For example, suppose a variable *I* is given a type that takes a range of values, say the allowed instruction set of a microprocessor. Such a type can be conveniently represented as an enumerated type in many languages. With VHDL, one can, for example, loop over all possible values for *I* with a loop starting with a statement of the form:

for I **in range** I' RANGE   **loop**

The ability to specify the range of the variable *I* by simply using the attribute 'RANGE is a great convenience which many languages omit. The range is computed dynamically, that is, at runtime, and so may be applied to objects whose range varies dynamically. (An example of this is discussed under "Resolution Functions" in Chapter 2. See Chapter 6 ("Attributes") for a list of the information readily available about types, signals, variables, and so on, in VHDL.

VHDL: OVERALL STRUCTURE

VHDL at first glance might seem to be a bewildering array of entities, architectures, components, and configurations. Here we wish to
review the grand scheme of VHDL to put these things into perspec-
tive.

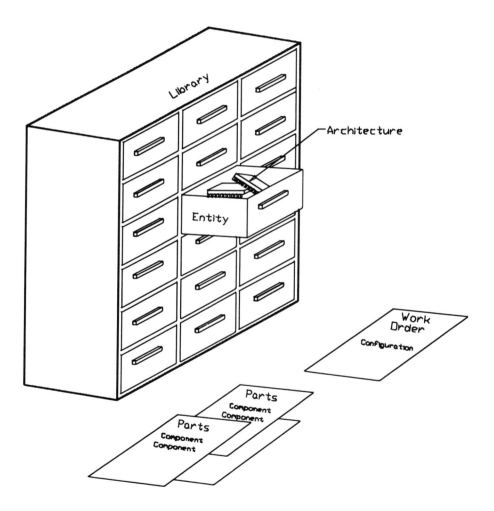

Figure 1.3 Technician's bench model for VHDL

The analogy we have come up with is that of a technician's
workbench (Figure 1.3). Consider VHDL as an industrious but
rather dim technician. It will do exactly what you tell it to do and

nothing more. It follows directions literally. It demands strict adherence to procedures and protocols it is familiar with. It has access to part bins full of all the hardware building blocks that are needed. These may be created either by you or as libraries. Each bin in labeled by an entity declaration, which basically defines the way the component looks to the outside world. This is the "visible" part of the device in question. It may have parameters specifying clock speed, for example, resulting in "generic" devices that can represent a family, depending upon how these parameters are chosen.

The implementation of each device is in the "invisible" architecture specification. This may be behavioral or structural. In the latter case it would have to describe the device in terms of smaller functional units. The architecture specifies what the device actually does, and defines how it does it, allowing the compiler to produce a simulation of the device. The details are hidden from the user of the architecture, who does not need to be concerned with them (so long as the architecture faithfully does its job).

There may be a variety of architectures for a given entity. For example, there might be a basic RS latch or flip-flop entity, which would be built out of NAND gates for TTL implementation or NOR gates for an ECL implementation. There might be two different architectural descriptions, one intended for use with TTL synthesis as an ultimate goal and the other for ECL. (These might be in two packages, one for TTL and one for ECL.) While one entity may have a number of associated architectures, each architecture will have to have an associated entity. Otherwise, the VHDL technician will never find it. It will be as if the label has fallen off the bin. In our workbench analogy, the architectures are chips or devices ready to be used, with the entities the labels on the parts bins stocking them. These bins hold limitless supplies, and you can create new bins any time you choose.

Suppose you have, say, an RS latch or flip-flop defined through an entity specification and one (or more) associated architectures. This device is ready to use. To use it as part of any larger device, you have to specify how to wire it into the device. This is done through the component specification. The component specification

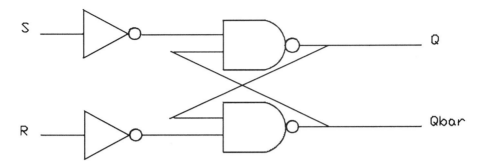

Figure 1.4 Latch using NAND gates

is part of the schematic you give to your technician when you say "build this." The technician will ultimately try to build it from the stuff in the parts bins. If the required entities can't be found, or its not clear which architecture is to used for a given entity, the technician is stymied.

Part of your job will be to turn this (potentially) many-to-one relationship between entities and architectures into a one-to-one correspondence. There will then be a unique relationship between any

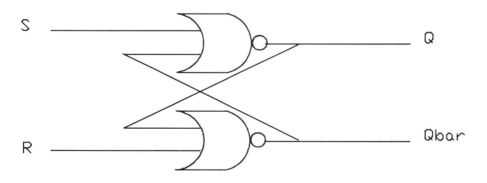

Figure 1.5 Latch using NOR gates

entity and the associated architecture that the compiler will use to implement it. This will be done by the configuration specification. Here, you specify which architectures to use for each corresponding entity. The configuration specification is like the final work order. Nothing is real, nothing gets wired into place, until this is in your technician's hands. The configuration specification makes the abstract concrete.

The package in VHDL allows grouping associated specifications in a useful manner. It makes sense, for example, to have the architectures for TTL simulation and synthesis together, not mixed in with the ECL architectures. Changes to the ECL architectures could then be accomplished without recompiling or otherwise affecting the TTL code. Your architectures for the RS flip-flop might correspond to those shown in Figures 1.4 and 1.5, depending on the technology. Both are shown as working on active high inputs for consistency. You may see different designs for an asynchronous latch or RS flip-flop, with different assumptions as to whether the inputs and outputs are active-high or active-low.

To make this all concrete, the code would be:

```
entity Latch is
      port( R, S: in Bit; Q, Qbar: out Bit);
end Latch

architecture RSLatch of Latch is
begin
... behavioral or structural description
  end RSLatch;

configuration FlipFlop of Latch
      for    RSLatch;
      end for;
end FlipFlop;
```

The entity declaration tells the world that there is such a thing as a Latch, with the specified ports, that is, tells the world how to interface with it. The architecture specifies a possible internal structure to this entity. The configuration specification binds the architecture to the entity declaration. We will flesh out this architecture later, explaining the port statements, and modifying it for greater flexibility.

DECLARATIONS, SPECIFICATIONS, AND EXECUTABLE STATEMENTS

As embodied in the title of Niklaus Wirth's very influential book (1976) *Algorithms + Data Structures = Programs*, it is fair to say the program statements may be divided into these two categories. In the latter category are the declarative statements that define the data objects of the language. VHDL is unusually rich in these. There are three basic types of data objects: signals, variables, and constants. In addition, there are various structural declarations necessary to represent hardware components. Specifications in VHDL are statements that add information about previously declared objects. VHDL has four types of specifications: the attribute, initialization, configuration, and disconnection specifications. These specifications are declarative in nature. It is the behavioral descriptions that most resemble the algorithms of classical programming languages. Even here, VHDL is richer than most languages in that it provides for both sequential and concurrent statements. The former are similar to conventional languages constructs, while the concurrent processes of VHDL are similar to the concurrent tasks of Ada.

Modern languages give users the ability to define their own compound data structures. VHDL gives users the opportunity to define signals of composite types, and to specify an enumeration of allowed signal values. Modern languages also allow users to dynamically allocate and free memory space. VHDL has this feature as well, modeled after the Ada new reserved word and the Deallocate() function. Use of this feature precludes hardware simulation, however, as silicon cannot be dynamically allocated and returned. It is therefore of most interest in functional simulations.

The remainder of Section I reviews the various declarative and executable statements of VHDL. The LRM has the luxury of describing the former and then the latter, since it does not have to be a comprehensible introduction to the language features. Our approach will be to introduce the basic structural elements and show how VHDL programs are built from them. In this tutorial section, only small code fragments will be presented. As the book progresses, larger modules will be developed until a prototype simulation of a microprocessor interacting with a real-time interface is modeled.

REFERENCES

Design Automation Standards Subcommitte of the the Standards Subcommittee of the Design Automation Technical Committee of the Computer Society of the IEEE and Automatic Test Program Generation Subcommittee of the IEEE Standards Coordinating Comittee 20, *IEEE Standard VHDL Language Reference Manual*, IEEE Std 1076-1987, Institute of Electrical and Electronics Engineers, Inc., 345 East 47th St., New York, N. Y. 10017.

Dolin, M., "Top-down Methodologies Infiltrate Systems Designs," *Computer Design*, Jan. 1992, pp. 61-68.

Egan, B. T.," VHDL: Standardizing a Standard," *Computer Design*, March 1992, p. 48.

Goering, R., "AF mandates VHDL design," *Electronic Engineering Times*, November 4, 1991, p. 14.

Wirth, N., *Algorithms + Data Structures = Programs* (Englewood Cliffs, N. J.: Prentice Hall,1976).

Chapter 2

Signals

SIGNALS IN VHDL

While VHDL has variables like other high-level languages, signals are the primary data items of the language. The LRM distinguishes between the two by defining variables as data "objects with a current value," while signals have a time history of values. This history is called the waveform. Signals may to some extent be thought of as the values of the data on signal lines or wires. You might think of the waveform as the sequence of values that might read off the signal line. VHDL has a very rich repertoire of different varieties of signals. Signals need not be individual values, as might be carried by a single wire. Signals should be thought of as cabling rather than individual wires. Signals can have integer or floating-point values, a value from an enumerated type (a specified set of values), TIME values, in fact any value a variable can have. Signals may have a number of different kinds of components, which will be explored next. Furthermore, the connection between elements of a VHDL model, such as between components or blocks, is by means of ports, and ports are signals (LRM 1.1.1.2). A port declaration will implicitly declare the associated signals. Other signals can be explicitly declared. A typical signal declaration will look something like this:

signal   Delay , Tick :   TIME;

This declares the signals Delay and Tick to be of type TIME. TIME is a data type defined in the STANDARD package to represent time (naturally!). As in strongly typed languages, attempting to assign a value to Delay of some data type other than TIME will produce an error. A simple signal assignment will be of the form:

Delay <= 1 ns ;

Here Delay has been assigned a value of 1 nanosecond(ns). The STANDARD package defines a number of units of time (see below). The precise semantics of this assignment statement, that is, just how and when the signal delay will have the value assigned to it, will depend upon the context of the statement. There are two types of assignment statements, the sequential and concurrent assignment statements. The former is contained within a process (see below); the latter is implicitly a process in and of itself. We will discuss this fully when we discuss processes in Chapter 8.

The assignment statement shown above produces a *transaction* for the associated signal at the time value it is executed. Various more complicated options are possible, such as this one:

Delay <= 1 ns **after** 100 ps ;

which will assign the new value to delay 100 picoseconds after the current time. Note that omitting the **after** clause is equivalent to **after** 0 ns. One can also assign waveforms, for example:

Delay <= 1 ns **after** 100 ps,
  2 ns **after** 200 ps,
    null after 300 ps ;

Note the assignment of a **null** value to the signal. This assignment turns off the signal driver associated with this assignment statement.

When we consider concurrent statements, we will encounter more complicated forms of signal assignments that in fact are shorthand notations in VHDL for processes.

A signal has a unique history of values, that is, an implied list of (time, value) pairs. Each signal driver has a similar list of projected future pairs it intends to attempt to assign to the signal.

BUS AND REGISTER

Signals are of two types, bus and register, the former being the default type. The crucial difference is that register signals have memory. They retain the value they were last assigned by a driver. It will be seen that, from the point of view of a VHDL compiler developer, the difference between the two types of signals is a relatively small change in the semantics and hence the implementation of the signal. However, note that in synthesizing circuits from VHDL, memory elements will have to be provided for register signals. Therefore, the register declaration should be used only when needed.

INITIALIZATION

Signals may be given initial or default values in their declarations, as in:

signal Signal1, Signal2 : INTEGER:=0;

If the initial value is omitted, the signal is given the leftmost value of the type, that is, the result that Signal1' LEFT would return (see attributes, Chapter 6). For example, if the signal is of the predefined type BIT, it will be initialized to ′ 0′ , as the header STANDARD defines BIT to be the enumerated type (′ 0′ ,′ 1′). This initial assignment is done at an indefinite time before the simulation starts. Asking for the time of the last transaction for the signal when that transaction was the initialization will produce garbage or an error message.

SIGNAL SOURCES AND DRIVERS

For each signal assigned a value by assignment statements within a process, there is an associated driver. A driver may be thought of as a "projected output waveform," according to section 9.2.1 of the LRM. This means that it is a list of transactions, or pairs of values of time and signal, that is, a list (or vector) of two component vectors of the form (time, new_signal_value). The time values are the times at which the signal value changes to the new value indicated. The driver always contains at least one transaction, which is initially the default value specified for the signal, and has exactly one transaction giving the current value of the signal at any time. Note that **null** values for the signal are perfectly legal. The word "projected" occurs in this definition because at any time the driver constitutes our best guess as to what the future waveform will look like. The actual future history of the waveform may be altered by other assignments.

While each driver has exactly one value for the current time, there may be more than one driver driving any signal at a given time. The sources of a signal (LRM 4.3.1.2) consist of the drivers and of any ports connected to the signal which may assign values to it, that is, any ports of type **out, inout, buffer,** or **linkage**. Ports will be discussed extensively in Chapter 3. There are numerous restrictions on how ports may be interconnected, and on what may be connected to them.

There is one driver per signal for each process. A concurrent signal assignment is equivalent to a process. The next section, on resolution functions, describes how the actual waveform is determined from the projected waveform(s) of the driver(s).

If a procedure that is called by a process makes a signal assignment, then there is an associated driver for that procedure. The details are discussed in Chapter 9.

RESOLUTION FUNCTIONS, DISCONNECTION

Suppose a signal line has one or more sources (drivers and/or ports). This is typical for a bus, which may have a number of drivers (the CPU, the DMA, etc.). Often, bus logic prevents a true conflict from occurring. For example, with TTL the drivers are usually tri-state buffers that are arranged so that only one should be driving the bus at any time, while the others are in their high-impedance states. But often, wired-OR or similar logic is used. How is the compiler to know? How is VHDL to know what the value of the signal should be? The answer is simple. VHDL requires you to resolve such ambiguities with an appropriate function. This function is called as needed with an array of values for each of the associated drivers. In the case of **register**-type signals, if all of the values are **null**, then the resolution function is not even called. Instead, the signal value is unchanged. That's all there is to simulating a register in VHDL. For type-**bus** signals, the resolution function is called whatever the values of the drivers are. Obviously, a clever programmer could outsmart VHDL and write a resolution function for a **bus**-type signal that would leave the signal value unchanged from its current value if all of the sources were **null**. There just is no need to.

It is possible to explicitly disconnect drivers. The assignment

```
Signal_name   <= null ;
```

will effect such a disconnection. In addition, it is possible to specify in a **disconnect** statement a finite time delay for the disconnection of drivers to take place. This is only for guarded signals, and will be discussed in Chapter 4 where blocks are discussed. For now, it suffices to note that there are guarded signals and guarded signal assignments. A guarded signal requires a guarded assignment. Other signals may be given assignments under the control of a guard. The difference between guarded and unguarded signals is that drivers for the former are disconnected automatically by VHDL, whereas unguarded signal assignments require the user to explicitly disconnect them if a disconnect is desired.

There are two ways to specify a resolution function. One is when the signal is declared:

```
type TTL5 is (' 0' ,' 1' ,' Z' ,' X' ,' U' );
signal Resolved_sig1,Resolved_sig2 :
     Wired_And TTL5;
```

This defines the two named signals to be of type TTL5, a four-valued signal type intended to represent TTL values (where 0 and 1 represent logic levels, Z the high-impedance state, and X is the don't-care state, and U the uninitialized state). It is possible to wire TTL gates with open-collector outputs together, tying this point with a pull-up resistor, so as to achieve an AND function of the gate output. Of course, totem-pole and tri-state outputs cannot be used to implement a wired-AND.

The other way is to define a subtype of a signal and specify the resolution function:

```
subtype Open_Collector is Wired_And TTL5;
signal Resolved_sig1 : Open_Collector;
```

The resolution function is invoked in any simulation cycle in which the corresponding resolved signal is *active*, that is, it has undergone a transaction. It is passed an array, each element of which is determined by a corresponding source, but excluding the drivers that are *off*, that is, those that have null transactions. It is therefore possible for the resolution function for a signal of a type **bus** signal to be passed a null array, if all of the associated sources are off. This is not possible for a signal of type **register**, for the resolution function will not be called in such a case.

An example of a resolution function would be:

```
function Wired_Or ( Source_Array :

          BIT_VECTOR) return BIT is
   constant Default: BIT :=' 0' ;
```

```
-- Default value if floating, i.e. no ac-
tive drivers


  begin
  if Source_Array' LENGTH = 0 then
                   return Default;
  else
     for I in Source_Array' RANGE loop
        if Source_Array(I) =' 1' then
           return ' 1';
           -- if any source values are ' 1',
           -- that is bus value.
           -- No need to look at others
           -- Short-circuited OR.
        end if;
     end loop;
  return ' 0';
-- if we are here, all sources are ' 0'
  end if;
  end;
```

Because we used the predefined BIT and BIT_VECTOR types, this function was particularly simple to code. In most applications, there will be more cases to consider, as the allowed signal values will often be richer than just ' 0' and ' 1'. In such cases, it can be useful to do a table look-up in the resolution function. Note we can assume within the function that no source has the **null** value, as these are filtered out when the Source_Array is constructed by the run-time simulation system. Note the object-oriented nature of VHDL; we need not expect variables defining the length of Source_Array or the allowed indices to access its elements. These are attributes of the data object Source_Array and may be easily obtained by the built-in attributes of VHDL. Note that these attributes are determined dynamically, since the length of the Source_Array passed to the resolution function may differ with each call, depending on what drivers are active. This should illustrate the expressive power of VHDL. It should also, perhaps, give a hint as to the difficulties of efficiently implementing VHDL while providing for all this functionality.

TRANSPORT AND INERTIAL DELAY

Here, we discuss how sequences of assignments to the same signal affect that signal's waveform. The reserved word **transport** may be used in any signal assignment:

```
Signal_1 <= transport '1' after 200 ns;
```

If this reserved word occurs, the signal is taken to have transport delay. If this word is not used, the signal is assumed to have *inertial* delay. There is no reserved word **inertial** in VHDL-87, but there is one in VHDL-92, as discussed here and in Chapter 10.

Transport delay means that transactions previous to that scheduled by the signal assignment are unaffected. This behavior corresponds to that of a transmission-line, for example. Transport delay was sometimes called *pure* delay. If a waveform f(t) suffers a pure or transport delay of D, the delayed waveform is f(t-D).

VHDL did not invent inertial delay, either. Many electronic devices do not respond immediately to input changes. For reliable operation, they require the input signal to be maintained for a minimum "set-up" time, S. If so, the output will be determined by this new value and will appear at the output after a total delay, usually called the propagation delay, P. Of course, P must be greater than or equal to S. In VHDL, the implicit assumption is that P = S. This assumption is often used in digital logic analysis, but it is an approximation and may not always be accurate. To remedy this, VHDL-92 adds the reserved words **inertial** and **reject** (the reserved word **use** was initially suggested in place of the new reserved word **reject**). There is now a third form of signal assignment:

```
Signal_1 <= reject  10 ns inertial'1' after
200 ns;
```

Transients shorter than 10ns will be rejected and will not appear as transactions.

Inertial delay is appropriate to electronic devices that have inertia, that is, that do not respond to transients or short-duration inputs. A signal assignment with inertial delay will delete from the projected waveform all those assignments that transport-delay assignments will, and in addition will delete any scheduled transactions before the current assignment. Section 8.3.1 of the LRM gives the precise algorithm for signal assignment.

For all signal assignments, VHDL-87 specified:

1. Delete all old transactions projected to occur at or after the new transaction.

2. Append new transactions to the projected waveform in time order.

For inertial delay signal assignments only (VHDL-87):

3. Mark:

a. all new transactions;

b. any old transaction that immediately precedes a marked transaction and assigns the same value as the marked transaction

c. the transaction that determines the current value of the driver.

4. Delete all unmarked transactions.

Notice that while it may be some additional work to implement an inertial delay assignment, such an assignment will generally delete more scheduled transactions, resulting in fewer transactions and hence fewer simulation cycles. Rule 3b is to ensure that signal attributes such as ′STABLE correctly report the time for which the signal has been constant (attributes are discussed in Chapter 6).

For the VHDL-92 form of inertial assignment with a reject clause, there is a finite time horizon in the deletion of transactions, specified in the reject clause. A new step 3b is inserted, and steps 3b and 3c become steps 3c and 3d, respectively. The new step is that old transactions are marked "if the time at which it is projected to occur is less than the time at which the first new transaction is projected to occur minus the pulse rejection limit." In other words, if the time difference between the new transaction and the old scheduled transaction is less than that specified in the reject clause, the old transaction is not marked and will be deleted, unless it determines the current value of the driver, or immediately preceeds a marked transaction and assigns the same value.

Note that this procedure is followed, separately, for each driver of a signal. The transaction that determines the current value of the driver is obviously marked because, if it were deleted, the current value of the signal could be lost.

Note that signal assignment does not happen immediately. If the value of Signal_1 is ' 0' , the sequential statements

```
Signal_1 <= ' 1' ;
if Signal_1 = ' 1' then
    some VHDL statements;
endif;
```

would not (immediately) execute the statements shown. When this if test is first encountered after the signal assignment, Signal_1 is still ' 0' . There is effectively an infinitesimal delay, generally called a *delta* delay, before the assignment occurs. Then the signals that need to be are all updated by their new resolved values. The evaluation cycle repeats until the system is stabilized. The simulation has then found the new state of the system at the assigned time, and may continue to the next scheduled transaction. This simulation cycle will be discussed in more detail in the next chapter.

Note also that, whatever delay is used, transactions that were scheduled by signal assignments made at an earlier time to occur at a later time than those scheduled by a driver at the current time are deleted. If at a simulation time of 100 ns a transaction is scheduled at 500 ns, and if at 200 ns a transaction is scheduled to occur at 400 ns, the transaction at 500 ns is deleted from the waveform. This may be quite reasonable for electronic signals. It means, however, that signal waveforms cannot be used as a general event queue. Implementing such event queues will be discussed in the next chapter.

Consider the example:

```
signal Signal1 : INTEGER;
process
begin
```

```
   Signal1 <= 1 after 1 ns;
   Signal1 <= 2 after 1 us;
   Signal1 <= 3 after 1 ms;
end process;
```

Here all of the assignments refer to one driver. The resulting projected waveform of that driver, because of the inertial delay of the assignments, will be the single transaction (1 ms, 3).

On the other hand, the assignment of a waveform via:

```
signal Signal1 : INTEGER;
process
begin
   Signal1 <=  1 after 1 ns,
               2 after 1 us,
               3 after 1 ms;
end process;
```

would be a single assignment and would result in the three transactions shown being scheduled in the projected waveform. The process:

```
signal Signal1 : INTEGER;
process
begin
   Signal1 <=  1 after 1 ns;
   Signal1 <= transport 2 after 1 us;
   Signal1 <= transport 3 after 1 ms;
end process;
```

would, likewise, result in three scheduled transactions because of the transport delay specified for the last two transactions. If the first of the three transactions were given transport delay, this would have no effect on the behavior of the process shown.

Now consider:

```
signal Signal1 : INTEGER;
process
begin
   Signal1 <=  1 after 1 ns;
   Signal1 <= transport 3 after 1 ms;
   Signal1 <= transport 2 after 1 us;
end process;
```

This code sample would behave differently from its predecessor. The third assignment would remove the "old" assignment (1 ms, 3) from the projected waveform because it occurs at a later time than the (1 us, 2) transaction it schedules. Inertial delay assignments would behave similarly.

If this seems complicated and confusing, it is. VHDL is very sophisticated in its event scheduling. If you are totally lost, go back and reread the four-step algorithm for signal assignment and apply it to the examples, to check it out.

Note once again that VHDL's model of inertial delay in the preceding example assumes that the device producing the signal assignment does not have some physical "inertia," such as a fixed setup time, but has whatever delay is implied by each assignment. Inertial delay is intended to simulate a device that ignores any "spike" or transient at its input. Physically, a device that has an inertial period ranging anywhere from 1 ns to 1 ms would be noteworthy.

GUARDED SIGNAL ASSIGNMENT

There are guarded signals and guarded signal assignments. The former always require the latter. It is possible to make a guarded signal assignment to an unguarded signal, however.

Whenever there is an explicit declaration of signal type, either bus or register, the signal is taken to be guarded. Note that register-type signals are always guarded, while bus-type signals may either be guarded or not. Guarded signals must be assigned by guarded signal assignments, of the form:

```
Delay <= guarded 1 ns ;
```

This assignment will take place only if an implicitly defined boolean variable, called the guard, it true. The next section discusses how these guard variables are defined and used. These guarded assignments are actually a form of concurrent statement, that is, they behave as a concurrent process. What is a VHDL process? You might want to think of a process as the analog of a block except that the block encapsulates concurrent statements while the process encapsulates sequential statements. Blocks and guards are discussed immediately below, while processes are discussed later in Chapter 8, Concurrent statements.

As noted above, if `Delay` is a guarded signal, that is, if its declaration contained either of the reserved words bus or register, then any assignment to it must be a guarded one. One the other hand, it is perfectly legal to do a guarded assignment to an unguarded signal. If the guard is false, the assignment doesn't occur.

The fundamental difference between guarded and unguarded signals is that drivers of the former disconnect "automatically," while the latter do not. The time it takes to effect the disconnect is 0 ns by default, but a finite delay may be specified in a **disconnect** specification. See Chapter 4 for examples.

TRANSACTIONS AND EVENTS

In VHDL, a signal is said to have had a *transaction* if an assignment has occurred for that signal. The signal is then said to be *active* during that simulation cycle. An *event* is a transaction that alters the value of the signal. Thus, all events are transactions, but only some transactions are events.

For reasons of efficiency, VHDL activates processes sensitive to signals only on events on those signals, that is, only when they change value. Sometimes it is necessary to respond to every transaction, whether it causes a change in the signal value or not. One common example would be an interrupt handler, which may have to stack a number of similar interrupts. A special case of this might be a timer or clock tick. VHDL recognizes this possibility and provides a convenient mechanism for converting transactions into guaranteed events. This is the predefined attribute signal TRANSACTION, which will be discussed fully under attributes.

THE SIMULATION CYCLE

To clarify the concept of a *delta* time increment, let us briefly discuss how time proceeds in a VHDL simulation. The LRM, section 12.6.3, is explicit as to just how a VHDL simulation is to proceed. Here, we present a modified discussion of the simulation cycle. postponing full discussion to when the reader may be expected to better understand the terminology peculiar to VHDL. In the next chapter there will be a detailed discussion of this process as it would apply to our simple asynchronous latch example.

The definition of the simulation cycle has been altered somewhat by the VHDL-92 standard.

There is an initialization phase, in which the simulation time is set to 0 ns, and initial values are assigned to all signals and are presumed to have existed for all negative times. If there are implicitly defined signals of the form S′ STABLE(T) or S′ QUIET(T), these are all initialized to TRUE (see Chapter 6 for a discussion of these implicit signals). The values of each GUARD signal is also initialized. (There is a final initialization step, executing each process until it suspends, which will be clarified when processes are discussed in Chapter 8.) The time of the next cycle, which will be the first, is computed according to the rules of step 6 of the simulation cycle.

Each simulation cycle now consists of the following steps:

1. The current time is set equal to the new time. If this is TIME'HIGH and there are no active drivers or process resumptions, the simulation is complete.

2. Each active signal is updated.

3. Each implicitly defined signal is updated. Such signals are defined by guards and by attributed signals, such as S' DELAYED(20ns). Here S is a user-defined signal and the signal shown is the value this signal had 20ns previous. Attributes are discussed in Chapter 6 and guards in Chapter 4.

4. Steps 2 and 3 may have generated events. For each process P, if it is sensitive to a signal S and an event has occured on S in this cycle, P resumes.

5. Each process that has resumed in the current cycle and was not declared **postponed** is executed until it suspends. (Postponed processes are new in VHDL-92.)

6. The time of the next cycle is set to the earliest of TIME' HIGH, the next time any driver becomes active, the next time a process resumes, or, if the time is unchanged, the next cycle will be a *delta cycle.*

7. If the next cycle is not a delta cycle, then each resumed postponed processes that has not been executed since its last resumption is executed until it suspends, and then the time of the next cycle is computed as in Step 6. It is an error if any of the postponed processes cause a delta cycle. Obviously, this step is only of interest in VHDL-92 with postponed processes.

Note that postponed processes resume according to the rules of Step 4, but don't actually execute until the time of the next cycle is determined and found to be different from that of the current cycle. When a process resumes, it is added to one of two lists, depending upon whether it is postponed or not. No process begins to execute until all of the signals have been updated, and all executed processes for the current simulation cycle have been identified and placed on the appropriate list.

Note that time is not advanced each cycle, but only if there are no active signal drivers. The result is that, if any event occurs, that is, if any signal changes during a simulation cycle, there will be another cycle executed at the same clock time, but at an infinitesimal *delta* time later. The VHDL simulation advances in time only when the system has stabilized at the new state, and all signal values are constant for at least one delta.

As discussed earlier, signals are not updated during the execution of any process, which occurs in step 4. The updating will take place as step 2 of the next simulation cycle. Thus, the assignment of a new value to a signal will not alter the value of that signal if it is used in a subsequent statement on the right-hand side of an assignment, for example, during the same simulation cycle. Nor will it cause the process to pass through a **wait on** S; statement for signal S. The transaction will take place at the start of the next simulation cycle, an event will then be noted if the value of the signal has changed, and the process will proceed through the wait statement if an event has been noted on the signal of interest.

VHDL-92 permits concurrent processes to be declared as **postponed**. They will execute once for any time, at the end of all the deltas. Such processes are prohibited from performing a signal assignment that would force another delta cycle. See Chapter 10.

Signal Value Updating

In each simulation cycle, new values of signals will have to be determined and assigned to the signals. This is done, in general, according to the procedure given by LRM 12.6.1. For signals implicitly defined by the predefined attributes ′STABLE, ′QUIET, ′TRANSACTION, different procedures are followed and these will be discussed in Chapter 6 on attributes. This updating is done at the end of the simulation cycle for all signals.

VHDL defines the *driving value* of a signal to be the value that signal provides as a source to other signals. Its *effective* value is that obtainable by evaluating a reference to the signal within an expression. These values may not be the same. Roughly speaking, the effective value of a signal is that which may be read internal to the component, while the driving value is that which is visible to the external world through the ports of the component. There is, therefore, no effective value defined for ports of mode **out** or **linkage**, as these may not be read.

The driving value of a signal S is determined as follows:

1. If S has no source, then it is the default value. Note that if the user does not supply an explicit default value, VHDL will determine one from the type specified for the signal.

2. If S has a single driver, and is not a resolved signal, it is the value of that driver.

3. If S has a single port as a source, and is not a resolved signal, then it is the driving value of the formal port.

4. If S is a resolved signal, then the resolution function will be called with an array of all the drivers whose current value is not determined by a null transaction, unless the signal is declared to be of type **register** and all of the associated sources have null transactions, in which case the current value is not changed.

The effective value is determined as follows:

1. If the signal is declared in a signal declaration, is a port of mode **buffer**, or is a port of mode **inout** which is unconnected, the effective value is the same as the driving value.

2. If it is an unconnected port of mode **in**, then it is the default value for signal S.

3. If it is a connected port of mode **in** or **inout**, then it is the *effective value of the actual* associated with the signal S (as expressed in the LRM). Put more simply, for ports of these modes the system assumes it may expect *input* due to some source, from whatever is connected to these port-defined signals. The simulation runtime kernel must then check to see what is connected to the "other side" of such ports to determine what the appropriate signal values are.

In any simulation cycle, the VHDL simulation evaluates the driving and effective values of the signal. It then updates the current value of the signal with the newly determined effective value, after first checking that the effective value of S belongs to the subtype of S.

Chapter 3

Entity, Architecture, Configuration Statements

THE ENTITY

The very first sentence of the VHDL LRM states that the "primary hardware abstraction" is the *design entity*. Entities are declared in the entity declaration. An entity represents a component of a system, such as a logic gate, a chip, or a PC board. The entity declaration generally defines the external view of the component in question. It is still effectively a "black box" with ports that may be connected to and parameters that may be specified, but no information as to what it does, that is, how it maps inputs to outputs. This is supplied by the architecture specification. VHDL cannot do its job of simulating an entity's behavior without one architecture bound to each entity. VHDL offers considerable flexibility in the specification of architectures. The architecture may specify the behavior of the entity, or it may build the entity by connecting together one or more entities, which are declared in **component** statements and then "wired together." Finally, a **configuration** specification must exist to cause the actual binding of components to the design entities (but see Chapter 10 for a discussion of VHDL-92's direct instantiation). Here again, there is flexibility in the ability to defer specifying such bindings or to specify bindings locally.

One might view the entity declaration as the hand, the architecture declaration as the glove. You can have many gloves in your closet, but they must all fit your hand, and you must select the gloves you wish to use at any given time. Some people might prefer the analogy reversed, with the entity as the glove fitting the achitectural body of the component. This analogy has merit as well, since the architecture defines the body of the entity while the entity provides the externally visible interface between the architecture and the universe. The configuration declaration actually inserts the hands in the gloves. It is permissible to associate a given entity with one architecture for one instance of a component and with another architecture for another instance. You might have a variety of, say, memory cells, all with the same external interface and entity declaration, but some might be SRAMs for speed and others DRAMs for reduced power consumption. It would be useful to use the same entity if you were experimenting with the trade-offs in different mixes of the memory types.

ENTITY AND ARCHITECTURE DECLARATIONS

The general form of the entity declaration is:

```
entity name is
    generic specifications
    port specifications
begin
    passive statements

end name;
```

The port specification provides the means for connecting the entity to other components in the design. Generics are parameters that permit customizing a generic design. For example, you might have a generic design for a NAND gate that takes as a parameter the propagation delay:

```
entity NAND_Gate is
  generic (Prop_Delay: TIME);
  port(X,Y: in BIT; Z: out BIT);
end NAND_Gate;
```

Here the propagation delay is specified as being of type TIME, a predefined type available through the use of the STANDARD package, as is type BIT. BIT is defined to take on the values ' 0' and ' 1' . The entity specifies the public or visible portion of the design entity NAND_Gate. It specifies how to connect to it. It in no way constrains what it does or how it is to be simulated. That's the job of the associated architecture, for example:

```
architecture SimpleNAND of NAND_Gate is
  generic (Prop_Delay:= 20 ns);
begin

  Z <= not (X and Y);
end SimpleNAND;
```

Here Z, which is a *signal* implicitly defined by the port specification, is assigned its value. Furthermore, the generic parameter is given a default value. This could have been done in the entity declaration as well. The signal assignment is the only executable statement in this simple model. This is a behavioral model, as it specifies the behavior of the NAND gate rather than building one up from simpler components. To illustrate these variations, let us consider and expand upon the simple latch or RS flip-flop mentioned earlier. The entity declaration as given above is repeated, with a fleshed-out architecture to simulate the latch:

```
entity Latch is
    port( R, S: in BIT; Q, Qbar: out BIT);
end Latch;
```

```
type State is BIT;

-- it is illegal to have both R(eset) and
S(et) inputs true or '1'

architecture Behave_Latch of Latch is
signal LatchState: State;
begin
LatchState <= '1' when (S = '1')
  else '0' when (R = '1')
  else LatchState;
Q<=Latchstate;
Qbar notLatchState;
end Behave_Latch;
```

This is at present a very simplistic and very likely inadequate design. For one thing, the illegal input condition is not handled correctly. At the very least, a warning should be generated. In this design, the ordering of the condition clauses in the conditional signal assignment to LatchState would cause such an input state to be equivalent to S=' 1' , R=' 0' , with the latch being set. For another thing, the latch instantly sets the values of the outputs, without any propagation delay. Clocking or enabling signals, for example, might be desired. The latch might be edge-triggered by the appropriate signal.

Let's make a structural architecture for this latch, using as components our two-input NAND gate. To do so, we have to address some of the inadequacies of the previous simplistic declarations.

```
entity Latch is
-- N. B.:  Q, Qbar now type inout!
--   This permits them to be read.
port( R, S: in BIT; Q, Qbar: inout BIT);
begin
assert not(R=' 1' and S=' 1')
report "R=' 1' and S=' 1' in Latch" severity
ERROR;
```

```
-- it is illegal to have
-- both R(eset) and S(et) inputs true or '1'

end Latch;

type State is (Set,Reset);

architecture Behave_Latch of Latch is
signal LatchState: State;
begin
LatchState <= set when (S = '1') else reset
when (R = '1') else LatchState ;
Q<='1' when LatchState = Set else '0' ;
Qbar not Q;
end Behave_Latch;
```

We have made two changes to the entity declaration. One change is the addition of the **assert** statement to report whenever the illegal condition exists. Note that the error message is triggered if the asserted condition is false. That is, we assert how things should be and get an error message if this assertion is wrong. By placing this statement in the entity declaration, it will be in effect whatever architecture is used. Only certain statements, namely passive concurrent processes, may be so placed. A passive process is one that does not make any signal assignments. Note that this assert statement is a concurrent process and as such is always monitoring the validity of the asserted condition. This is appropriate for the asynchronous latch design entity of this example. For most logic designs, a synchronous or clocked circuit will be used and it will be of interest only to check for such error conditions if the latch is enabled for input by the clock. In that case, a process would be used and a sequential form of the **assert** would be employed for the purpose. This will be discussed fully with examples in Chapter 7 on sequential statements. We have also altered the type of State to an enumerated type. This will make the model somewhat more transparent and "self-documenting." Enumerated types are discussed fully in Chapter 5. Note that BIT is an enumerated type, defined by the system package STANDARD.

The other change is to alter the declarations of d Qbar in the port statement to make these of *mode* **inout** instead of mode **out**. Without this change, we could only assign values to these signals, not read them. It will be useful to be able to read the value of these signals when we construct a structural model of the latch, as they are inputs to the component gates as well as the outputs of the entity. The declaration of these signals as of mode **out** gives us this flexibility, but at the price of losing some automatic error checking capability. Port modes are discussed in more detail shortly. (Let us note in passing that one text on VHDL has a similar example in which mode **buffer** is used instead of **inout**. This will generate an error, as has been confirmed with the Vantage VHDL compiler. The moral is that port modes can be tricky.)

For a structural model of the latch, we will use the two-input NAND gate behavioral model along with a behavioral model of the inverter or not gate:

```
entity Inverter is
-- Need inverter for out latch model
generic (Prop_Delay: TIME :=0 ns);
port (Input: in BIT; Output: out BIT);
end Inverter;

architecture Behave_Inv of Inverter is
begin
Output <= '1' when (Input = '0') else '0'
  after Prop_Delay;
end Behave_Inv;
```

This model included a generic parameter, the propagation delay for the latch, which can be specified as desired when the component is *instantiated*, that is, actually turned into a real instance of the component device within the model of the complete system being modeled.

The structural model for our Latch will then be:

```
architecture Struct_Latch of Latch is
signal Link1, Link2: BIT;
   component NAND_G
      port(X,Y: in BIT; Z: out BIT);
   end NAND_G;
   component NOT_G
      port(Input: in BIT; Output: out BIT);
   end I;
begin
U1: NOT_G generic map (20 ns);
port map (S, Link1);
U2: NAND_G port map (Link1, Qbar, Q);
U3: NOT_G generic map (30 ns);
port map (R, Link2);
U4: NAND_G port map (Link2, Q, Qbar);
end   Struct_Latch;
```

In the declaration section, we have told the compiler what components will be used to build up the device. These specifications have to correspond to a visible entity for the compiler to be able to build the device from these components. We then "wire" the two inverters and two NAND gates to the external ports of the latch as well as to one another. The two signals defined in the architecture may be thought of as these wires.

The model given above is appropriate for later synthesis in TTL or CMOS technologies. For ECL, where NOR gates are more natural than NAND, a more appropriate structural model might be:

```
entity NOR_Gate is
   generic (Prop_Delay: TIME);
   port(X,Y: in BIT; Z: out BIT);
end NOR_Gate;

architecture SimpleNOR of NOR_Gate is
   generic (Prop_Delay:= 20 ns);
begin
```

```
    Z <= not ( X or Y );
  end SimpleNOR;

  architecture ECL_Latch of Latch is
    component NOR_G
      port(X,Y: in BIT; Z: out BIT);
    end NOR_G;
    end I;
  begin
  U1: NOR_G port map ( S, Qbar, Q);
  U2: NOR_G port map ( R, Q, Qbar);
  end ECL_Latch;
```

Note that we have given each component a unique *label*. This is optional. It is useful when it is necessary to distinguish between the two inverters, for example. There is no need that the two inverters, for example, have the same architecture, even though they have the same entity name. It is possible to instantiate different architectures for U1 and U3. Note that the component declaration references the entity declaration, not the architecture. So far, the architecture to be used has not been referenced. The architecture will be specified and bound to the use of the **configuration** declaration. This is not used in this design, but examples of reference to the label, for example in attribute statements, will be presented below.

The propagation delays of the two inverters have been assigned through the **generic map**. Different values have been specified, to illustrate that this can be done. This might be done in practice to determine the sensitivity of the design to such asymmetries and possible race conditions or other hazards. Variables or constants can be used to specify such parameters as well as explicit values, giving the designer flexibility in such testing. The use of such parameters in *back-annotation* will be discussed in Chapter 3.

Note the need to declare two signals to actually wire together the inverters and NAND gates. These signals are not visible outside of the latch. References to Link1 in another architecture body, for example, will not refer to this signal. Other architectures may therefore use the same term without conflict. If the other architecture does not declare such a signal, the result will be an error message.

The declaration:

```
entity Silent is
end Silent;
```

is perfectly legal. It defines an entity that has no generic parameters and does not have any external connections. Such an entity may be encountered as the top-level of a "test-bench" architecture that supervises a simulation. Such an entity might read input and write output files to communicate with the universe, and might drive signals specified within its architecture to control the simulation.

Port Modes

VHDL is a strongly typed language. That means that objects are declared with restrictive specifications that limit what may be legally done to them. The intent is to prevent erroneous usage by allowing the compiler to check for proper usage to the greatest degree. One example of this approach is in the declaration of ports. There are five possible modes for ports: **in**, **out**, **inout**, **buffer**, **linkage**. The signals declared as mode **in** by a port can only be read, and cannot be the left-hand side of a signal assignment. This will prevent the user from unintentionally wiring a device that can drive signals to such a port. Mode **out** ports are the opposite. Mode **buffer** ports are those which to the external universe behave as an **out** port, but may be read from internally. These signals are restricted, however, in that only a single driver, such as a single signal assignment statement or a single component that may drive the port, are connected to it. A port of mode **buffer** has another subtlety, which is generally not important, in that the value of its associated signal when read is always the value of the source, even if there are type conversions specified as part of its "buffering" role as viewed externally. Mode **inout** ports are not limited. Mode **linkage** ports are intended to serve as a "pass-through" for the entity, that is, the intent is that the entity in question merely passes the signal between a lower-level component and a higher-level one. Thus, the entity should neither read nor write to such a signal.

When a **component** is declared as being used in the declaration portion of an **architecture**, the port names are called the *formal* ports. They are merely used to reference the associated ports we wish to connect to. All formal port signal names must be associated with an actual signal.

There are special rules for interconnecting ports. These are intended to prevent errors, such as wiring one of the inverters backwards in the above model. This would be precluded because VHDL would catch the error when we tried to wire the formal mode out to the actual mode in signal defined by latch. Note that the component specification and the associated port maps define formal signals, whereas actuals are defined by the architecture itself. These actuals correspond to waveforms that take up storage in simulation codes and get values assigned to them. Note that signals defined in architectures, etc., explicitly, that is, not through ports, do not have a mode. They may freely be wired to any ports. Thus, the VHDL compiler will not look over our shoulder and second-guess our internal connections. If we wired a number of output ports together with no input port connected to that signal, it would probably go unnoticed. (We would, however, have to tell the VHDL simulator how to assign the signal value when more than one output driver is active. This is discussed in Chapter 2 under Resolution functions.)

The rules for wiring between signals defined by ports is discussed in the LRM, section 1.1.1.2. They are summarized here in Tables 3.1 and 3.2.

Table 3.1 Permissible actuals for a given formal Mode	
formal	permissible actuals
in	in, inout, buffer
out	out, inout
inout	inout
buffer	buffer
linkage	in, inout, out, buffer, linkage

Table 3.2 Permissible formals for a given actual Mode	
actual	permissible formals
in	in, linkage
out	out, linkage
inout	in, inout, linkage
buffer	in, buffer, linkage
linkage	linkage

These may be understood in regard to our simple Latch as follows. First, consider the connections between the ports of the NAND gates and inverters and the Latch itself. Here, the actuals are the signals Link1 and Link2, and the ports of the Latch. The formal parameters are those of the internal component gates. There are no restrictions on connections to signals defined by the **signal** declaration, so it is safe to use such a signal to "connect" the mode **out** output of the inverter to such a signal and then connect this signal to the mode **in** port of the NAND gate. VHDL uses the term *associate* for the intuitive *connect*. For the inverters, the formal mode **in** ports are connected to the actual mode **in** port of the Latch, which is legal. Both mode **in** and mode **out** formals are connected to the actual Q and Qbar signals. Mode **inout** is the only legal mode for this port.

Now assume that the Latch entity is used as a component in some other architecture. Its ports now become the formals. Its mode **in** ports, R and S, can be connected to signals declared in that architecture, and to ports of mode **in**, mode **inout**, or mode **buffer**. Its mode **inout** ports Q and Qbar may be connected to signals declared in that architecture, and to mode **inout** ports.

Port and Generic Mapping Revisited

In the Latch example given above, ports were mapped by position. It is also possible to map by name, that is, by explicitly writing the association between formal and actual signal names. This is done by means of the syntax: formal => actual. (The terms formal and actual are defined in the previous section.) Thus, instead of:

```
U1: Inverter generic map (20 ns);
port map (R, Link1);
U1: Inverter generic map (20 ns);
port map (Input =>R, Output =>Link1);
```

or

```
U1: Inverter generic map (20 ns);
port map (Output =>Link1, Input => R);
```

may all be used. We could also have used the same syntax for the generic mapping:

```
U1: Inverter generic map (Prop_Delay = > 20 ns);
port map (R, Link1);
```

These specifications are somewhat easier to read, but less compact.

Port Defaults

It is possible to specify default values for input ports, that is, ports of mode **in**. This is shown in the Inverter architecture specification given above. Such default values are assigned to the associated signals before the beginning of the simulation, but do not have a definite time value associated with them.

It is an error to provide an initial or default value for a port of mode **linkage** (LRM 4.3.3).

In the absence of an explicitly supplied default value, the system will provide a default value from the type of the signal, in the same manner that it assigns such default or initial values to signals.

Ports are assumed to be of mode **in** by default if the mode of the port is not explicitly specified.

Open Ports

It is generally an error to leave a port unconnected. However, in special circumstances, this is desired and it may be done through the use of the reserved word **open** being used in the port map. A formal port of mode **in** may be unconnected only if its declaration includes a default. Any other port mode may be unconnected so long as its type is not that of an unconstrained array, since such an array needs to obtain its length by being associated with an actual to supply such information.

DELTA DELAY REVISITED

Consider the structural architecture Struct_Latch of Latch we have used as our example. The NAND gate we have used has no propagation delay specified. For simplicity, let us assume zero delay as well for the inverters. Suppose the Latch is set, that is, suppose Q = ′ 1′ , Qbar = ′ 0′ , R = ′ 0′ , S= ′ 0′ . Now suppose that at some time T the assignment R <= ′ 1′ takes effect. What happens, exactly? The event on signal R will cause the process associated with inverter U3 to become active. This process is implicitly defined by the concurrent signal assignment in the inverter architecture. This will result in inverter U3's output signal Link2 being scheduled to become '0' at the next delta. This event will then cause the process defined by the signal assignments in NAND gate U4 to become active. This NAND gate will duly switch its output, Qbar, to ′ 1′ , at the end of this delta. The next delta will see

NAND gate U2 respond to the event on Qbar at its input, resulting in the assignment Q <= ′ 0′ . The next delta will have NAND
gate U4 responding to the altered inputs it sees due to the change in
Q. This will not, however, alter its output Qbar. Therefore, no
additional events will be scheduled by this entity. The simulation
can then proceed to the next scheduled occurrence (event or process
resumption), assuming of course that the changes in other parts of
the model, such as are due to the changes in Q and Qbar, do not
cause additional simulation cycle deltas.

If we had not used gates with zero propagation delay, the ultimate effect would be the same. No simulation deltas would be
needed, as the changes in signals would occur at finite time increments into the future. There would presumably be some additional
overhead compared with the instantaneous propagation, as scheduling the events presumably has additional overhead compared with
executing a simulation cycle.

CONFIGURATION SPECIFICATION

The configuration specification performs the actual instantiation of
components. It associates the architectures to the entities. Without a
configuration specification, nothing has been made into actual objects that could be simulated. VHDL-92 modifies the configuration
binding by permitting the configuration to be defaulted, without an
explicit specification, in some cases. See Chapter 10.

Configuration specifications can be collected in one location, or
the configurations of components can be separately made. There
must be at least one configuration specification for the highest level
entity to produce something that may be simulated.

It is possible to delay specifying the generic map parameters,
such as propagation delays, in the configuration specification, and
to remap the ports if the desired model in the library has a different
port naming convention.

There are a great many varieties of configuration specifications.
Configurations may be used to bind to for blocks or to specify ge-

neric parameters component by component. The latter will be discussed later in this chapter, the former in the next chapter.

A typical configuration specification is of the form:

```
configuration identifierofentity_name is
use library_specification;
-- repeat above as needed
for component_specification use binding;
-- repeat above as needed
end identifier;
```

The identifier is a name for later reference of the configuration, that is, the object created by the entity. If this is the highest level configuration, it will likely be the name to be specified when you request the simulation to be executed and the system asks you "what do you want to simulate?"

The construct **for ... end for** is called a "component configuration" in the LRM and in the Backus-Naur productions used in the syntax summary therein. The *component_specification* is a list of component instances to be bound to. Labels can be provided to distinguish between different instances of the same component.

The use clauses specify the libraries that will be used, while the for statements specify the architecture bindings. The bindings can specify generic and port mappings as well as architectures, configurations, or the reserved word **open** to indicate that no component is actually connected.

As we compile a project, the various entities, architectures, and configurations are put into a library called *work*. Reference to any item X in this library may be made as work.X. The syntax for references to other libraries is similar.

Our full behavioral latch model could be:

```
entity Latch is
-- N. B.:   Q, Qbar now type inout!
--   This permits them to be read.
port( R, S: in BIT; Q, Qbar: inout BIT);
```

```
begin
assert not(R=' 1'  and  S=' 1' )
report  " R=' 1'  and  S=' 1'  in  Latch"  severity
     ERROR;
-- it is illegal to have
-- both R(eset) and S(et) inputs true or ' 1'
end Latch;

type State is BIT;

architecture Behave_Latch of Latch is
signal LatchState: State;
begin
LatchState <= ' 1'  when (S = ' 1' )
     else ' 0'  when (R = ' 1' )
     else LatchState ;
Q<=LatchState;
Qbar not LatchState;
end Behave_Latch;

library work;
   configuration BehavioralRS of Latch is
   for Behave_Latch
   -- use default.  nothing more needed!
   end for;
end BehavioralRS;
```

No additional **for** or **use** clauses are necessary because Be-have_Latch does not use any components.

The code for the structural model of the latch will be more complicated, as there are components with architectures of their own. For clarity we collect all of these together because we will be making modifications to many portions of the latch description to illustrate the many varieties of configuration specification. Starting with our entities and structural architectures as above:

```
entity Latch is
    port( R, S: in BIT; Q, Qbar: out BIT);
end Latch;

architecture Struct_Latch of Latch is
Bsignal Link1, Link2: BIT;
   component NAND_G
     port(X,Y: in BIT; Z: out BIT);
   end NAND_G;
   component NOT_G
     port(Input: in BIT; Output: out BIT);
   end NOT_G;
begin
U1: NOT_G generic map (20 ns);
port map (R, Link1);
U2: NAND_G port map (Link1, Qbar, Q);
U3: NOT_G generic map (30 ns);
port map (S, Link2);
U4: NAND_G port map (Link2, Q, Qbar);
end   Struct_Latch;

entity Inverter is
-- Need inverter for out latch model
generic (Prop_Delay: TIME :=0 ns);
port (Input: in BIT; Output: out BIT);
end Inverter;

architecture Behave_Inv of Inverter is
begin
Output <= '1' when (Input = '0') else '0'
 after Prop_Delay;
end Behave_Inv;

entity NAND_Gate is
   generic (Prop_Delay: TIME);
```

```
   port(X,Y: in BIT; Z: out BIT);
end NAND_Gate;

architecture SimpleNAND of NAND_Gate is
   generic (Prop_Delay:= 20 ns);
begin

   Z <= not (X and Y);
end SimpleNAND;

 library work;
configuration Nand_1  of NAND_Gate is
for Simple_NAND
-- Default sufficient
end for;
end Nand_1;

configuration Not_1  of Inverter is
for Behav_Inv
-- Default sufficient
end for;
end Not_1;

configuration StructuralRS of Latch is
for Struct_Latch
   for all NAND_G use
      configuration work.Nand_1;
   end for;
   for all NOT_G use
      configuration work.Not_1;
   end for;
   end for;
end for;
end StructuralRS;
```

The reserved word **all** specifies that all of the NOT_G components are bound as shown. One can also specify various individual

components and use the reserved word **others**, similarly to **all**, to specify the other component instances not individually named.

Here we have used separate configuration specifications for each entity. Assuming all of the entities and architectures in question are in, say, one user file or that the simulation environment has been told somehow that they are all part of one simulation project, it would not be necessary to specify any libraries, as in this example:

```
entity Latch is
     port( R, S: in BIT; Q, Qbar: out BIT);
end Latch;

architecture Struct_Latch of Latch is
signal Link1, Link2: BIT;
   component NAND_Gate
     port(X,Y: in BIT; Z: out BIT);
   end NAND_Gate;
   component Inverter
     port(Input: in BIT; Output: out BIT);
   end Inverter;
begin
U1: Invertergeneric map (20 ns);
port map (R, Link1);
U2: NAND_Gate port map (Link1, Qbar, Q);
U3: Inverter generic map (30 ns);
port map (S, Link2);
U4: NAND_Gate port map (Link2, Q, Qbar);
end   Struct_Latch;

entity Inverter is
-- Need inverter for out latch model
generic (Prop_Delay: TIME :=0 ns);
port (Input: in BIT; Output: out BIT);
end Inverter;

architecture Behave_Inv of Inverter is
begin
```

```
Output <= '1' when (Input = '0') else '0'
  after Prop_Delay;
end Behave_Inv;

entity NAND_Gate is
   generic (Prop_Delay: TIME);
   port(X,Y: in BIT; Z: out BIT);
end NAND_Gate;

architecture SimpleNAND of NAND_Gate is
   generic (Prop_Delay:= 20 ns);
begin

   Z <= not (X and Y);
end SimpleNAND;

  library work;
configuration StructuralRS of Latch is
for Struct_Latch
   -- Defaults sufficient
   end for;
end for;
end StructuralRS;
```

The configuration information can also be included in the declarative portion of the architecture:

```
entity Latch is
     port( R, S: in BIT; Q, Qbar: out BIT);
end Latch;

architecture Struct_Latch of Latch is
signal Link1, Link2: BIT;
   component NAND_G
     port(X,Y: in BIT; Z: out BIT);
   end NAND_G;
   component NOT_G
     port(Input: in BIT; Output: out BIT);
```

```
    end NOT_G;
    forNAND_G use
       configuration NAND_1; end for;
    forNOT_G use
       configuration NOT_1; end for;
begin
U1: NOT_Ggeneric map (20 ns);
port map (R, Link1);
U2: NAND_G port map (Link1, Qbar, Q);
U3: NOT_G generic map (30 ns);
port map (S, Link2);
U4: NAND_G port map (Link2, Q, Qbar);
end   Struct_Latch;

entity Inverter is
-- Need inverter for out latch model
generic (Prop_Delay: TIME :=0 ns);
port (Input: in BIT; Output: out BIT);
end Inverter;

architecture Behave_Inv of Inverter is
begin
Output <= '1' when (Input = '0') else '0'
 after Prop_Delay;
end Behave_Inv;

entity NAND_Gate is
   generic (Prop_Delay: TIME);
   port(X,Y: in BIT; Z: out BIT);
end NAND_Gate;

architecture SimpleNAND of NAND_Gate is
   generic (Prop_Delay:= 20 ns);
begin

   Z <= not (X and Y);
end SimpleNAND;
```

```
  library work;
configuration Nand_1  of NAND_Gate is
for Simple_NAND
-- Default sufficient
end for;
end Nand_1;


configuration Not_1  of Inverter is
for Behav_Inv
-- Default sufficient
end for;
```

This still does not exhaust all of our options! The entity and the architecture may be specified together in the form of *library.entity (architecture)*. Thus:

```
entity Latch is
      port( R, S: in BIT; Q, Qbar: out BIT);
end Latch;


architecture Struct_Latch of Latch is
Bsignal Link1, Link2: BIT;
   component NAND_G
     port(X,Y: in BIT; Z: out BIT);
   end NAND_G;
   component NOT_G
     port(Input: in BIT; Output: out BIT);
   end NOT_G;
begin
U1: NOT_G generic map (20 ns);
port map (R, Link1);
U2: NAND_G port map (Link1, Qbar, Q);
U3: NOT_G generic map (30 ns);
port map (S, Link2);
U4: NAND_G port map (Link2, Q, Qbar);
end   Struct_Latch;
```

```
entity Inverter is
-- Need inverter for out latch model
generic (Prop_Delay: TIME :=0 ns);
port (Input: in BIT; Output: out BIT);
end Inverter;


architecture Behave_Inv of Inverter is
begin
Output <= '1' when (Input = '0') else '0'
  after Prop_Delay;
end Behave_Inv;

entity NAND_Gate is
   generic (Prop_Delay: TIME);
   port(X,Y: in BIT; Z: out BIT);
end NAND_Gate;

architecture SimpleNAND of NAND_Gate is
   generic (Prop_Delay:= 20 ns);
begin

   Z <= not (X and Y);
end SimpleNAND;

library work;
configuration StructuralRS of Latch is
for Struct_Latch
   for all NAND_G use
     entity work.Nand_Gate ( SimpleNAND );
   end for;
   for all NOT_G use
     entity  work.Inverter ( Behave_Inv);
   end for;
end for;
end StructuralRS;
```

So far, all the NAND gates and inverters of our model have been identical. This need not be a general rule. For example, suppose the two inverters are different. This may be due to variations in nominally identical components, which we wish to simulate to check for possible race conditions or logic hazards, or due to the use of different components for similar logic functions in different portions of the higher-level device. As a simple example, the TTL hex inverter 7404 has various other "models" such as 74LS04, 74S04, 74HC04, 74HCU04 (an unbuffered version of the CMOS version, for example). Due to price and power consumption considerations, we might find it desirable in some designs to use the 74LS04 for most of the inverters required and use the 74HS04 for one particular component where greater speed is essential.   Let us first assume that the differences between the various inverters can be modeled by merely altering the generic parameter values.

```
entity Latch is
    port( R, S: in BIT; Q, Qbar: out BIT);
end Latch;

architecture Struct_Latch of Latch is
Bsignal Link1, Link2: BIT;
  component NAND_G
    port(X,Y: in BIT; Z: out BIT);
  end NAND_G;
  component NOT_G
    port(Input: in BIT; Output: out BIT);
  end NOT_G;
begin
U1: NOT_Gport map (R, Link1);
U2: NAND_G port map (Link1, Qbar, Q);
U3: NOT_G port map (S, Link2);
U4: NAND_G port map (Link2, Q, Qbar);
end   Struct_Latch;

entity Inverter is
-- Need inverter for out latch model
```

```vhdl
generic (Prop_Delay: TIME :=0 ns);
port (Input: in BIT; Output: out BIT);
end Inverter;


architecture Behave_Inv of Inverter is
begin
Output <= '1' when (Input = '0') else '0'
  after Prop_Delay;
end Behave_Inv;

entity NAND_Gate is
   generic (Prop_Delay: TIME);
   port(X,Y: in BIT; Z: out BIT);
end NAND_Gate;

architecture SimpleNAND of NAND_Gate is
   generic (Prop_Delay:= 20 ns);
begin

   Z <= not (X and Y);
end SimpleNAND;

  library work;
configuration Nand_1  of NAND_Gate is
for Simple_NAND
-- Default sufficient
end for;
end Nand_1;

configuration Not_1  of Inverter is
for Behav_Inv
-- Default sufficient
end for;
end Not_1;

configuration StructuralRS of Latch is
```

```
for Struct_Latch
  for   U2 NAND_G use
    configuration work.Nand_1;
  end for;
  for U1 NOT_G use
    configuration work.Not_1;
    generic map (35 ns);
  end for;
  for others NOT_G use
    configuration work.Nand_1;
    generic map (Prop_Delay => 25 ns);
  end for;
  end for;
end for;
end StructuralRS;
```

In this last example, we have put the generic mapping, in both formats, into the final configuration instead of embedding it in the architecture. This is probably the most convenient place for back-annotation. It allows us to set the propagation delay separately for each gate. This is logical, as the propagation delay will be determined not only by the internal characteristics of the hardware implementation, but also on the fan-out and other characteristics of what the gate is connected to. It makes sense to collect these specifications together for the most convenient updating of these values.

The use of configurations for block will be discussed in the next chapter.

Chapter 5 will discuss the **generate** statement, which may be used to generate components in a regular fashion. Such a command will be useful in specifying structures such as shift registers and memories, as well as the PLDs and FPGAs that feature a number of similar or identical structures.

This chapter is a long one because of the great variety of options available to the user, an illustration of the flexibility of VHDL.

Chapter 4

Blocks and Guards

THE BLOCK

There are two fundamental concurrent statements in VHDL. The process collects together sequential statements that run concurrently as independent processes. The block collects together concurrent processes. For example, the **generate** declaration, when elaborated or turned into effect, results in a block of code. (This is somewhat analogous to how a concurrent signal assignment becomes in effect a process, although that is not called elaboration in the terminology of VHDL because the signal assignment is not viewed as a declaration.) If the body of an architecture is not written as one or more processes, but rather as a number of concurrent statements, it is equivalent to a block. Blocks are also implicitly created by **generate** statements, which are discussed in the next chapter. It is possible in VHDL-92 to use block labels in a hierarchical specification of individual items; see Chapter 10.

Blocks have a structure typical of VHDL constructs:

```
block_label : block   optional_guard
     block_header
     declarative statements
```

```
begin
    concurrent statements
end block block_label;
```

Blocks may be used to organize separately written program units. Blocks may be nested in a hierarchical manner. The user typically may wish to use the block construct only to define a guard or to use the *block_header* portion of the statement to define a generic mapping or a port mapping. Finally, blocks may be labeled, in a manner similar to components, and these labels may be used to distinguish blocks and thereby specify different bindings for the different blocks. Consider this example:

```
OuterB: block
    signal X,Y: BIT; begin
    X <= '0';    Y <= '0'; InnerB: block
        signal Y,Z: BIT
        begin
        Y <= '1'; -- same as InnerB.Y <= '1';
        OuterB.Y <= '1';
        X <= '1';
        end block InnerB;
        --    Z <= '1' would be an error here. In-
ner2: block
        signal Y,Z: BIT
        begin
        Y <= '1'; -- same as Inner2.Y <= '1';
        OuterB.Y <= '1';
        X <= '1';
        end block Inner2;
    end block OuterB;
```

This illustrates a number of aspects of blocks. First, blocks may be nested in a hierarchical manner, as the block labeled InnerB is within that with label OuterB. Note also that declarations, such as those for variables and signals, have visibility and scope limited by the defining block. The signal Z is defined within the inner block only. It would be a mistake to refer to it in any way outside of the defining block. Note that signal X, defined by the outer block, is visible within the inner blocks. Finally, note the signals y. There are actually three distinct signals with that name defined in the example. There is a signal visible throughout the example, which may be referred to as y without ambiguity outside of the nested blocks, but needs to be referred to as OuterB. Y within the blocks to resolve the ambiguity. Within each inner block, a local signal Y is defined. Without additional qualifications, a reference to Y will refer to one of these local signals within the block. Once we have left block InnerB, the local InnerB.Y is no longer defined, and may not be referred to anywhere. The Y local to Inner2 is unrelated to that of InnerB. This example illustrates *overloading* of a symbol, in this case Y. Such overloading is permitted if the potential ambiguities are resolvable at compile-time, that is, using static information.

The previous example was one of a number of hierarchical blocks constructed explicitly by the user. Consider now the unseen blocks that VHDL creates. Suppose you have produced a model device with:

```
entity Entity_Name is
port(Clk, Data inout BIT);
begin
-- concurrent, passive statements allowed
here
CheckSetup(Clk, Data, SetupTime);
CheckHold( Clk, Data, Holdtime );
end Entity_Name;


architecture Implement of Entity_Name is
signal Link: BIT;
begin
Data <= Clk ;
Internal_Block1 : block
   signal Deep: BIT;
   begin
```

```
      Deep <= Clk xor Data ;R? end block;
end Implement;
```

with the declaration:

```
component Comp_Name port ( Clock, Info:
inoutBIT);
```

and the associated configuration specification:

```
for C: Comp_Name use
    -- bind architecture to entity.
    -- See Chapter 3
    entity Entity_Name ( Implement )
    -- map entity formals Clk,
    -- Data to component
    port map ( Clk = Clock, Data = Info );
  end for;
```

and the component instantiation:

```
MyLabel : Comp_Name port map ( Clock = My-
Clock, Info = MyInfo ) ;
```

Here the formals in the component declaration have been mapped to actual signals defined for the section of code containing the instance of component Comp_Name. The following will produce an equivalent instantiation:

```
MyLabel : block
-- component block
port (Clock, Info :inout BIT);
-- bind to actuals
port map (Clock =MyClock, Info =MyInfo);
begin
  Entity_Name:block --design entity block
  port (Clk, Data :inout BIT);
  -- map entity formals port map (Clk =Clock,
Data =Info);
  -- entity declarations would be here
  -- architecture declarations
```

```
   signal Link: BIT;
   begin   -- from entity CheckSetup(Clk, Data,
SetupTime);
   CheckHold( Clk, Data, Holdtime );
   Data <= Clk ;
   Internal_Block1 : block
      signal Deep: BIT;
      begin
         Deep <= Clk xor Data ;R? end block;
   end block;
end block MyLabel;
```

GUARDS

The guard is a boolean expression that defines the signal GUARD. This signal is not permitted to have a source, that is, the user cannot assign values to it. However, the user can employ the boolean signal GUARD, passing it to functions and subroutines, for example. As noted earlier, assignments to guarded signals (those declared with the reserved word **bus** or **register**) must be done with guarded assignments, such as:

```
block_1: block (Enable=' 1' )
   begin
    Signal_1 <= guarded transport ' 1'  after
200 ms;
   end block block_1;
```

Here we have given the block and optional label. The assignment will take place only if GUARD is true, that is, if Enable=' 1' is true. In Chapter 13 on finite-state machines, a **register** signal will be used to retain the state of the machine. This will necessitate the use of guarded signal assignments, and hence the use of block statements to define the guards. Note that processes are not used, since the guarded signal assignment is a concurrent signal assignment, while the signal assignments within processes are sequential statements.

THE DISCONNECT SPECIFICATION

One declarative specification of interest is the **disconnect** statement mentioned previously.

> **disconnect** Signal_1, Signal_2 : Resolved_Type **after** 100 ns;

Here the two signals listed in it are to be disconnected after the given delay time. The default disconnect time is 0 ns. Thus, the guarded assignment will immediately disconnect if the signal GUARD is false. A disconnected signal produces a **null** transaction for the purposes of resolution. This is discussed more fully in Chapter 8.

A guarded assignment to a guarded signal can be viewed as equivalent to a process of the form:

```
process ( guard signals)
begin
    if GUARD then
    signal_assignment;
    else
    disconnection_statement;
    endif;
end process;
```

It is possible to perform a guarded assignment to an unguarded signal; in this case, the else clause is not present, and no disconnection takes place.

Note that if the GUARD is false, the block is not skipped or ignored. Only the behaviors of the guarded signal assignments within are affected. Unguarded, concurrent signal assignments, other processes, etc. may all be within the block and these will be executed whatever the value of GUARD.

BLOCK MAPPINGS

Generic Mapping

Another reason for the use of a block construct is to define generic parameters, such as propagation delay times. Different sets of gates might have different parameters, and might be enclosed with different block headers giving them different properties. The generic map permits assigning values to the generic parameters of a design entity. Thus, it is possible to write:

```
B1: block
generic map(Prop_Delay = 20 ns);
begin
   U1: NAND_Gate port map ( ...); end block;
B2: block
generic map(Prop_Delay = 25 ns);
begin
   U2: NAND_Gate port map ( ...); end block;
```

Port Mapping

A final reason for employing a block statement is to rename port signals. This could be desirable if we were using a number of libraries with inconsistent naming conventions, for example. Remember the *formal => actual* syntax convention. Here, the mapping is of the form *formal => local*. This is illustrated in to some degree in the example given previously showing the elaboration of the entity and architecture within a block. To reinforce this, consider:

```
architecture Blocked of  DEntity is
signal Actual: BITbegin
Bouter:block
port ( OuterP : inout BIT);
port map (OuterP  = Actual);
begin
   Binner:block
   port ( InnerP: inout BIT);
```

```
   port map ( InnerP  = OuterP );
   begin
   U1: Buffer ( InnerP );
   ...
   end Binner;
end Bouter;
```

BLOCK CONFIGURATIONS

It is possible to have configuration statements refer to block labels, and thereby make the instantiation of components different for different blocks. For example:

```
entity Something is
   port ( X: in BIT; Z: out BIT; );
end Something; architecture  Varied ofSometh-
ingis
component Device1
 port ( Input: in BIT; Output: out BIT; );
end component;
signal A,B,C: BIT; begin
 B1: block
begin
   U1: Device1 port map ( X, A );
   U2: Device1 port map ( A, B );
end block
 B2: block
   U1: Device1 port map ( B, C );
   U2: Device1 port map ( C, Z );
begin
end block
end Varied

configuration Embody of Something is
for Varied
```

```
for B1
  for all Device1 use
      configuration My_Lib.Device
          end for;
  end for;
  for B2
    for U2:Device1 use
      configuration Buf_Lib.Device
          for others:  Device1 use
      configuration My_Lib.Device
          end for;
  end for;
end for;
end Embody;
```

This would enable the use of a special buffer model of Device1 as, for example, U2 in block B2.

Chapter 5

Data

DATA IN VHDL

VHDL supports signals, variables, and constants, all of which may have any number of predefined or user-defined data types.

VHDL, like other modern languages, comes with predefined data types, such as integers, and permits users to define their own data structures. It is particularly flexible in permitting the definition and initialization of arrays and similar aggregates. These permit the definition of complicated busses as a single signal.

VHDL-87 specified four classes of data types: *scalar, composite, access,* and *file*. In VHDL-92, files are no longer variables but become their own type of objects, along with signals, variables, and constants. See Chapter 10.

Scalar types have single values and include integers, floating-point, types given physical units such as TIME, and enumerated types. Composite types are either arrays or record types. The latter are data structures defined by the user. Access types are *pointers* to other data objects and are used to refer indirectly to other objects. File types are used to refer to data files. (VHDL has rather limited file input/output abilities.)

Given any data type, it is possible to define subtypes by restricting the values through a *constraint*.

VHDL-92 supports the new reserved word **private**, with which variables and types may be protected from user manipulation except through the use of public subprograms specified in the package. This is similar to the declaration private as used in Ada, C++, and other object-oriented approaches.

PREDEFINED TYPES

A number of types are predefined for user convenience in the STANDARD package. These are INTEGER, REAL, NATURAL, POSITIVE, BIT, BIT_ARRAY, BOOLEAN, CHARACTER, and STRING. These types should generally be familiar to the user, but will be discussed regarding their traits peculiar to VHDL.

NUMBERS AND BASE

The range of allowed integer values is guaranteed to be at least $2^{31} - 1$ to $- (2^{31} - 1)$, that is, -2147483647 to 2147483647. (As a minor point, note that the usual twos-complement representation of numbers will encompass this range and additionally the value -2147483648. Thus, it would be sufficient to use 32-bit twos-complement arithmetic to implement a VHDL simulation.) The standard package goes on to define two subtypes:

subtype NATURAL **is**INTEGER **range** 0 **to INTEGER'HIGH;**

and

subtype POSITIVE **is**INTEGER **range** 1 **to INTEGER'HIGH;**

(Here INTEGER'HIGH uses the predefined attribute 'HIGH to return the largest INTEGER value supported by the implementation. See Chapter 6.) It is interesting to note that a mathematician would call the natural numbers the positive integers, that is, they do not include zero. The usage of this term in VHDL is therefore different from customary usage.

Similarly, floating-point numbers are the predefined REAL type, and must extend to a magnitude of at least 10^{38}, with a precision of at least six decimal digits. Thus, IEEE-Std-754 implementations for single-precision floating point numbers suffice to implement a VHDL simulation. Such numbers have eight bits allocated to the exponent, one sign bit, and 23 additional bits devoted to the mantissa.

The features in Ada to specify base and to segment numbers have been borrowed. Thus, n#m# is the number represented in base m. That is,

15 = 8#17# = 2#1101# = 16#F# = 12#13#

shows a variety of ways to represent the decimal value of 15. A colon (:) may be used in place of the sharp # sign if it is done consistently, for example, 8:17: but not 8:17#. This is intended to permit the use of VHDL with older equipment that might not support the full ASCII character set. Similarly, the vertical bar (|) can be replaced by exclamation mark (!) as a delimiter in choice expressions, and the quotation marks (") may be replaced by the percent sign (%) in character and bit string literal declarations.

The underscore may be used the way the comma is used in English-speaking lands and the period is used in continental countries to break up long digit sequences:

123_456
3.141_592_653_589_793_238462643383279

The underscore is ignored within the number and so its usage is arbitrary.

Because VHDL is strongly typed, automatic type conversions do not occur. It is an error to assign an INTEGER to a REAL or vice versa. There must be an explicit type conversion. This is done in a manner similar to the typecast in the C language.

Range and Subtypes

Types based on integers may be defined as in the example:

type OpCode **is** INTEGER **range**   0 **to** 255;

Note that this is not a subtype declaration, although it could be:

subtype OpCode **of** INTEGER **is** **range**   0 **to** 255;

The difference between these two declarations is that with the latter, OpCode is considered a version of integer and can be used in arithmetic with integers or assigned to an integer variable or signal, while with the former OpCode is a new type and would need a type conversion to do arithmetic with an integer or be assigned to an integer or have an integer assigned to it. This distinction could be useful in preventing erroneous assignments. One use of defining a number of different types would be to prevent accidental misuse. For example, the definitions:

type Address **is** INTEGER **range**   0 **to** 32767;
signal Adrbus: Address;
signal Instrbus: OpCode;

would prevent errors in which a value of type OpCode were assigned to Adrbus, even though it would be within the allowed range. It would be an error to use POSITIVE instead of INTEGER.

Now consider the type definition:

type OpCode2 **is** INTEGER **range**   255 **downto** 0;

This type would have a range spanning the same values as OpCode, but it would behave somewhat differently. In the loop:

for I **in** Instrbus' RANGE **loop;**
... **end loop;**

the loop index variable I will sequence through the values 0, 1, 2, . . . whereas if Instrbus were defined to be of type OpCode2 it would sequence through the values 255, 254, . . . down to zero.

It is an error if one attempts to change the direction of a subtype from its base type. It is also an error if the subtype does not fit within the range constraints of the type from which it is derived.

Operations and Expressions

The usual operators +, −, *, / are supported for the REAL type and, with the exception of /, for the INTEGER type. The exponentiation operator ** is defined for type INTEGER exponents. In addition, for INTEGERS, the **mod** and **rem** reserved words determine the modulus and remainder. The reserved word operator **abs** is also predefined for numeric types such as INTEGER and REAL.

The **rem** operator is defined by a = (a/b)*b + a **rem** b, where a **rem** has the sign of A and an absolute value less than that of b. The same operator is present in Ada. For example 7/5 =1 = −7/(−5), −7/5 = 7/(−5) = −1, therefore:

```
 7 rem  5 =  2
-7 rem  5 = -2
 7 rem -5 =  2
-7 rem -5 = -2
```

The a **mod** b operation, on the other hand, has the sign of b and an absolute value less than that of b, such that a = b*n + a **mod** b for some integer n. Thus:

```
 7 mod  5 =  2 (n =  1)
-7 mod  5 =  3 (n = -2)
 7 mod -5 = -3 (n = -2)
-7 mod -5 = -2 (n =  1)
```

ENUMERATED TYPES

An enumerated type is a set of values. The STANDARD package gives us a number of predefined enumerated types. The most familiar is:

```
type BIT is ('0', '1');
```

type BOOLEAN **is** (FALSE, TRUE);

Another predefined enumerated type in the standard package is type CHARACTER. Type BIT makes use of two of the characters in type CHARACTER.

We have used such types already, such as:

type State **is** (Set, Reset);

which was used in one of our models of latch in Chapter 3.

Enumerated types are of great utility in making code more readable and self-documenting. They make it possible to assign meaningful English words or mnemonics, such as machine opcodes, to a set.

See Chapter 6 for a discussion of the various attributes that may be used with enumerated types. For example, if we want to construct a loop over all the possible values of an enumerated type, we could use:

for   I **in** State' RANGE   **loop**
. . .
end loop;

Here the variable I is automatically defined within the scope of this loop and will take on the values of the enumerated type. In addition, there are attributes for use with enumerated types such as ' FIRST, ' LAST, ' NEXT, ' POS (X), ' VAL (X).

The definition of BOOLEAN was chosen with FALSE first so that it would be assigned the integer value 0, that is, BOOLEAN' POS (FALSE) =0. Also, BOOLEAN' POS (TRUE) =1, BOOLEAN' NEXT (FALSE) =TRUE, BOOLEAN' VAL (0) =FALSE are examples of attributes applied to enumerated types.

In C, it is possible to assign the values of each type, that is, they are not necessarily integers based at 0 and increasing by one between successive elements. Thus, if the enumerated type were to represent opcodes, the actual hexadecimal values could be assigned to them, with gaps in the sequence skipped. In VHDL, this flexibility is not present.

VHDL-92 provides shift operations for arrays of BIT and BOOLEAN values; see Chapter 10. These binary operators are:

sll   shift left logical
srl   shift right logical
sla   shift left arithmetic
sra   shift right arithmetic
rol   rotate left logical
ror   rotate right logical

The operand to the right of the operator is an INTEGER, while the value to be shifted must be a one-dimensional array whose element type is either BIT or BOOLEAN. The integer is the number of bits to shift, and need not be positive. Fill values are T'Left. The sla operator preserves L'Right, the rightmost element of the array, while the sra operator preserves the value of L'Left, the leftmost element, as well as using this element value to fill the adjacent element as the shift progresses.

LOGICAL OPERATIONS AND TYPE BOOLEAN

VHDL supports the type BOOLEAN discussed above through the STANDARD package. It supports a number of logical operations on BOOLEAN, BIT, and BIT_VECTOR operands, indeed on any one-dimensional array whose element type is BIT or BOOLEAN (LRM 7.2.1). The operations supported are **and, or, nor, nand, nor, not, xor**.

The operators **and, or, nand, nor** are all short-circuited. This means that if the value of the expression can be determined from the first operand only, the second operand is not evaluated. Thus, in the expression A **and** B, if A is FALSE or ' 0' , the expression is FALSE or ' 0' without reference to the value of B.

VHDL-92 adds the negated exclusive or, or **xnor** operator. It is true whenever the two variables have the same truth value, either both TRUE or both FALSE.

Relational operators, such as = (equality), /= (inequality), <, <=, >, >= return BOOLEAN results.

UNITS

VHDL provides the feature of *physical* variables, that is, variables
that have units. The predefined TIME in the STANDARD package is
an example. Presumably, it was felt that for little extra effort in
compiler development, this could be made a general feature. One
can define variables that have units such as length, area, and so on.
For example, TIME is defined via:

```
type time is range implementation_defined
units
    fs;             -- femtosecond
    ps = 1000 fs;   -- picosecond
    ns = 1000 ps;   -- nanosecond
    us = 1000 ns;   -- microsecond
    ms = 1000 us;   -- millisecond
    sec = 1000 ms;  -- second
    min = 60 sec;   -- minute
    hr = 60 min;    -- hour end units;
```

Because of the strong typing of VHDL, the utility is somewhat
limited. You cannot multiply a velocity by a time to get distance,
or two lengths together to obtain an area, for example. Here seconds
are the *base type*, and the other units are *secondary units*. The secondary types must be integer multiples of the base type. One can
multiply physical types by pure numbers, type REAL or INTEGER,
and divide by type INTEGER. One can also use the type conversion feature to convert physical types to pure numbers, and then
convert back to a physical type by the same technique. Aside from
being unaesthetic, such computations are probably of limited use.

ARRAY TYPES

Arrays are composite objects. They consist of elements of a single
type. A particular element within an array may be selected by specifying an index value, which belongs to a discrete type such as INTEGER
or an enumerated type. Example array definitions of an array are:

```
type Word is array ( 0 to 31 ) of BIT;

type Word2 is array ( 31 downto 0 ) of BIT;

type General_Word is array (INTEGER range
<> ) of BIT;
```

The declaration of General_Word is an *unconstrained* array. The symbol <> is called a *box*. The size will have to be specified for each variable or signal declared to be of this type, for example:

```
variable Cray_Word: Word ( 1: 64) ;
```

Needless to say, it is an error to fail to give such a dimension to an instantiation of such an array.

Multi-dimensional arrays are allowed, with syntax as in Ada:

```
type Word2d is array ( 31 downto 0 , 0 to
19 ) of BIT;
```

which may then be used in statements such as

```
Word2d ( 5, 3) := 1;
```

Array Initialization

Array initialization is the same as in Ada. Thus,

```
type Day_of_Week is
(Mon,Tues,Wed,Thur,Fri,Sat,Sum);
type Date_Array is array (
Day_of_Week' RANGE ) of INTEGER;
constant Dates : Date_Array := (
0,1,2,3,4,5,6,7);
```

The data on the right-hand side of the assignment operator := is an array *aggregate*. Aggregates are collected values used to produce a composite value of a record or array type.

The following code fragment illustrates three different methods of using array aggregates.

```
type MVL5 is ( ' 0' , ' 1' , ' X' , ' Z' , ' U' );
type MVL5Array is array ( MVL5 ) of BIT;
constant A_MVL5: MVL5Array :=
( ' 0' ,' 1' ,' 1' ,' 0' ,' 0' );
constant A_MVL5: MVL5Array :=
( ' 0' =>' 0' ,' 1' =>' 1' ,' X' =>' 1' ,Z=>' 0' ,' U' =>' 0' );
constant A_MVL5: MVL5Array :=
( ' 1' |' x' =>' 1' , others=>' 0' );
constant A_MVL5: MVL5Array := (" 01100" );
```

Note the use of the vertical bar (|) to "or" choices, the use of the reserved word **others**, and the use of an enumerated type as the index of the array. The length of the range of the enumerated type gives the range of allowed indices for the array. The final example uses a string literal to specify an array of type CHARACTER, which is a shortcut legal in VHDL.

For a two-dimensional array, the data is stored row by row:

```
type Date_Array2 is array (
Day_of_Week' RANGE , 0 to 2 ) of INTEGER;
constant Dates2 : Date_Array2 := (
    (0,1,2),
    (3,4,5),
    (6,7,8),
    (9,10,11),
    (12,13,14),
    (15,16,17),
    (18,19,20),
    );
```

The order is similar to that in C, with the first index changing the most slowly. However, it is described as array aggregates, that is, sub-arrays (vectors in this case) of lower dimensionality, not as individual elements as in C. It is unlike the FORTRAN DATA statement in which the ordering is "row-major," i. e., the first index varies most rapidly, and which treats the array as a collection of elements instead of as a collection of sub-arrays.

Type STRING

The STRING is a predefined array of CHARACTERs:

type STRING **is array** (POSITIVE **range** <>)
of CHARACTER;

Thus, we can create strings such as:

variable NAME: STRING(30);
   subtype WORD **is** STRING(25);
   variable Words, Message: WORD;

Because of the strong typing of VHDL, attempting to set

Message:=NAME;

will fail.

Concatenation

The & operator may be used to concatenate any array type with either another array of similar type or with an element of that array. Thus, it is possible to add a CHARACTER to either end of a STRING, or join two STRINGs together. Note that care has to be taken because of VHDL's strong typing to insure that the resultant string is assigned to a STRING of the correct length.

Slices

It is possible to refer to contiguous portions of an array as a *slice* of the array. Thus

type IEEE754 **is array** (31 **downto** 0) of BIT;
type Mant754 **is array** (23 **downto** 0) of
BIT; **variable** FloatNum: IEEE754;

```
variable Mantissa: Mant754;
variable Sign: BIT;
Mantissa := FloatNum (23 downto 0 );-- Man-
tissa slice:
Sign := FloatNum (31 downto 31 );-- slice
of 1 element
Sign := FloatNum (31);-- single element as-
signment
```

Applications of One- and Two-Dimensional Arrays

Arrays have a great many uses in VHDL. One-dimensional arrays are useful in applying the **generate** statement, which will be discussed at the end of this chapter.

Multi-dimensional arrays are useful in a number of circumstances. One is in modeling gates in a multi-valued logic (MVL), which will be discussed. For a gate with two inputs, a simple table look-up in a two-dimensional array will provide an efficient implementation of such a gate. A table look-up for an n-input gate obviously requires an n-dimensional array. This approach becomes impractical for large values of n, as a great deal of storage is needed and the array will likely have to be generated automatically. Such a description is obviously behavioral, which makes perfect sense because the logic levels are often representations not of physical levels, such as voltage or current, but of situations, such as *don't care* or *uninitialized*.

Another use of arrays is in state tables for finite state machines, which will also be discussed in Chapter 13. A look-up table based on a two-dimensional array, with the two indices being current state and input, will provide an implementation method that can be quite efficient in computer and personnel time. A state table is generally a necessary step in the design of a finite state machine, so no additional work is needed except to transfer the information into a VHDL model.

In each of these suggested applications, the use of **constant** arrays is recommended. Examples will be given as discussed, where appropriate. The bottom line is that arrays can be very useful.

ACCESS TYPES, NEW

Many languages permit the definition of variables that refer to other variables. These variables contain the address or memory location of the variable being referenced. VHDL and Ada call these variables *access* types. Languages such as Pascal, C/C++, and FORTRAN 90 call them pointers.

Access types are of interest only for behavioral simulation. There is no hardware equivalent to them; silicon real estate cannot be allocated and deallocated from a heap of sand! Their major use will be seen to be in higher-order behavioral simulation, for modeling event queues and other constructs for which dynamic data structures are indispensable.

A typical declaration would be:

```
type DATUM is INTEGER:=0;
 type DATUM_PTR is access DATUM;
variable DATUMPointer: DATUM_PTR;
```

This would be employed by executing the sequential code:

```
DATUMPointer := new DATUM;
```

which creates a new DATUM, that is, it allocates storage for an object with the appropriate size, and initializes it as specified. DATUMPointer points to that variable; it contains its address and may be used to reference it. Here, we can refer to the single value associated by DATUMPointer by constructs such as:

```
DATUMPointer.all := 3;
```

In general, access types will not be pointers to scalar types but rather will refer to records. This will be discussed in the next section.

The procedure DEALLOCATE() is automatically defined by the declaration of the associated access type. Thus, the sequential statement:

```
DEALLOCATE( DATUMPointer );
```

will free the storage allocated to the datum and erase the pointer value.

Obviously, attempting to use an uninitialized pointer, such as using DATUMPointer before the assignment or immediately after the DEALLOCATE and before a reallocation, should result in an error. The value **null** is implicitly defined for any access type, and any attempt to access through a null-valued pointer will result in an error. The value **null** may be assigned to an access variable (pointer).

Note that only variables, not signals, may be access types.

Access types to arrays are allowed. For example, the predefined TEXIO package, discussed in Chapter 10, uses a pointer to a STRING, which is a predefined array. Thus, one could write

```
type DATA is array (INTEGER range 0 to8 )
of INTEGER;
 type DATA_PTR is access DATA;
variable DATAPointer: DATA_PTR;
```

with usage such as:

```
 DATAPointer := new DATA; @CODE =   DATAPoin-
ter.all(2)  := 3;
```

RECORD TYPES

VHDL, like Ada and Pascal, supports the record type, which is similar to the *struct* concept of C. The version in VHDL is less general than that of Ada, as it does not support discriminants or variant parts. Thus, it is much closer to the C *struct*.

A typical record declaration would be:

```
type Customer is
   record
      variable Name, Address: STRING(30);
      variable Income: INTEGER;
   end record;
```

with typical usage:

```
type Customer_Ptr is access Customer;
 variable New_Acct, Old_Acct: Customer_Ptr;

New_Acct := new Customer;
New_Acct.Income := 15000;
New_Acct.Name :="
Mark";
Old_Acct :=New_Acct
```

Incomplete Type Declarations

Often, we need a data structure with records containing pointers to other, similar records. This happens whenever we use linked lists, doubly-linked lists, queues and double-ended queues (dequeues), stacks, and any of the various forms of tress. How can we define a pointer to an object that has not been declared yet? Obviously we can't. The solution is a mechanism provided in most languages called the incomplete declaration. Here we merely declare the object type exists, with the details contained in a full declaration that is promised to come later. Thus, our problem is solved by code of the form:

```
type Node ; -- the incomplete declaration
type Node_Ptr is access Node;

type Node is
   record
      variable Name, Address: STRING(30);
      variable Income: INTEGER;
      variable Next: Node_Ptr; end record;
```

We could then form a linked-list or a stack of Nodes. Examples of the usage of such data structures will be given in Chapter 11. They are typically called *dynamic* data structures as they are dynamically allocated and deallocated with time, in contrast to *static* structures which do not change during the simulation.

VARIABLES

Variables, unlike signals, have only a current value associated with them. Furthermore, assignments to variables occur immediately. Finally, variables are much simpler and more easily dealt with than signals. A variable with multiple assignments would not require a resolution function that a signal with multiple sources would require. Thus, if a signal could be replaced by a variable, the resultant code would compile faster, occupy less storage, and probably execute more rapidly (depending on how well the compiler optimized). Variables have little role in structural simulations, however, as they do not correlate well with hardware constructs. Therefore, variables are of most interest in behavioral, high-level simulations. Properly used, they can increase the speed and efficiency of such simulations.

Variables have limited scope. Processes live forever, so variables defined in a process do not lose their value. However, a variable defined in a function or procedure will not be remembered between calls to that procedure.

CONSTANTS

A constant may be declared and used where a variable or signal might occur. An example is included above in the initialization of a two-dimensional array. Obviously, constants must be assigned a value at compilation time. This value may not be altered by an assignment, directly or indirectly. VHDL will carefully enforce this constraint.

For each access type defined, the function Deallocate() is implicitly defined for this type. This permits the deletion of newly allocated objects of the type, allowing users to do their own memory management.

LABELS

In Chapter 3, we gave many examples of components carrying labels to distinguish them from other components. In Chapter 4, blocks were shown to be capable of being labeled as well, for similar purposes. Labels are not strictly data types in VHDL. They can arise as data in an attribute statement, where a construct such as:

attribute POSITION **of** U2:**label is** Position1;

would assign the value Position1 as the attribute POSITION of the component with label U2. This is apparently the only situation in which the declarative reserved word **label** might occur. It is used here to alert VHDL to the fact that U2 is a label, and is needed because the label itself will follow the code with the attribute specification. Thus, U2 in the previous example will not have been encountered previously, and it is an aid to the compiler as well as another consistency check to have it declared to be a label.

Labels can also be assigned to sequential statements, such as loops. The major benefit of this is to make the code more readable, particularly if there are a number of nested loops. These sequential statements will be discussed in Chapter 7.

Aliasing, Big- and Little-endian

The alias declaration permits renaming objects or parts of objects. A common use might be to rename portions of the instruction as to opcode, address, and so forth. A different alias might be useful for each instruction format. Consider, for example, the instruction formats of the MIPS R2000-R4000 architectures. Define:

variable Instruction: BIT_VECTOR(31 **downto** 0);

Then:

alias Op: BIT_VECTOR **is**
    Instruction(31 **downto** 26);

```
alias Rs: BIT_VECTOR is
Instruction(25 downto 21);
alias Rt: BIT_VECTOR is
Instruction(20 downto 16);
alias Im: BIT_VECTOR is
Instruction(15 downto  0);
alias Target: BIT_VECTOR is
Instruction(25 downto 0);
alias Rd: BIT_VECTOR is
Instruction(15 downto 11);
alias shamt: BIT_VECTOR is
Instruction(10 downto  6);
alias funct: BIT_VECTOR is
Instruction( 5 downto  0);
```

Note that we are using the **downto** reserved word to specify a little-endian bit ordering. We follow the terminology of Dewar and Smosna, who discuss this processor and define little-endian bit ordering to be one in which the least significant bit is the 0 bit on the right-hand side of a linear representation of the data word. In the present example, the original variable and the alias are both in little-endian order. The alias declaration may be used to effect a conversion from little-endian to big-endian order. The MIPS R2000 is an interesting example on this topic since its address ordering is determined by an input signal at reset time. The Intel i860 has a software instruction to change the data ordering. This does not change the bit field numbering in the ordering in instructions, as defined above. That data ordering can be a concern when serial data transfer is occurring between machines, for example. Ethernet, for example, specifies little-endian or least significant bit first. The XDR protocol for data exchange specifies a big-endian data ordering. The Motorola 68030 uses big-endian byte and bit-field ordering, but according to Dewar and Smosna the documentation is little-endian in its representation.

An example of such a use would be:

> **variable** XDRInteger: BYTE_VECTOR(0 **to** 3);

Then:

> **alias** LEInteger: BYTE_VECTOR **is**
>   XDR(3 **downto** 0);

defines a little-endian ordered integer. The most significant byte of this integer datum may be addressed as either XDRInteger(0) or LEInteger(3).

Aliases are not permitted for arrays with multiple dimensions (LRM 4.3.4). Note also that the identifier aliased must be a static name denoting an object. We cannot, for example, define a type to be the little-endian version of another, big-endian type.

Alias provides another name for an object which has been declared already. It is unlike the FORTRAN *equivalence*, which connects two previously declared objects, or the C *union* declaration, which declares the overlaying of structures in storage, and which will precede the declarations of any actual objects of the type defined by the union.

VHDL-92 generalizes the permitted usage of alias. See Chapter 10.

TYPE CONVERSION

Because of VHDL's strong typing, one cannot simply multiply numbers of type REAL and type INTEGER, for example. Many languages, such as FORTRAN and C, automatically make such a conversion, but not VHDL. The solution is an explicit type conversion (LRM 7.3.5), which is of the form:

type_mark (*expression*)

It is therefore possible to write code such as:

```
variable X : REAL;
variable Rounded : INTEGER;
...
Rounded := INTEGER ( X + 0.5 )
```

THE GENERATE STATEMENT

According to the LRM, Section 9.7, "A generate statement provides
a mechanism for iterative or conditional elaboration of a portion of
a description." The generate statement was intended to reduce the
tedium and effort required to define a device with a repetitive pattern. Because of its ability to handle conditional expressions to control the generation, it can be useful in other situations. VHDL-92
introduces hierarchical pathnames to permit the specification of individual objects generated; see Chapter 10.

Arrays and the Generate Statement

Consider, for example, the construction of a shift register from a
number of connected D-type flip-flops. These have one input, D,
instead of two as in the RS latch, and are clocked or synchronous
devices. In addition, they are often edge-triggered, that is, they latch
the value of D at the clock transition, and do not respond to changes
in the D input thereafter.

```
entity Shift_Register is
     generic (Stages: POSITIVE:=8); port (   In-
put, Clock :   in BIT;
        Output: out BIT);
     end Shift_Register;


architecture Serial_Reg of Shift_Register is
component DFlipFlop
   port ( D, Clk: in BIT;
        ( Q, Qbar: out BIT);
end component;
signal Links : BIT_VECTOR ( 0 to Stages);
begin
Links(0) <= Input;
-- Prepare to Connect input to
-- first flip-flop
```

```
U1: for Index in 0 to ( Stages - 1 ) gener-
ate
   Regff: DFlipFlop
      port map ( Links(Index), Clk = Clock, Links
(Index + 1) , open);
end generate;
Output <= Links ( Stages);-- connect to out-
put end Serial_Reg;
```

Note that we have left the Qbar outputs **open** (unused) in this
simple design. Note the use of the generic parameter Stages to allow our design to use an arbitrary number of stages. To illustrate
the use of conditionals, the former design may be altered slightly:

```
entity Shift_Register is
     generic (Stages: POSITIVE:=8);
     port (  Input, Clock :  in BIT;
        Output: out BIT);
     end Shift_Register;


architecture Serial_Reg of Shift_Register is
component DFlipFlop
   port ( D, Clk: in BIT;
        ( Q, Qbar: out BIT);
end component;
signal Links :
   BIT_VECTOR ( 0 to ( Stages - 2 ));
begin

U1: for Index in 0 to ( Stages - 1 )
   generate
   if Index = 0 generate
   -- connects Input to D, Q to Links(0)
     RegIn: DFlipFlop
        port map ( Input, Clock,
           Links ( Index ) , open);
   end generate;
```

```
if (( Index /= 0 ) and (Index /= ( Stages -
1 )) )
generate
   RegIn: DFlipFlop
   -- internal connections only
   -- first time, Index =1,
   -- D= Links(0), Q = Links(1)
      port map (Links ( Index - 1) , Clock,
         Links ( Index ) , open);
end generate;

if Index = ( Stages - 1 ) generate
   -- connect last flip-flop Q to Output;
   RegOut: DFlipFlop
         port map ( Links (Index -1) ,Clock,
            Output , open);
end generate;
end generate;
end Serial_Reg;
```

Note that it is allowable to label blocks (component instantiations in this example) in a **generate** statement. This does not produce multiple declarations of the label (LRM 12.4.2). Instead, these are taken as "multiple references to the same implicitly declared label." Thus, a reference to this label would be a reference to all of the generated devices in our example. We have given our flip-flops connected to device ports different labels, as we might want to instantiate different architectures here. The internal D flip-flops have fan-out and fan-in counts of 1, whereas the flip-flop used for the RegOut component might have to be a different model, with higher fan-out capacity, or perhaps tri-state output and different propagation delay as a result. Similarly, it might be desirable to specify a different model flip-flop for the input, with lower input capacitance for lower loading of any devices connected to it. Such a device might again have different propagation delays or other characteristics.

For completeness, we provide a behavioral description of a D-type flip-flop. If you are curious about the **process** statement, see Chapter 8. This flip-flop is edge-triggered; it will only change state when Clk transitions to ' 1' from ' 0' . It is left as an exercise for the reader to include generic parameters for propagation delay, and to enforce setup and hold times. Such refinements will await the discussion of attributes in Chapter 6 and the process statement in Chapter 8.

```
entity DFlipFlop is port ( D, Clk: in BIT;
          ( Q, Qbar: out BIT);
end DFlipFlop;
architecture DFF of DFlipFlop is
variable State: BIT; begin
process (Clk) -- explicit sensitivity list
   -- Only activated for event on Clk, i. e.
edge triggered if (Clk=' 1' ) then
   -- only when clock is high are inputs active
   State := D;
   Q <= State;
   Qbar <= not State;
end if;
end DFF;
```

Note that the code generated must be concurrent code, that is, processes or blocks. It can be behavioral, as with processes, or structural, as in the instantiation of components.

Conditional Compilation with the Generate Statement

While VHDL does not have the powerful C preprocessor, with its #define, #ifdef, and so forth, conditional compilation can be implemented with the generate statement. An obvious application for this is to insert various diagnostic or debugging statements that may be activated only as needed. The conditional **generate** statement may be used for this purpose. The highest level design entity or test-bed could include generic parameters or constants to turn on debugging. Thus:

```
type Verbose is BOOLEAN;
variable Slack: TIME; constant Holdtime:
TIME:= 3 ns; entity Object is
   generic  ( Debug: Verbose; ...
end Object;

. . .
wait on Data; Diagnose1: if Debug generate
-- User-implemented trace with additional in-
formation:d
WRITE(L," At label Diagnose1 at ");
WRITE(L,NOW);WRITELINE(L);
Slack := (NOW-Clock' LASTEVENT)  - Holdtime;
WRITE(L," Slack is ");
WRITE(L,Slack);WRITELINE(L);
end generate;
```

If Debug is TRUE, this code will tell us where we are and how
much leeway we have to meet the minimum hold requirements on
the Data signal of interest. This quantitative information may be of
use in early design stages where we are optimizing design trade-
offs. In later stages, the extra output might be undesirable, and a test
merely to insure that proper setup and hold conditions are being met
would suffice.

REFERENCE

Dewar, R., and Smosna, M., *Microprocessors*, (N.Y.: McGraw-Hill,
1990).

Chapter 6

Attributes

An attribute is a characteristic of a variable or type. VHDL permits the user to easily determine such attributes. Ada pioneered the use of attributes for various types. It is a feature that C/C++ would benefit from. Attributes have the syntax T'ATTRIBUTE where T is the name of the object for which the attribute is to be obtained. Some attributes have an additional parameter, which may be optional, with a form T'ATTRIBUTE(X). A number of examples will make this clear. The user can define attributes. These are somewhat limited in power because they are only local data. Attributes have associated declarations and specifications. The former define the data type; the latter assign the values of the attribute for the associated object.

VHDL-92 introduces the *group* declaration, which collects objects that may be assigned the same attribute. It also introduces the implementation-dependent attribute ' FOREIGN. The attributes ' PATH_NAME and ' SIMPLE_NAME are introduced for use with hierarchical pathnames. ' DRIVING and ' DRIVING_VALUE provide information on signal drivers. ' IMAGE creates a type STRING value for a scalar type, and could be used for TEXTIO. ' VALUE(X) is the inverse of ' IMAGE, returning a value for the type given by the string X. ' ASCENDING(N) returns a Boolean value for a constrained array subtype depending which is TRUE if the Nth index has an ascending range. See Chapter 10.

PREDEFINED ATTRIBUTES

Attributes for Enumerated Types

There are a number of attributes of value for use with enumerated types. Suppose we have defined:

type Five_State_Logic **is**
   ('0' ,' 1' ,' Z' ,' X' ,' U');
   variable State: Five_State_Logic;

Then we have an attribute for the successor of a value in the enumeration list, 'SUCC, for which:

Five_State_Logic' SUCC (' 1') =' Z'

for example. This illustrates the general form. There is an attribute for the predecessor:

Five_State_Logic' PRED (' 1') =' 0'

Attempting to find the predecessor of' 0' or the successor of ' U' will produce errors. A few other attributes of interest:

Five_State_Logic' LOW=' 0'
Five_State_Logic' HIGH=' U'
Five_State_Logic' LEFTOF (' 1') =' 0'
Five_State_Logic' RIGHTTOF (' 1') =' Z'

The ' LEFTOF and ' RIGHTOF attributes are not redundant with the ' PRED and ' SUCC attributes respectively, although they are for the enumerated type. They will be opposites; ' LEFTOF will correspond to ' SUCC instead of ' PRED for types defined with ordering specified by the **downto** reserved word. There are attributes ' LEFT and ' RIGHT that behave similarly with respect to ' LOW and ' HIGH.

Two attributes that are the inverse of one another are ′ POS and ′ VAL, which enable us to go between enumerated types and integers:

```
Five_State_Logic' POS (' 1' ) =  1
```

```
Five_State_Logic' VAL (1) =' 1'
```

Note that, for an enumerated type T, T′ VAL (T′ LOW) = 0. For subtypes of integers, this will not be the case; instead, the integer-valued types T'VAL(X)=X. The attributes will often be of value for input and output purposes, for which integer values are required.

The attributes 'RANGE and 'REVERSE_RANGE may be applied to array objects, and return a range value. These attributes allow constructing loops that index through all values in the range of the object.

The attribute 'LENGTH may be applied to an array object to get the size of the array, that is, A'HIGH-A'LOW+1 for a one-dimensional array. For a multi-dimensional array, use 'LENGTH(N) to find the length of the Nth index of the array. The utility of this for constructing loops and dimensioning array slices is obvious.

Attributes for Signal Types

VHDL allows the attribute prefix to be a signal in some cases. This enables the user to easily determine a number of characteristics of interest, without the user having to keep track. For a given signal S,

S'TRANSACTION

defines a signal that has an event whenever S has had a transaction. This is clearly the purpose of the signal, to turn transactions into events. It is implemented as a signal of type BIT, which toggles between the values of '0' and '1' whenever there is a transaction on the signal S. It is not defined at the beginning of the simulation. Therefore, you should not check its value, but rather use it to signal transactions on S by changing them to events of the implicitly defined signal S′ TRANSACTION.

S′ TRANSACTION is implemented by defining a signal that is updated by performing a signal assignment equivalent to

S′ TRANSACTION <= **not** S′ TRANSACTION;

Obviously, only one such assignment must be done per simulation cycle, if we are not to nullify the effect of toggling the signal value.

The attribute

S′ EVENT

defines a Boolean value that is true if an event (a transaction that changes the signal's value) has occurred during the current simulation cycle. Because of the *delta* time advances possible in VHDL at any time, there may have been an event at the current time, but not during the current cycle if one or more *deltas* have transpired. The principal application of the ′ EVENT attribute is model edge-triggered devices. Clk′ EVENT will be true only for the simulation cycle on which signal Clk has had an event, say a transition from ′ 0′ to ′ 1′. As Clk continues to be ′ 1′, no matter how many simulation cycles follow, S′ EVENT will be FALSE and when used in a guard expression will prevent recalculation of signals.

The S′ ACTIVE Boolean corresponds to S'EVENT except that it refers to transactions rather than events. It differs from S'TRANS-ACTION in that the latter is of type BIT and toggles, whereas S'ACTIVE is, like S'EVENT, of type BOOLEAN. One can find similar attributes for a specified period of time instead of merely for the current simulation cycle, using:

S′ STABLE (T)

to return a Boolean value that is true if there has been no event, (that is, no change of value) within the specified time interval T, and

S′ QUIET (T)

to return the same information regarding transactions on S.

S'STABLE(T) is implemented in a manner equivalent to the VHDL code:

```
wait on S;
  S' STABLE(T) <= FALSE;
  S' STABLE(T) <= TRUE after T;
```

Therefore, S'STABLE (0 ns) = **not** S'ACTIVE.

S'QUIET(T) may be implemented in a similar manner:

```
wait on S' TRANSACTION;
  S' QUIET(T) <= FALSE;
  S' QUIET(T) <= TRUE after T;
```

Notice that if a number of signals of the form S'STABLE(T) or S'QUIET(T) are required for different values of T, these in general will require the same number of different implicit signals to keep the event queues separate.

The TIME-valued functions

```
S' LAST_EVENT S' LAST_ACTIVE
```

return the elapsed time since the last event and the last transaction, respectively. Note that time intervals, not the simulation time of the last event or transaction, are returned.

```
S' DELAYED(T)
```

returns the value of the signal S delayed by a time interval T, that is S(NOW-T) where the function S(t) gives the time behavior of S. It is equivalent to the user defining a process of the form:

```
process(S)
  begin
  S' DELAYED <= transport S after T;
end process;
```

Notice that, if and event has occurred on S in the current simulation cycle, S' DELAYED(0 ns) /= S. In fact, S' STABLE(0 ns) = (S = S' DELAYED(0 ns)). Some care should therefore be taken if ' DELAYED(X) is used in a manner in which X might be zero. Because X must be of type TIME, it cannot be negative; non-causal delays cannot be specified, and negative values of TIME are not allowed in VHDL.

Finally, the attribute:

S' LAST_VALUE

returns the previous value of the signal, that is, the most recent value it had that was different from the current value, if there is such a value. If not, S' LAST_VALUE = S.

For a composite signal, these functions generally do the obvious thing. A transaction or event on a portion of the signal is accounted as such an occurrence on the signal as a whole.

These Boolean attributes were of interest in VHDL-87

Label' BEHAVIOR
Label' STRUCTURE

These may be applied to the architecture name of any entity or to a block label. 'BEHAVIOR is true if there is no component instantiation statement within the specified object, otherwise it is false. 'STRUCTURE is true if the object contains neither a non-passive process nor a concurrent statement that is equivalent to a non-passive process; otherwise it is false. Note that these two attributes are not antonyms, for they can simultaneously be true or false. They were probably not of great utility, and were dropped from VHDL-92.

USER-DEFINED ATTRIBUTES

Users are permitted to define their own attributes. User-defined attributes are "constants of arbitrary types." User-defined attributes are therefore much more limited in power than many of the predefined attributes. On the other hand, attributes may apply to an entity, architecture, configuration, procedure, function, package, type, subtype, constant, signal, variable, component, or label. Omitted from this list are access types, which cannot have attributes, and file types, which could not have attributes in VHDL-87. VHDL-92 adds literals, and the keyword **literal**, to allow literals to be assigned attributes. VHDL-92 also permits attributed to be assigned to units, groups, and files.

Consider as an example the version number of a microprocessor. The Intel 80386 came in a number of versions or "steps." The B0 step implemented the instructions XBTS (Extract Bit String) and IBTS (Insert Bit String). At step B1 these instructions were deleted because of a need to free up area on the mask. The opcodes were later assigned to the CMPXCHG instruction. In current 486's and 386's, XBTS and IBTS opcodes will cause an invalid opcode exception. Suppose we were to define an enumerated type for the step value of the CPU:

```
type Version is (B0,B1,D0,Later);
```

Suppose now we had a variety of 386's in a multiple-CPU simulation. Perhaps we are concerned about the compatibility of these different processors and that concern motivates the simulation. Then we might have code of the form:

```
attribute Step : Version;
architecture DifferentSteps of MultiCPU is
component i386
port ( CPUStep: in Step; ...)
   ...end component
attribute Step of CPU1:label is B1;
attribute Step of CPU2:label is D0;
  attribute Step of CPU3:label is B0;
begin
CPU1: i386 port map  (CPUStep => CPU1' Step,
...);
CPU2: i386 port map  (CPUStep => CPU2' Step,
...);
CPU3: i386 port map  (CPUStep => CPU3' Step,
...);
end;
```

This architecture will enable us to tell each i386 model to behave differently based on which component it is. The attribute i386'Step may be passed to the component by a signal, for example, informing it which step it is.

Note that when the attribute is first encountered, the names CPU1, CPU2, CPU3 are not yet defined. VHDL must be informed in the attribute statement that this will be a label to be encountered later if it is to make the attribute assignment.

Although we have used the Intel 386 as an example, this sort of variation occurs with many microprocessors, and it is often sensible to handle the relatively minor differences without resorting to different models for each CPU version. For example, the MIPS x000 family is implemented by a number of different manufacturers with different chip sets: there will be variations in the behavior of each version of, say, a MIPS R3000. As another example, the MIL-STD-1750A processors are allowed to have additional instructions, called built-in functions, beyond the mandated instruction set. Different manufactures implement different built-in functions. This, and other options and variations such as the clock count for instructions, will vary among manufacturers. The variations are probably largest for the 1750A family, but there might be some advantage in a single model for a number of versions even for this CPU.

An Imperfect Example

Another example might be to associate an area with each architecture employed in the design. This would enable us to check the footprint of the device. Such a check might help us spot errors in complex designs in which a functional unit is repeated many times, as in a PLA, memory, and so forth. Such information is most naturally associated with the architecture specification, since a given entity might have a number of associated architectures, each embodying a different technology or implementation strategy (one optimized for speed, another for space, etc.). Thus:

```
type Area is   units
   nms;
-- 10**(-12) meters-squared = 1 sq. micron
   hms= 100nms;
-- 10**(-10) or 10 microns by 10 microns
   tms = 100 hms ;
```

```
-- 10**(-8) or 100 microns by 100 microns
   sms = 100 tms ;
-- 10**(-6) or 1 mm x 1 mm
   cms = 100 sms ;
-- 10**(-4) or 1 cm by 1 cm
   ms  = 10000 cms; -- 1 square meter!
   end units;


attribute Footprint:Area;
   attribute Footprint of
Nand_Gate:architecture is 1 hms;
```

At this point, there is a strong temptation, due to the limitations of VHDL, to say "the remainder of this example is left as an exercise for the reader." According to section 5.1 of the LRM, "User-defined attributes represent local information only and cannot be used to pass information from one description to another." In other words, associating this architecture with an entity (necessarily through a configuration declaration), associating that entity with a component, and instantiating each component instance as a labeled component, will not let us get at the attribute values! Only variables and signals can be used to pass such values. Aside from some aesthetic appeal, giving a signal the area value and propagating it through the design without using attributes is the practical approach. If you would prefer to assign the signal its value by way of an attribute, go right ahead.

There are other examples of user-defined attributes to be found in various texts, but these seem to be of dubious utility because of the limitations placed upon user-defined attributes. The LRM gives an example of an attribute LOCATION, intended to apply to a component instance and therefore associated with the **label** of the instance. This is certainly a valid usage, but the location of a device is probably not of great interest in its simulation. Presumably, the device is already synthesized if the component locations are all known. The generation of the associated attribute statements for all instances of components must have required automatic generation of the VHDL if the device is not to be a trivial toy. If the device characteristics were sensitive to its coordinates on the chip, it would surely be a peculiar design. There should be better ways than a VHDL simulation to check for device overlap or other flaws. Such an example seems highly artificial.

The moral is that while the predefined attributes are truly valuable and sorely missed in other languages, user-defined attributes are apparently of dubious utility because of their limitations.

Chapter 7

Sequential Statements

Sequential statements are those found within subprograms (functions and procedures) and those found within processes. They execute one after the other, as in familiar programming languages. They therefore allow the user to control the sequence of events, to wait for events, the passage of time, or other occurrences of interest.

THE ASSERT STATEMENT

The **assert** statement is a useful tool for error checking and debugging. It enables the user to assert what the correct situation is. If this is not the situation when the assert is executed, there occurs an "assertion violation." This may cause a message to be printed, or the simulation to terminate, or both. The assert statement comes in both sequential and concurrent forms. Both are of the form:

```
assert Boolean_condition report Msg severity
    Severity_level;
```

The STANDARD package contains the definition:

```
type SEVERITY_LEVEL is (NOTE,WARNING,
    ERROR,FAILURE);
```

These are the choices for an assert error level. The semantics of these messages are dependent on the VHDL compiler and user options. Typically, by default an ERROR will terminate a calculation while WARNING will not. The report clause, if present, will print the desired message. If it is absent, the message is taken to be an *assertion violation*. The LRM specifies the minimum error message to contain an indication that the message is due to an assertion violation, the severity level, the message string, and the name of the design unit containing the assertion. Note that a full traceback specifying the precise entity that incurred the violation is not given.

We have already used a simple version of a concurrent assertion statement in the simple, asynchronous latch discussed in Chapter 3. This simple assertion will report a problem whenever the illegal input condition is true, as is appropriate for such a latch. Generally, however, clocked or synchronous logic is used. Is such cases, we want to check for such erroneous inputs only under certain conditions, such as when the gate is enabled by the clock input. This requires the use of a process with a sequential assertion. Great power and flexibility can be obtained with increased efficiency through this approach.

```
CheckSetup: process
  begin
  if ( Enable' EVENT
  --Enable has just transitioned
    and ( Enable=' 1' ) ) -- to active
  then
    assert ( Data' LAST_EVENT >= Setup_Time)
      report " Setup Violation "
      severity ERROR;
  end if;
end process;
```

Note again some of the limitations of employing **assert**, compared with custom coding. You cannot conveniently learn, for example, by how much the setup violation occurred (i. e., did we just miss by 1 ns?).

The compiler short-circuits the logical expression in the **if** conditional; that is, if it concludes that the result is false without evaluating the second term in the conjunction because the first is false, it makes sense to make the first test less likely to be true than the second. It is likely that there will be fewer deltas during which the Enable signal has transitioned than those on which it is true. That is why we have chosen the ordering of terms shown above.

Additional checks may be inserted in the same process or as other processes. Any number of processes may be used. Checks on other signals should be inserted in other processes in order to limit the sensitivity of each process (see Chapter 8 for a discussion of processes).

A statement of the form **assert** FALSE **report** ... will produce a warning message. VHDL-92 supports this by providing the **report** statement, which is simply the construct given above without the need to write **assert** FALSE.

ANSI C supports an **assert** statement, which produces an error message and aborts the program. ANSI C does not support a variety of severity levels.

FUNCTIONS AND PROCEDURES

VHDL supports two types of subprograms: functions and procedures. Functions return values, procedures do not, although the latter can alter parameters that are specified to be of **inout** mode. They are discussed here because they incorporate sequential statements. Obviously, **return** statements in procedures have no arguments, whereas in functions they must have a legal expression corresponding to the function's return value.

VHDL-87 goes to some length to prevent "side-effects." VHDL-92 permits **impure** functions, which are allowed some side-effects; see Chapter 10. Functions are only permitted to have formal parameters of mode **in**, and the class of the object must be either **signal** or **constant**. A **variable** may of course be a function argument, but internal to the function, the value of that variable cannot be altered. If the class is not specified, **constant** is assumed. For procedures, allowed modes are **in, inout**, or **out**. If no mode is specified, **in** is assumed and if no class is specified, **constant** is assumed. For other modes, the class is assumed to be **variable** if no class is specified.

For a formal of class **signal**, the actual must be of class **signal**. For a formal of class **variable**, the actual must be of class **variable**. For a formal of class **constant**, the actual can be an expression, which would of course include a single **variable** as a special case.

If a signal is passed into a subprogram, the predefined attributes ′STABLE, ′QUITE, and ′DELAYED may not be used ("read" in the language of VHDL). As discussed in Chapter 6, the use of these attributes results in the simulation system emulating a process to keep track of the value of the attribute signal. The bookkeeping would get very complicated to dynamically create and evaluate such information. If these attribute values are needed, they can be sent as arguments (parameters) to the subprogram in question.

Just as the assignment to a signal in a process creates a driver associated with that signal and that process, so does the assignment to a signal within a procedure. Assignments to the signal in the procedure are equivalent to assignments by other drivers. In particular, as emphasized by the LRM, the procedure need not return to the caller for the assignment to take effect. It is therefore practical to write procedures that contain mixtures of assignments, **wait** statements, and so forth.

VHDL permits overloading of the names of functions and procedures. Different subprograms with the same names must be distinguishable by having different numbers of arguments, or different argument types, or returning different types of values if they are functions. If this does not resolve the ambiguity, it may still be possible to do so if the similarly named subprograms are in different packages, say package A and B. Then the two subprograms might be referred to as A.X and B.X, where X is the function name. For more on packages, see Chapter 9.

Because packages can define "global" signals (see Chapter 9), and subprograms can read and procedures can assign to this signal, side-effects are possible with subprograms.

THE wait STATEMENT

The **wait** statement is the key to effecting the synchronization necessary in any collection of concurrent processes. VHDL in effect inserts wait statements in processes with sensitivity lists, and converts concurrent assignments into such processes, so there are effective wait statements inserted into user code without explicit waits.

This is the general form of the wait statement, where all of the **on, until**, and **for** clauses are optional:

```
wait on signal_sensitivity_list
   until  boolean_expression
   for maximum_time;
```

This statement will wait until a signal in the sensitivity list has an event. It is also sensitive to changes in other signals that might occur, for example, in the boolean_expression. The until clause, if not present, is effectively fixed at TRUE. If present, the process will wait at this point until the clause evaluates to TRUE. The for clause specifies a maximum time for the wait.

A special case of such a statement, which is legal, is:

```
wait;
```

When encountered, this statement will cause a process to suspend indefinitely, that is, for the remainder of the simulation. It is therefore dead. Such statements might be used in some cases, as in simulating the failure of a component. It may also be used in a process or component that performs some initialization function and then is no longer needed.

The statement:

```
wait until   (Signal_1 = '1');
```

would suspend until the boolean expression was true, that is, until the signal `Signal_1` took on the boolean value of `'1'`. The boolean expression need not involve signals, of course. Finally, the form:

wait on   `Signal_1, Signal_2;`

will wait until an event occurs on any of the signals in the sensitivity list. Note that a mere transaction does not count; the signal value must change. Of course, you can easily use the statement:

wait on   `Signal_1'` TRANSACTION, `Signal_2;`

with the predefined attribute TRANSACTION to cause the process to wake up upon any transaction on Signal_1.

The statement:

wait on `Signal_3` **until**   (`Signal_1 = '1'`)
    for `100 us;`

will "sleep" until an event occurs on Signal_1 or on Signal_3, or until 100 us has elapsed. If 100 us has not elapsed, if Signal_1 has the value `'0'` it will continue to sleep. Thus, there are three ways for the code to proceed to the next statement: (1) 100 us elapses; (2) Signal_1 changes to `'1'` (from `'0'`, the only other possible value a signal of predefined type BIT can have); and (3) and event occurs on `Signal_3`, and `Signal_1='1'`.

VARIABLE ASSIGNMENTS

Variable assignments have been used throughout this VHDL tutorial. The assignment operator is :=. It is illegal to assign to a variable of type FILE.

THE If, then, elsif, else, end if CONDITIONALS

VHDL supports the usual structured conditional, of the form:

```
if BOOLEAN_Expression then
   . . .
   -- zero or more optional elsif clauses
   elsif  BOOLEAN_Expression then
   . . .
   -- Optional else clause
   else
   . . .
   end if;
```

This is the most general conditional structure in VHDL. It is therefore the least structured of the conditional constructs. The VHDL syntax is the same as in Ada and behaves as the analogous constructs in Ada, PASCAL, C, and FORTRAN77. At least one of these should be sufficiently familiar to the reader that no further discussion is necessary.

THE case STATEMENT

The case statement corresponds to the case statement in Ada and the switch statement in C. A typical example, which illustrates overloading the reserved word **not** would be:

```
type MVL5 is (' 0' ,' 1' ,' ' Z' ,' X' ,' U' );
 function "not" ( X: in MVL5) return MVL5 is
case X is
   when ' 0'  => return ' 1' ;
   when ' 1'  => return ' 0' ;
   when ' Z'  => return ' Z' ;
   when ' X'  => return ' X' ;
   when ' U'  => return ' U' ;
   when others  => return ' X' ;
end ;
```

When a number of values of the expression should result in the same action, these values may be collected together in a single **when** clause by using the vertical bar (|) to specify the choice:

```
case Expression is
  when value1 | value2 =>
  . . .
  when value3 | value4 =>
  . . .
  when others =>
    -- default choice
  . . .
end case;
```

The **others** reserved word may be used to specify a default case, as in Ada, and similar to the *default:* clause in C switch statements. The use of the others clause is optional, but usually a good idea.

THE loop, next, exit STATEMENTS

There are two major types of loops, the **for** and the **while** loops. The **for** loops are typified by the following:

```
for Index in 0 to 31 loop
. . .
end loop;
```

This statement declares the variable Index, which in the example is of type INTEGER. The variable need not be declared elsewhere, and its scope is that of the loop. Enumerated types can also be used, and a range may be used:

```
type Etype is ( up, down, right, left);
for Index in EType' RANGE loop
. . .
end loop;
```

In this example, **Etype** will run through the four enumerated values as declared.

```
while ( Index < 32 ) loop
. . .
end loop;
```

In this case, the loop will be executed while the BOOLEAN condition is true. The loop may be executed anywhere from zero to an infinite number of times. The variable Index in the case shown must be defined explicitly.

Loops can be labeled:

```
L1: while ( Index < 32 ) loop
. . .
end loop L1;
```

Labeling loops increases the readability of the code by enabling others to quickly find the **end** statement for each loop, and is therefore useful when a number of loops are nested.

The **next** statement is similar to the *continue* statement in C, and effectively causes the loop to go to the **end loop** statement, that is, to go on to the next iteration of the loop, if any. The code:

```
variable Sum: INTEGER:=0;
for I in Data' RANGE loop
if DataItem(I) < 0 then next;
Sum := Sum + DataItem(R):
end loop;
```

will find the sum of the non-negative values of the DataItem array.

There are two forms of the **next** statement, the simple form shown above and a conditional form with a **when** clause:

```
variable Sum: INTEGER:=0; for I in
Data' RANGE loop
next when DataItem(I) < 0 ;
Sum := Sum + DataItem(R):
end loop;
```

This would accomplish the same thing as the previous example. The following code, with the loop label specified and used in the **next** statement, would also be legal:

```
variable Sum: INTEGER:=0;  L1:
for I in Data'RANGE loop
next L1 when  DataItem(I) < 0 ;
Sum := Sum + DataItem(R):
end loop L1;
```

The **exit** statement is similar to the *break* statement in C, and causes an immediate exit from the loop, to the statement immediately after the **end loop**.

The loop:

```
while TRUE loop
. . .
if Condition then exit;
end loop;
```

will execute an indeterminate number of times, possibly infinite, until *Condition* is TRUE.

The **exit** statement also comes in a conditional form with a **when** clause:

```
while TRUE loop
. . .
exit when Condition;
end loop;
```

THE null STATEMENT

It is occasionally useful to have a statement that does nothing. Such a statement may occupy some clause of an **if** . . . **then** . . . **else** . . . **end** sequence or a **case** statement. Languages such as Ada and VHDL require you to explicitly use the **null** statement reserved word. Other languages such as C are happy to accept a sequence such as *;;;* which contains two null statements as well as the closing parenthesis of a previous statement.

Chapter 8

Concurrent Statements

Concurrent programming statements are natural to hardware, but relatively uncommon to software. Hardware elements naturally operate in parallel, simultaneously. Simulations, by contrast, emulate concurrent processes sequentially. If two processes proceed from time T to T+ delta-t, one is executed, then the other, and finally the clock is advanced to the later time. Each process "thinks" it has been run concurrently.

Table 8.1 illustrates the correspondence between concurrent and sequential language features.

Table 8.1 Corresponding Concurrent and Sequential Features	
concurrent	sequential
process	function, procedure
signal	variable

It will be seen that many concurrent statements are merely short-hand notations for processes that contain the equivalent sequential statements. On the other hand, guarded signal assignments, which are discussed fully in Chapter 2, must be concurrent assignments. Some formats of concurrent signal assignment, such as the selected signal assignment, do not exist in sequential form, although they are equivalent to process statements with sequential assignments.

PROCESS STATEMENT

The process statement is the fundamental concurrent statement. All other concurrent statements are effectively processes. Each process runs concurrently with the others. Each process establishes a driver for every signal to which it may assign values.

There are two basic forms of process statements, those with an explicit *sensitivity list* and those without. The sensitivity list enumerates the signals to which the process is sensitive. An event on any of these signals will cause the process to execute. Consider the process with the sensitivity list:

```
signal X,Y,Z: BIT;
Or: process (X,Y)
   begin
      if X = '1' then
         Z <= '1';
      elsif Y = '1' then
         Z <= '1';
      else
         Z < ='0';
      end if;   end process;
```

This process is precisely equivalent to the following process:

```
signal X,Y,Z: BIT;
Or: process
   begin
      if X = '1' then
         Z <= '1';
      elsif Y = '1' then
         Z <= '1';
      else
         Z < ='0';
```

```
      end if;        wait on X,Y;
    end process;
```

Note the **wait on** statement, which takes the place of the explicit sensitivity list. It is located at the end of the process, not at the beginning, in order to permit initialization at the beginning of the simulation. At that time, 0 ns, all processes are started and run until they suspend. This will happen at the **wait** statement, which will cause the process to suspend until there is an event on signals X or Y. Note that the process is in effect an infinite loop between the begin and **end process** statements.

If a process has an explicit sensitivity list, **wait** statements are not permitted. The sensitivity list will completely specify the signals whose events control the awakening of the process. No other condition nor the passage of time with regard to a **wait for** may alter this. If you see the sensitivity list within the **process** statement, you need not look through the process to make certain you have found all the things that would activate the process.

Now consider the alternative process:

```
signal X,Y,Z: BIT;
Or: process
  begin
    if X = ' 1'  then
       Z <= ' 1' ;
       wait on X;
    elsif Y = ' 1'  then
       Z <= ' 1' ;
       wait on Y;
    else
       Z < =' 0' ;
       wait on X,Y;
    end if;    end process;
```

This process is functionally equivalent to the previous processes, although its precise behavior is different. If X=' 1' , then by the nature of the logical or, the value of signal Y is of no concern. Z will continue to be ' 1' , however Y may change. It therefore makes sense to ignore changes on Y under these circumstances. The process therefore suspends until X changes. It then will update Z based on the current values of X and Y. This revised process will therefore ignore events on signals that do not matter, instead of responding to all events on X and Y. It should therefore be more efficient than the previous two processes. Almost certainly, it will take more time to compile and occupy more storage, because it is more complex with more statements. Such hand tuning of the sensitivity through **wait** statements can speed simulations, but they also enhance the risk that an error will be made and that a signal that should be in the sensitivity list of the **wait** statement will be overlooked.

BLOCK STATEMENT

Block statements are covered in Chapter 4. Their primary application is in defining guard signals that can then be used to control guarded signal assignments, which are concurrent statements. Guards are discussed in Chapter 2, concurrent signal assignments are discussed later in this chapter.

CONCURRENT PROCEDURE CALL

A concurrent procedure call "represents a process containing the corresponding sequential procedure call." The equivalent process does not have a sensitivity list or a declarative part. Instead, its final executable statement is a **wait on** statement containing actual signals corresponding to formal signals that are of mode **in** or **inout** in the parameter list of the procedure call. Thus, if:

```
TestProc ( X: in BIT; Y:out BIT);
```

then:

```
signal A,B: BIT;
TestProc(A,B);
```

is equivalent to:

```
signal A,B: BIT;
process
begin
TestProc(A,B);
wait on A;
end process;
```

CONCURRENT ASSERTION

Concurrent assertions are equivalent to passive processes containing an **assert** statement within. It is generally more practical to use a process containing the assertion with an appropriate sensitivity list and conditionals, in order to have the assert test performed only under appropriate conditions.

CONCURRENT SIGNAL ASSIGNMENT

As noted previously, a concurrent signal assignment is in effect a process with the appropriate sensitivity list that performs the required (sequential) signal assignment. It is also discussed in Chapter 2. A simple concurrent signal assignment can be of the following forms:

```
  Sig <=   WavForm1;
@CODE  =   Sig <= transport WavForm1;
@CODE  =   Sig <= guarded WavForm1;
@CODE  =   Sig <= guarded transport WavForm1;
```

Only concurrent signal assignments may be guarded, or be of the conditional or selected formats described below. The reserved words **guarded** and **transport** may each be optionally inserted after the <= operator in any of these concurrent signal assignments (LRM 9.5). The former is for a guarded assignment, and the latter is used if transport instead of inertial delay is desired. See Chapter 2 for a complete discussion of these options. Here Wavform1, and so on, are of the form of a list containing one or more elements, separated by commas, of the form of a signal value (including **null**) and the optional **after** Delay_Time.

VHDL-92 introduces the **unaffected** keyword. This word, in an waveform list, produces a **null** transaction. The keyword **unaffected** may not be used in a sequential signal assignment.

Conditional Signal Assignment

Note that there are two forms of concurrent signal assignments. The first is the conditional signal assignment:

```
Sig <= Wavform1 when Condition1 else
   ...
```

Examples are:

```
Sig <= '1' after 20 ns,
   '0' after 40 ns,
   null after 60 ns  when X = '1' else
   '0' after 20 ns;

Sig <= transport '1' after 20 ns,
   '0' after 40 ns,
   null after 60 ns  when X = '1' else
   '0' after 20 ns;
```

The conditional signal assignment is equivalent to a process with signal assignments within an **if** ... **elsif** ... **else** ... **end if;** construct.

Selected Signal Assignment

The other form for concurrent signal assignments is the selected signal assignment:

```
Sig <= with Expression  select Wavform1
   when Value1
   ...;
```

The selected signal assignment is equivalent to a process with signal assignments within a **case** ... **when** ... **others** ... **end case;** construct.

POSTPONED PROCESSES

In VHDL-92, any of the concurrent processes, signal assignments, assertions, and procedures can be preceded by the new reserved word **postponed**. These will execute only once for any given time, after all of the deltas (infinitesimal time increments) have been performed and the simulation is ready to advance to the next finite time into the future. See Chapter 10.

Chapter 9

Packages, Libraries, Input/Output

DESIGN UNITS

VHDL calls constructs that may be dealt with independently from others *design units*. A file may contain a number of such units. Design units include packages, entities, architectures, and configurations. Within a library, there are primary and secondary library units. The primary unit is the declaration, such as a package declaration, or entity or configuration declaration. The secondary unit would be the package body corresponding to the package declaration, or an architecture corresponding to an entity declaration. Within a given library, the primary names must be unique to prevent ambiguity, and all of the architectures corresponding to the same entity must be uniquely named, although different architectures corresponding to different entities may have the same name.

PACKAGES

VHDL supports an encapsulation of data, procedures, functions, and so forth, in a form borrowed from Ada: the *package*. The package STANDARD has already been encountered. It embodies the basic data types of VHDL. In this chapter, we will discuss the other important system-supplied package, TEXIO. We will also discuss user-defined packages, and the other facility for encapsulating information in VHDL, the *library*.

A package has, in general, two parts: the package declaration and the package body. The package declaration provides the definition of the visible aspects of the package. The package body contains the implementation of this functionality. This information in the body is hidden from the user. The hidden information can include constants, functions, or procedures that users are not permitted to call directly; indeed, they may not even know they exist. This encapsulation can preserve the validity of the simulation by preventing users from making errors.

The package body is not required. If the package exists merely to define constants, for example, there is no need for a package body. The body will contain the subprograms, that is, functions or procedures, that make up the package.

The package declaration may contain a *deferred* constant declaration, similar to an incomplete type declaration. If so, the constant must be assigned an actual value within the package body; this is called the **full** declaration of the constant. Within the package declaration and before the full declaration, the deferred constant is only allowed in the default expression for a local generic, local port, or formal parameter. The constant value is not defined before elaboration.

The package declaration can contain declarations for any of the following: types, subtypes, constants, signals, files, alias declarations, components, attribute declarations and specifications, disconnection specifications, and use clauses. The package body can contain declarations for types, subtypes, constants, files, alias declarations, use clauses, and subprogram bodies. Items declared in the body of the package cannot be made visible outside of the package (LRM 2.6). Thus, the hiding or encapsulation of data or subprograms is supported. Note that signals may be declared in the package declaration. This permits the use of "global" signals that will be visible to any design entity that uses the package. Variables cannot be declared or used in this global manner, however. Because subprograms may reference or assign values to this signal, there is the opportunity for various side-effects.

LIBRARIES

Packages may be thought of as libraries of subprograms. Libraries may in general contain design entities. We might have separate libraries for TTL, CMOS, ECL, and other technologies. We could then simulate the same device, implemented in different technologies, simply by changing the reference in the library statement to the appropriate library. (This assumes, of course, that component names, port names, etc., are the same, although the architectures, generic values, etc., will differ.)

VHDL supports the reuse of code through the use of libraries. There are two declarative statements associated with libraries: the **library** and **use** statements. These correspond to the *with* and *use* clauses of Ada.

Every design unit is assumed to contain the following part of its *context clause* (see LRM 11.2):

library STD, WORK; **use** STD.STANDARD.**all**;

This context clause contains two kinds of statements, which is typical. The **library** statement names the library we wish to use. The **use** statement selects the elements within that library that we wish to make visible to the design unit under compilation. It may be useful to use multiple libraries with identically named components, so VHDL insists that, by default, we specify precisely which elements in each library we wish to use, each and every time we use them, unless the default is specified. The default **all** is often used to reduce the tedium of specifying precisely which elements from the library are to be used. Without the **use** statement, statements of the form:

signal Sig: STD.STANDARD.BIT;

would have to be used whenever type BIT, from package STANDARD of library name STD was used. The **use** statement can therefore save a tremendous amount of typing, along with improving read-ability. In VHDL terminology, BIT would be the *suffix* and STD.STANDARD the *prefix* in the name of the type. It is the suf-fix that becomes directly visible.

It is, of course, possible to use a number of libraries at a time. Such libraries are called *resource libraries* in the VHDL LRM.

Library STD contains the packages STANDARD and TEXTIO. Library WORK denotes the current working library, that is, the VHDL code currently being compiled. Although the LRM 11.2 rec-ommends that STD contain only those library units defined in the LRM, compiler vendors appear to ignore that admonition.

Libraries can refer to other libraries via context clauses. The code must be arranged such that a referenced primary unit can be analyzed prior to the analysis of the corresponding secondary.

STANDARD PACKAGE TEXTIO

The ability to input and output data is relatively limited in VHDL-87. VHDL-92 enhances the flexibilty somewhat (see Chapter 10). The standard package TEXTIO provides the ability to read from and write to files with text. Only sequential operations are sup-ported. If the data is to be used in any other manner, it presumably must be read into a data structure in memory and accessed from there. Binary data cannot be read, even as sequential data. Thus, memory dumps must be preprocessed in some manner if they are to be used as data in a simulation. Files are declared as type INPUT or OUTPUT only.

There are no OPEN or CLOSE operations for files in VHDL-87; these are introduced in VHDL-92 (see Chapter 1). Thus, you can-not, for example, associate a number of files in sequence to a single data stream in VHDL-87, except by opening each with an associ-ated file and successively assigning these to a single file-type signal. Assignment to variables of type file are illegal (LRM 8.4), so a variable may not be used for such purposes. All files are in effect opened when the simulation begins and presumably closed when it terminates. The Vantage compiler opens output files by default for appending data, and will add new data to the end of the file rather than over-writing the previous data. This should not be assumed to be a general rule for all VHDL environments, however.

VHDL input/output is line oriented, as is FORTRAN. Information is passed to or from the file as a line. The lines are read in with the READLINE procedure or written with the WRITELINE procedure. These transfer data between the file and a type LINE, which is a pointer to a STRING, as defined in the TEXTIO package:

```
type LINE is access STRING;
type TEXT is file of  STRING;
```

Thus, a simple form of buffered I/O is implemented in VHDL. To read from a file, a line at a time is read from the file into a text buffer, which is specified by the user. READ operations may then be undertaken by the user from this buffer. In addition, users can employ the BOOLEAN functions ENDLINE and ENDFILE to determine whether they have reached the end of the line, or the end of the file, respectively. In addition, the attribute ' LENGTH may be applied to the buffer text string in order to determine the current length of the line being processed. For a line being read, this is the number of characters that remain to be read. The function ENDLINE is equal to (LineBuffer' LENGTH = 0), where LineBuffer is the access type to the line buffer specified in the READLINE or WRITELINE. For a line being written, it is the number of characters that have already been stored in the line buffer with the WRITE procedure. Note that READ and WRITE operations may alter the value of the ' LENGTH attribute of the buffer, and can even cause the deallocation of the buffer. This can cause a dangling reference and possible errors if the ' LENGTH is not checked before referencing. These functions are of the following form:

```
procedure  READLINE ( F: in TEXT; L: out
LINE );
```

procedure WRITELINE (F: **out** TEXT; L: **in** LINE);

There are READ and WRITE functions for BIT, BIT_VEC-TOR, BOOLEAN, CHARACTER, INTEGER, REAL, TIME, and STRING. Note that there are none possible for user-defined enumerated types, although the ' POS (X) attribute may be used to obtain an INTEGER to write to a file. When this integer is read, it may be converted back to the enumerated type with the ' VAL attribute.

There are two READ functions for each data type; here is an illustration:

procedure READ (L: **inout** LINE; VALUE: **out** BIT); GOOD: **out** BIT);
procedure READ (L: **inout** LINE; VALUE: **out** BIT);

The final value, GOOD, returns TRUE if there was no error and FALSE if there was any error, such as a type mismatch between the requested data item and the text in LINE, or if the LINE buffer is empty. This permits a graceful recovery from such errors. If you use this form, it would be inexcusable not to check the value of GOOD and take appropriate action if it were FALSE.

There is one WRITE procedure for each type, each with a number of optional parameters for formatting purpose; they are typically in this form:

type SIDE **is** (RIGHT, LEFT);
type WIDTH **is** NATURAL;

 procedure WRITE (L: **inout** LINE;
  VALUE: **in** TIME); JUSTIFIED: **in** SIDE:=RIGHT;
  FIELD:**in** WIDTH:=0;
  UNIT: **in** TIME);

For WRITE operations of type TIME data, it is possible to specify the units to be used. The default is nanoseconds (ns). It is also possible to specify the width of the field, and whether the value printed in right- or left-justified within this field. For BIT, BIT_VECTOR, BOOLEAN, CHARACTER, STRING, and IN-TEGER data the form for this procedure is the same, except that the UNIT parameter is absent. For REAL type data, the UNIT parameter is replaced by the parameter DIGITS: **in** NATURAL:=0, which specifies the number of digits to the right of the decimal point that should be printed. In its default value of 0 it specifies an exponential format: 2.99792458E+08. If DIGITS is nonzero, then it is output as 3.14159 or in a similar manner.

The default input and output files are typically of this form:

```
file INPUT: TEXT is in "STD_INPUT";
file OUTPUT: TEXT is out "STD_OUTPUT";
```

One can define files of types other than TEXT. However, the usage of such files might not be portable. It is recommended that TEXIO be used exclusively, at least until other forms of input/output become standardized in VHDL.

Chapter 10

VHDL-92 and Miscellaneous Topics

VHDL-92

This chapter will review the major innovations of the VHDL-92 revision. The modifications to VHDL-87 have been collected for your convenience in one chapter. The appropriate tutorial chapters briefly discuss the new features and refer to this chapter for details.

New Keywords

VHDL-92 introduces a total of 19 new keywords:

```
allow element group impure inertial literal
postponed private pure reject rol ror
shared sla sll sra srl unaffected xnor
```

There are new arithmetic operators: shifts `rol  ror  sla  sll  sra  srl` and the negated exclusive or **xnor**. The new keywords **inertial reject unaffected** are for use with signal assignments. Functions may be declared **pure** or **impure**. Processes may be **postponed** to run only once per time, attributes may be **literal**, variables may be **shared**, objects may be **private** with specific permissible actions granted by an **allow** clause, possibly on an **array element**, **record element**, or **file element**. Finally, **groups** may be declared.

Groups

VHDL-92 supports groups and group types. One can build groups of groups. This capability makes it possible to collect individual items, for the purpose of, say, assigning them the same attributes. An example is:

```
group type Channel is (signal <>);
group Group1: Channel(S1,S2,S3);
attribute Hold_Time: Time;
attribute Hold_Time of Channel is 10 ns;
```

This first defines the group type Channel, which groups together an arbitrary number of signals, and then is used to collect the signals S1, S2, and S3, which is then made use of in assigning the common attribute to all of the signals. This declaration groups together two signals:

```
group type Channel is (signal,signal);
```

Private

The idea of information hiding is popular in object-oriented programming, and C++ provides the option of declaring variables and procedures private. VHDL-92 now allows similar hiding of implementation details in packages. Private portions of packages are not available to users, but may be used within the package. For example:

```
package Limited is
type PType  is private;
function Doit(XY: PType) return Integer;
...
private
...
```

```
type PType is Integer ;
end Limited;
```

Here the user is allowed to declare variables of type `PType`, but is not allowed to make use of the face that such variables are integers. Because the type declaration for `PType` precedes `private` reserved word, it is visible to users of the package, as is the function `DoIt`. Functions, types, and so forth which are in the private section of the package, following the `private` reserved word, are not visible to the user. The incomplete definition of `PType` given in the public part of the package declaration must be completed in the private type.

A clause beginning with **allow** is called a *contract* and specifies the permissions available to users of the type. The contract provides a list, separated by commas, of any of the following:

```
constant
variable
shared variable
signal
array element
record element
file element
```

In the next example the user is permitted to define variables and constants of type `AType` (pointers):

```
package Limited is
typeAType is private allow variable;
...
private
type AType is INTEGER range 1 to 255;
...
end Limited;
```

This code permits the package user to declare variables of type `AType`. Composite types and file types declared outside of the package may have subelements of the private type only if the contract clause contains the appropriate permission, such as **array**

element. A variety of limitations apply to using private types with allow permission. For example, if **constant** is specified in the allow clause, then the private part of the package must declare the item as a constant, and the user may not declare an access type to that item. Similarly, the user cannot define access types to point to signals and shared variables specified as a private type. See the LRM for a complete list of limitations.

Shared Variables

As noted in Chapter 3, variables in VHDL-87 are local, and cannot be used to communicate information. Because signals cannot be access types, access types must be local variables. It was felt that the extra flexibility gained by permitting global variables outweighed the dangers, so they were adopted for VHDL-92. A new reserved word is used, **shared**, in variable declarations:

shared variable A, B: Integer;

in any declarative region. Because VHDL represents concurrent processes, modifying shared variables has to be carefully controlled so that consistent results are obtained. Shared variables may not be access types or have components that are access or file types.

It had been proposed (see Dunlap and Ussery 1992) to introduce the *protected region*, which behaves as a critical section (see Chapter 11). This would have enabled VHDL users to have the simulation system assume the burden of ensuring shared variables were consistently updated. This feature has not made it into the draft standard. The techniques of Chapter 11 will have to be used if a number of sections of code modify shared variables.

Shared variables correspond to globals in C, and variables in COMMON in FORTRAN. Though often though to reduce function call overhead, their use often produces *slower* code by inhibiting optimization. Functions which use shared variables should be declared **impure**, as their result can change due to a change in the shared variable, even though the arguments are unaltered.

Hierarchical Pathnames

Hierarchical pathnames enable easier specification of unique objects in referencing entities, architectures, labels, and **generate** statement index values. Predefined attributes ′ PATH_NAME and ′ SIMPLE_NAME, which yield strings are results, return the unique hierarchical and simple name, respectively, of appropriate items. Two separators are used in these specifications: ′ /′ when crossing external blocks (such as instantiations of entities within others), ′ .′ in internal blocks (e. g, for specifying the block or generate statement label within a specified architecture). Such pathnames may not be used for static objects, such as declared in subprograms. For example, given the architecture:

```
architecture Higher of Board is
begin
Gen: for Index in 1 to 5 generate
   Blck: block
   component Chip is
   end Chip;    for Chip use Dip; begin
     Chip;
   end block;
end architecture A;
```

the pathname of the second instance of Dip will be the string "/Board(Higher).Gen(2).Blck/Dip". An item in Dip could be referenced with further string concatenated to the end of this string as appropriate.

Foreign Languages

In order to facilitate the interface to other languages, a string-valued attribute FOREIGN may be supplied. It is defined in the standard package:

```
attribute FOREIGN: STRING;
```

It only applies to architectures and subprograms. The details are implementation dependent. This feature corresponds somewhat to the

PRAGMA feature in Ada insofar as that feature may be used to specify interface details.

Other New Attributes

Eight new attributes have been added to the language, including FOREIGN, PATH_NAME, and SIMPLE_NAME, which have already been discussed in this chapter. The others are:

ASCENDING[(N)]

which returns a Boolean value TRUE if the Nth index range of the associated array object is in ascending order, otherwise zero. If the parameter is omitted, it is assumed to be one. Ascending, without a parameter, may be applied to any scalar type or subtype.

IMAGE(X) VALUE(X)

This pair of attributes allows the user to convert between string representations of values and the variable type. The primary purpose of these attributes would be to allow editing of input and output in conjunction with TEXTIO. IMAGE(X) returns a STRING representation of the data, and VALUE(X) converts the data specified by the string X into the appropriate type. These attributes are therefore somewhat similar to the C library functions atoi(), itoa(), and so on.

DRIVING
DRIVING_VALUE

Driving returns a Boolean FALSE if the current value of the driver for the associated signal is determined by a NULL transaction, otherwise it returns TRUE. DRIVING_VALUE returns the value of the driver. These attributes are available only from within a process, subprogram, or a concurrent statement with an equivalent process (such as a concurrent signal assignment). If it is part of a subprogram, the associated signal must either be a formal parameter of the subprogram, with a mode of **inout**, **out**, or **buffer**, or the subprogram must be declared within the process. Note that it is an error if there is no driver for S in the process, and an error to call DRIVING_VALUE if DRIVING is FALSE. Therefore,

DRIVING_VALUE should generally be used in a protecting construct such as:

```
if S' DRIVING then
    X:=S' DRIVING_VALUE;
  else
    X:=null;
  endif
```

Generalized Aliasing

It is now possible to alias subprograms, types, units, and so forth.

Postponed Processes

The new reserved word **postponed** is added to the language. It may be used to declare processes (and implicit processes such as concurrent assertions, procedure calls, and signal assignments) to declare that the process should only be invoked once for any time, after all the deltas have occurred. Because such a process should not produce another delta time advance, a postponed process is forbidden to assign a signal **after** 0 **ns**, nor can it have a timeout clause in a wait statement that evaluates to 0 ns. The reserved word **postponed** is the first word of the declaration or statement.

Shift and Rotate Instructions

Six new operators have been added that operate on arrays of type Bit or Boolean. They are **sll**, **srl**, **sla**, **slr**, **rol**, **ror**, which are logical shifts, arithmetic shifts, and rotate operations, in right and left variants. The rotate operations are circular shifts. The other operations lose bits that are shifted out of the array. For arithmetic shifts, the value shifted in, the *fill value*, is the leftmost or rightmost value, for right and left shifts, respectively. For logical shifts, the fill value is '0' for Bit and FALSE for BOOLEAN variables. Negative shift values are allowed, and represent shifts in the opposite sense. See Chapter 5 for more details.

A standard library of mathematical functions is planned for the future.

Files and File Objects

Files are no longer a type of variable in VHDL-92. Instead, they are their own class of objects. The functions File_Open() and File_Close() now exist. Files may be opened for reading, writing, or appending.

Impure Functions

VHDL-87 sought to minimize the possibility of side-effects in functions. VHDL-92 is more permissive. *Impure* functions can read from files, or used shared variables, for example. They are declared with the reserved word **impure** preceding the word function. A function is considered impure if it may return different values even if called with the same arguments. Declaring such functions should permit compilers to perform more effective optimization by forsaking unnecessary calls to functions.

Recall that our random number generator, RANDOM16, had to be a subprogram in order to update the seeds. The impure function was inspired by similar problems. VHDL-92 offers a similar random number generator:

```
package UNIFORM_DISTRIBUTION is
   type RANDOM_RANGE is 0.0 to 1.0;
   -- the range is open on the right
   procedure SEED(Value: RANDOM_RANGE);
   impure function RANDOM return RANDOM_RANGE;
   end package UNIFORM_DISTRIBUTION;
```

Note that RANDOM will never return a value of 1.0. Note also that it is not portable, and might give different values on different machines for the same initial seed.

The NOW function is another example of an impure function. It is discussed later in this chapter.

Inertial Delay

As discussed in Chapter 2, there is now a third type of signal assignment delay, in addition to the transport delay and the inertial delay of VHDL-87. This new form of inertial delay more closely corresponds to actual device behavior, in which inputs must be stable for a specified hold time, which may not equal the propagation delay through the device as implicitly assumed by VHDL-87. The new assignment is of this form:

```
Sig <= reject 10 ns inertial '1' after 20
ns;
```

Note the two new reserved words. The time specified in the **reject** clause represents the required hold time. Assignments operate similarly to VHDL-87 assignments, except that the inertial assignment will only delete transactions that occur within the effective window specified by the hold time and alter the value of the signal from that of the later assignment. Such transactions, if they assign a value different from the later assignment, would not have been stable for the required hold time, and would not influence the output.

Miscellaneous Syntax Changes

Direct Instantiation is now possible, and refers to the ability to specify the instantiation of an `entity(architecture)` pair directly, without a component binding.

Configuration Binding has been introduced to eliminate the need for writing empty configurations.

Other small changes have been made. The reserved word **is** is now permitted (but, for upward compatibility with VHDL-87, not required) in some places where its use would be natural. Similarly, specifiers such as **function** and **architecture** are optional in the **end** clauses for the object declarations. It is now possible to use the backslash character to enclose *extended* identifiers, identifiers that would not normally be allowed as valid VHDL identifiers because they contain illegal characters, begin with a number, contain a blank, or conflict with a reserved word.

A number of issues remain under study and will likely be the subject of revisions to the standard, or new standards, at a later date. These include back-annotation and the format for the SDF (standard delay file), standard mathematical function package, analog simulation, and the specification for finite-state machines.

MISCELLANEOUS TOPICS

The NOW Function

The STANDARD package defines a function, NOW, which returns the present value of the time. This function is of obvious utility, and will be used a number of times in our simulation example in Chapter 15. For example:

```
signal Present: TIME;
Present <= NOW;
```

This will set Present to the current value of the time. ote that advancing by a simulation cycle will not change the present value of time.

The standard package of VHDL-92 contains the definintions:

```
subtype DELAY_LENGTH is TIME range 0fs to
TIME'HIGH; impure function NOW return DE-
LAY_LENGTH;
```

The new subtype DELAY_LENGTH constrains TIME and NOW is declared to be **impure** because it has memory, and will not return the same value every time it is called, even though it has no arguments that might change.

Overloading

As in languages such as Ada or C++, functions, operators, enumeration type values, and so forth, may be overloaded, or given different meanings based on context. For example, it may be desirable to have a number of functions named READ(), that are called to read a value in from a file. One would read integer values, another TIME values, etc. They could all be named READ. VHDL would distinguish between these functions based on the type of variable to be returned. Note that VHDL is only capable of "static binding"; it must be able to determine at compilation time which version of the function READ to call. An example of operator overloading might be the following:

```
function "+" (A,B: in BIT) return BIT is
    -- OR function
    begin
    return  A or B;
    end;
```

Note the use of the quotation marks (") to tell the compiler that the reserved operator (+) is not an operator here but a literal value, that is, a function name. Note the comment below about overloading short-circuited operators. One can of course overload the names of user subprograms, so long as there is no ambiguity.

To resolve possible ambiguities between functions with the same name, the *signature* of the overloaded function may be specified. This is the list of arguments and return values that must be matched, and should uniquely determine the function desired. For example:

```
attribute ShortCircuited of "or" (MVL9, MVL9
return MVL9) is TRUE;
```

Short-Circuited Operations

One feature of note is the "short-circuited" logical operation. Consider a logical expression of the form: A and B. Clearly, if A is FALSE there is no need to evaluate B, as the conjunction cannot be anything but false whatever B is. Similarly, in the expression A or B, if A is TRUE there is no need to evaluate B. In Wirth's Modula-2 language, all such logical expressions are short-circuited: if it is unnecessary to evaluate the latter portion of the expression, this evaluation is omitted. In Ada, these operators are not short-circuited. However, it is possible to use operators that are short-circuited, the *and ... then* and *or ... else* operators. The short-circuited operator does not have a hardware analog, as the synthesized logical operation would be performed in parallel by hardware. The logical operations in VHDL are short-circuited (LRM 7.2.1). Thus, **and** in VHDL corresponds to **and then** in Ada rather than Ada's **and**, with VHDL's **or** corresponding to Ada's **or else**. VHDL does not support non-short-circuited logical operations. This should not make a difference unless the evaluation of expression B has side-effects, which is usually not good programming practice. But such side-effects are allowed within VHDL, notably in procedures that can make signal assignments.

It should be noted that if a short-circuited operator, such as the **and** operator, is overloaded, the function overloading the operator should not be assumed to be short-circuited (LRM 2.3.1).

The goto Statement

The oft-maligned *goto* statement is not to be found in VHDL. In some circumstances, its use may be obviated by the use of short-circuited logical expressions discussed above, which are, however, also absent from VHDL. This omission might perhaps ease the task of synthesis tools that work from the behavioral description of a sequential function. If VHDL were intended to be a general-purpose language, I would deem the lack of a goto a mistake. Because VHDL is not such a language, and because the logical structure should be constrained so as to permit synthesis tools a chance of analyzing programs, the omission of the goto is probably a good design choice.

REFERENCES

Draft Standard VHDL Language Reference Manual, P1076-1992A, Oct. 7, 1992.

Dunlop, D., and Ussery, C., "An Introduction to VHDL-92," *VIUF Spring 1992*, May 3-6, 1992, Scottsdale, Arizona.

Section II

Using VHDL

Chapter 11

VHDL Programming

PURPOSE

This and the following chapters of this book assume fluency in VHDL. You should refer back to the first section of this book as necessary. Now that you understand the language, it is time to discuss how to apply the language. This chapter will introduce a number of useful simulation tools.

This chapter has two major sections. The first covers the basic data structures and algorithms of interest to VHDL users. It is intended to provide the foundation for VHDL tools developed in later chapters, and to provide concrete examples to reinforce the lessons of the first section of this book. The second covers methods for concurrency control and mutual exclusion. This is an important tool in both simulating and implementing multiprocessor systems. Even "simple" RISC processors have superscalar and pipelined architectures that have a great deal of concurrent activity, and current hardware evolution is in the direction of many processors tied together over busses and networks. For this reason, concurrency will become an ever-increasing factor in design and simulation. Concurrency in simulation will be discussed in the next chapter. Here its simulation is discussed, with reference to issues such as mutual exclusion and shared memory.

DATA STRUCTURE USE

Stacks and Pseudo-Stacks

People who have programmed the Intel 80x87 family of floating-point math coprocessors, or used RPN (Reverse Polish Notation) calculators, or seen a "lazy susan" probably know what a stack is. A stack, also called a first-in last-out (FILO) or last-in first-out (LIFO) queue, or a push-down stack, is a restricted form of memory in which only the most recently stored item is accessible. It is thus similar to stacking items one on top of the other, which allows only the topmost item to be removed, and additions to the stack may be made only by placing an item on top. The removal operation is typically called a "pop," while adding an item to the stack is generally called a "push."

In principle, the abstract data type (ADT) stack is of unlimited storage, and cannot be implemented in hardware. The Intel coprocessors emulate such a stack with a finite memory buffer of eight registers. These registers are never addressed directly, but always through an address relative to the top-of-stack register, which is stored in a register of three bits, holding values from 0 to 7. A circular buffer is used, so that up to eight data values may be stored, with the value in the register above the top-of-stack (if there is any such value) being the eighth value, or seventh value below the top-of-stack value. Associated with each register is a tag that shows whether the register is empty, and whether it contains a finite or infinite value. A "Stack overflow" error will be signaled when the top-of-stack moves up into a nonempty register. As the stack of the 80x87 is not a true stack ADT, we will call it a pseudo-stack. Simulation of this circular buffer will be discussed below. Micro-program sequencers, such as the IDT49C410, have a finite-length stack (33 deep in this case) to support subroutine calls and returns within microcode.

Stacks and pseudo-stacks are important in software and hardware. The use of operator precedence parsing produces postfix or reverse Polish notation expressions for arithmetical expressions, for example. These are relatively simply evaluated by a processor that uses a stack. Interrupt handling is typically done by stacking interrupts. This permits an interrupt handler to be interrupted.

Operating systems typically divide free memory into two sections, the stack and the heap. Often, one contiguous area is allotted to the user, with the stack building down from the top of the area and the heap building up. The heap area is then used to allocate memory requested by the user, such as with the **new** operation in VHDL. Every time a subprogram or interrupt handler is called, it obtains a portion of the stack, its stack frame, which is used for the storage of local variables and other information such as the return address. This permits recursive and re-entrant coding. At the end of the subprogram's execution, the stack frame is deallocated from the stack. This means that every time the subroutine is called, it gets a new stack frame, forgetting the values of local variables that were used in a previous call. This behavior has been the source of some grief to programmers who learned FORTRAN a long time ago when the implementation was different and such variables were remembered between calls. FORTRAN77 gave us the SAVE declaration which puts local subprogram variables into an area in the heap and so they are remembered, at the cost of preventing recursive or re-entrant use of such routines.

Simulating stacks (and pseudo-stacks) is therefore useful in simulating both hardware and interaction with the real world. For this reason, let us consider the following implementation of a stack package. The fundamental operations are the pop and push operations, which remove or add data to the stack, respectively. In addition, it may be desirable to create the stack explicitly, ask other questions about the stack, check for overflow on a finite stack, and so forth.

In Ada, with its *generic* facility, or C++ 3.0 with templates, it is possible to define a stack class (to use the C++ terminology) that will work for any data to be stored on the stack. This class is then

instantiated for each data type of interest. VHDL does not have that
facility. Generics in VHDL are parameters, not data types.

Consider the following package for stacking integer data elements:

```
package Stack_Int is
-- define visible portion of the code
-- set frame for stacking integer data
type Framedata is INTEGER;
-- rest of code is relatively generic
type Frame;
type FramePtr is access Frame;
type Frame is record
   Data: Framedata;
   Next: FramePtr;
end record;


-- generic stack:
--user can have multiple stacks
-- only Frame declaration need be changed
-- for other data types
type Stack;
type StackPtr is access Stack;
type Frame is record
   Top: FramePtr:=null;
   Size: NATURAL:=0;
end record;
-- allowed public operations:
-- First operation on any stack must be
-- its creation.
function  Stack_Create return StackPtr;
function  Stack_Size (MYStack: StackPtr)
    return NATURAL;
procedure Push(MYStack: inout StackPtr;
   Value: in Framedata);
procedure Pop(MYStack: inout StackPtr;
   Value: out Framedata);
```

```
procedure Stack_Destroy(MYStack:
   inout StackPtr);
end Stack_Int;

package body Stack_Int is
function Stack_Create return StackPtr is vari-
able NewStack: StackPtr;
 begin
   NewStack := new Stack;
   --initialize stack to empty
   NewStack.Size := 0;
   NewStack.Top := null;
   return NewStack;
end Stack_Create ;

function Stack_Size (MYStack: StackPtr)
   return NATURAL is
begin
   return MYStack.Size;
end Stack_Size;

procedure Push(MYStack: inout StackPtr;
Value: in Framedata) is
variable NewFrame: FramePtr;
begin
-- first, create new frame
NewFrame := new Frame;
NewFrame.Data := Value;
-- add new frame to top of stack
NewFrame.Next := MyStack.Top;
 MYStack.Size := MYStack.Size  +1 ;
-- New top of stack:
MyStack.Top :=NewFrame;
end Push;

procedure Pop(MYStack: inout StackPtr;
```

```
Value: out Framedata)is
variable Popped: FramePtr;
begin
Popped := MyStack.Top;
Value := Popped.Value;
MYStack.Top := Popped.Next;
Deallocate (Popped);
  MYStack.Size := MYStack.Size  - 1;
end Pop;


procedure Stack_Destroy(MYStack: inout
StackPtr) is
variable MYFrame,NextFrame: FramePtr
   :=MYStack.Top;
begin
-- first, get rid of all frames
MYFrame :=MYStack.Top;
while MYFrame /= null loop
  NextFrame :=MYFrame.Next;
  Deallocate (MYFrame);
  MYFrame := NextFrame;
end loop;
-- finally, destroy stack itself
Deallocate(MYStack);
-- MYStack is now null
end Stack_Destroy;


end Stack_Int;
```

Note the structure of the package declaration followed by the package body. The declaration makes available to the user the type declarations and the subprograms listed. In this example, there was no need for private subprograms in the body that are not directly callable by the user.

We have conformed to the convention, mentioned in Chapter 5, of naming access types by appending Ptr to the type they access.

This is a standard practice in Ada, and helps keep clear what points to what.

The package has been written to be easily modified. Altering the declaration for type `Framedata` would suffice to make the stack package suitable for any other data type, including records, instead of type INTEGER as used in the example. We named the package Stack_Int to emphasize that, as currently written, it is designed to stack integers.

Recall that access types must be variables, and that variables may not be declared in package declarations or as globals within packages. This means that such access-type variables must be passed in as arguments to the subprograms of the package.

First, we define the data, `Framedata`, to be stacked. We then define the stack frame or data element as a record to be stacked. This requires the use of an incomplete type declaration (Chapter 5) in order to define the pointer type and have such pointers included in the record. The pointers link together the elements on the stack. The ADT stack is therefore implemented through the use of another, somewhat more general ADT, the linked-list.

Each stack has a record that records the number of elements in the stack, and has a pointer to the top of the stack. Because this is the only frame or element of the stack that is visible to the user, this is all that is needed. The stack frames or elements then link down through one another via the Next pointer.

A stack is created by a call to `Stack_Create`. This initializes the stack explicitly, although the default values would not differ from the explicit values (0 is NATURAL' LEFT). Aggregates could also have been used to simplify the initialization if so desired, but it is more transparent (although it may be less efficient) to initialize as shown.

The `Push` operation creates a new frame, places the appropriate data in it, and then alters `MYStack` to point to this new frame as the new top of stack, as well as increasing the count of stacked elements by one. (It might be argued that the ADT stack should not support the function `Stack_Size`. You may delete the function

from your copy of the package, and then delete the references to the
Size variable, if you feel this way.)

Pop is the inverse operation. It obtains the data value to be
returned to the caller, adjusts the top of stack pointer and stack
count, and frees the storage used by the top of stack element for
reuse.

Stack_Destroy gets rid of all of the frames, and then deletes
the stack record itself. It will return a **null** value for the pointer to
the Stack record.

If you are a novice to the use of pointers, access types, and
records, you should review this example until it seems clear. Consulting a good book on Ada for examples of similar usage for access types and pointers. There are also numerous books on data
structures that might be of value. A number of these are listed as
references at the end of this chapter.

Lists, Buffers

As noted in the preceding discussion, a circular buffer is used to
emulate a stack in the Intel 80x87. A functional model of this
would be the following:

```
package Stack_8087is
type Register_Set is array (0 to 7 )
   of REAL;
type Tag_Set is array (0 to 7 ) of BIT;
type TOS is INTEGER range 0 to 7;
type Registers_8087 is
   record Registers: Registers_8087;
   Empty: Tag_Set;
   Finite: Tag_Set:
   TOS: Integer;
end record;
procedure Pop( Reg: inout Registers_8087;
   Value: out REAL);
procedure Push (Reg: inout Registers_8087;
   Value: in   REAL);
```

```
procedureInit(Reg: inout Registers_8087);
endStack_8087;

package body Stack_8087 is
begin
procedure Pop( Reg: inout Registers_8087;
   Value: outREAL)
begin
if Reg.Empty(Reg.TOS) =' 1' then
assert TRUE report
    " 8087 Access Empty Stack"
   severity WARNING;
else
   Value := Reg.Registers(Reg.TOS);
   Reg.Empty(Reg.TOS) := ' 1' ;
   Reg.TOS := (Reg.TOS - 1) mod 8 ;
end if ;
end Pop;

procedure Push (Reg: inout Registers_8087;
 Value: in REAL);
variable NewTOS: TOS; begin
NewTOS := ( Reg.TOS + 1 ) mod 8;
if Reg.Empty(NewTOS) =' 1' then
   Reg.Empty(NewTOS) := ' 0' ;
   if Value = 0.0  then
      Reg.Finite(NewTOS) := ' 1' ;
   else
      Reg.Finite(NewTOS) := ' 0' ;
   end if;
   -- tag now: 00 valid, 01 if zero.
   -- would become 10 if error
   --    (NaN or infinite)
   -- it is assumed here user would
   -- not Push such a value
   Reg.Registers(NewTOS) := Value;
```

```
    Reg.Empty(NewTOS)  :=  ' 0' ;
    Reg.TOS  :=  NewTOS ;
else
-- Error: value is stored in TOS
  assert TRUE report " 8087 Stack Overflow"
  severity WARNING;
end if;
end Push;


procedureInit(Reg:  inout Registers_8087);
begin
-- must set tags 11= empty.
for I in 0 to 7 loop
    Reg.Empty(I)  :=' 1' ;
    Reg.Finite(I) :=' 1' ;
end loop;
Reg.TOS  :=7;  end Init;


endStack_8087;
```

Access types are not required or used. As the register set is of fixed size, the use of an array is more natural and would permit synthesis. Pseudocode has been used where the test for an infinite value occurs.

Note the information hiding of VHDL is weaker than in some other object-oriented languages. In VHDL, it is not possible to prevent the user from, say, reading register Reg.Registers(3), whatever the top of the stack value is, because this data must be declared within the code that invokes the package. It is not possible to define data hidden in the package, as with Ada. Even if the data is assigned to a signal instead of a variable, it will still be visible outside of the package.

Circular buffers are usually implemented with indices or pointers to the head and the tail of the list. This was not done here in order to conform more closely to the usage of the 80x87 family.

QUEUES AND DEQUEUES

A queue is a sequence of objects waiting for service. The *queue discipline* is the way in which objects are prioritized. A general queue in which objects are prioritized by their properties is a priority queue. VHDL simulators must, in effect, use a priority queue to schedule transactions based on their time. A stack is a last-in, first-out (LIFO) queue. The first-in, first-out (FIFO) queue is the model for a waiting line at a supermarket checkout stand. The LIFO queue is what is meant when the word queue is unqualified by an adjective such as priority.

The Intel 80960MC supports process management with hardware support for a queue data type. As processes are suspended they are added to the end of the queue and the process at the head of the queue is removed from the queue and activated. The queue discipline is therefore first-in, first-out (FIFO), unlike the stack. Items are removed from the front and added to the end. This discipline corresponds to "round-robin" scheduling of processes.

Ada code for queues of various forms may be found in numerous books, including Booch (1987), and will not be covered here in detail. Two pointers must be maintained to point to the head (front) and tail (end) of a LIFO queue. In implementing such a queue as an abstract data type (ADT), with unbounded memory, a linked-list can be used. Such an implementation will use access types as pointers for both the head and tail as well as the links between queued clients. In a finite-memory situation, a circular list or array may be used, with pointers into the array being implemented as the integer addresses of the head and tail in the array. As in the stack implementation, checks must be made to ensure that additions to the queue do not cause the new tail to overwrite the head. For a C implementation, see, for example, the article (1992) by Jaeschke.

A dequeue is a double ended queue, or one in which additions or deletions may be made to either end. See, for example, Booch (1987), for Ada code.

CONCURRENCY, MUTUAL EXCLUSION

When a number of processors are operating concurrently, there could be problems when they modify or read the same data. For example, if there is a stack or circular buffer that may be accessed simultaneously by two processes, one might alter the top of stack index and, before using this modified index to access data, the other process could further modify the top of stack index, resulting in the first process producing erroneous results because it did not deal with the data item it thought it did.

To prevent different processors from tripping over each other, a method of *mutual exclusion* must be provided. Portions of code dealing with shared variables or that are otherwise hazardous are called *critical sections*. If only one of the processors is in its critical section at any time, then the situation is *safe*. But safety is not enough. It is also necessary to insure that a situation does not arise in which all the processes are *deadlocked*, that is, where each is politely saying "After you . . . No, please, after you . . . ."

Many of the solutions to the mutual exclusion problem that avoid deadlock and are safe permit *starvation*. If an unlucky process might possibly wait forever for permission to enter its critical section, the mutual exclusion method is not safe from starvation. Obviously, starvation prevention requires a mutual exclusion method that prioritizes processes in such a manner that a process that has been waiting for a long time will get preference over a newcomer. A general prioritized mutual exclusion method would subsume the starvation-free methods.

The implementation of hardware features such as atomic test and set instructions greatly simplifies the software designer's task. But the same sorts of mutual exclusion problems arise when a number of hardware units contend for a resource, such as processors sharing a bus. Consequently, these mutual exclusion considerations are relevant for hardware as well as software.

VHDL-92 introduces features for built-in mutual exclusion. These are discussed under "Shared Memory, Locks" in this chapter and in Chapter 10. While it may not be necessary to code your own control of access to shared variables with such features, it is still useful to provide the background for mutual exclusion methods.

Classic Mutual Exclusion Methods

We first present some of the classic mutual exclusion algorithms, translated into VHDL. Because of the behavior of signals and variables in VHDL, it is not completely straightforward to make the translation. However, precisely because of the way signals are resolved, mutual exclusion can be done in VHDL in a direct method. These classic methods may be of interest in some applications where their synthesis, perhaps in microcode, is required.

The classic algorithms generally use "busy waiting," whereby processes contending for access to the critical resource continually attempt to gain access. In a multitasking environment, it is much better to use another approach, such as discussed under monitors below, in which contending processes register their desire and then suspend until a supervisory process assigns them the required resource. Such a protocol requires a supervisor, of course, not a collection of peers.

One of the simpler and more popular mutual exclusion methods is that due to Peterson (1981). It is of the following form, in VHDL, for two processes:

```
variable Q1,Q2: BOOLEAN;
 variable Turn: INTEGER;
signal Wakeup:   WakeupRes BIT;
process P1 is
begin
   Q1 := TRUE; Turn := 1;
wait on Wakeup' TRANSACTION
   until ( not Q2 ) or ( Turn = 2) ) ;
   Critical Section;
   Q1 := FALSE;
   Wakeup <= ' 1' ;
    Non-Critical Section;
end P1;
```

```
process P2 is
begin
   Q2 := TRUE; Turn := 2;
   wait on Wakeup' TRANSACTION
   until ( not Q1 ) or ( Turn = 1) ) ;
   Critical Section;
   Q2 := FALSE;
   Wakeup <= ' 1' ; Non-Critical Section;
end P2;
```

Because signal assignments do not take effect until the next simulation cycle has begun, the use of signals in place of the shared variables here would not work! A process suspended by a **wait until** *condition* statement requires an event on a signal in the sensitivity set of the process to reactivate. As a process containing a **wait** statement, or calling a subprogram that contains one, cannot have a sensitivity list, it is assumed that other **wait** statements have appropriate sensitivity lists. The purpose of the Wakeup signal is to trigger the evaluation of the conditional in the wait statement. This will happen whenever a process leaves its critical section, and it becomes safe for another to enter its critical section. Wakeup must be a resolved signal, as it will have a driver and hence a source in each concurrent process. Because we only care about an assignment to Wakeup producing a transaction, which is then converted into an event by the ' TRANSACTION attribute, the nature of the resolution function is irrelevant.

The only way both processes could be in their critical sections at the same time is with Q1 = Q2 = TRUE. The **wait** statements would prevent this unless Turn evaluates to 2 in P1 and 1 in P2. Because each process sets Turn to a value that precludes its proceeding through to the critical section, this is not possible. P1, for example, cannot proceed into the critical section while Q2 is TRUE unless Turn = 2. Suppose P1 set Turn to 1 just before P2 assigned the value of 2 to it. Then P1 proceeds into the critical section. But then P2 cannot, during its test, find either Q1 = FALSE or Turn = 1. A more rigorous proof of safety is provided by

Axford (1989). Peterson (1981) proves *liveness*, the fact that neither process can be locked out indefinitely.

This method is not proof from starvation, however. It is possible for P1 to wait forever if it is unlucky and P2 is such that it keeps sneaking back into its critical section before P1 notices that Q2 is FALSE while it is FALSE, or that Turn = 2 while that is true and Q2 is TRUE.

The method generalizes to *N* processes:

```
variable Q: array ( 1 to N) of INTEGER:=0;
variable Turn: array
    ( 1 to (N-1) ) of INTEGER:=1;
signal Wakeup: BIT;
function Permission (I: in INTEGER )
    return BOOLEAN is
variable Permit: BOOLEAN:=TRUE;
begin
for K in 1 to N loop
  if K /= I then
    if Q(K) =J then
        Permit := FALSE;
    end if;
  end if;
end loop;
return
end;
-- Ith process
process P is
begin
for J := 1 to N-1 loop
  Q(I) := J;
  Turn(J) := I;
; wait on Wakeup' TRANSACTION
    until Permission(I) or (Turn(J) = I )) ;
end loop;
Critical Section;
Q(I) := 0 ;
```

```
Wakeup <= '1'; Non-Critical Section;
end P;
```

Notice that a **generate** statement could be used to generate a number of similar processes with different values for I.

Let us consider solutions to mutual exclusion that are *fair*, that is, that prevent starvation. There are a number of popular alternatives. One is Lamport's (1974) Bakery Algorithm. This method is so named because it simulates the manner in which customers are prioritized as they enter a bakery and wait for service. They obtain a ticket with their priority stamped on it, and get service when their number is called:

```
type ProcList is array ( 1 to N) of INTE-
GER; variable Choosing: ProcList:=0;
variable Number: ProcList:=0;
signal Wakeup: BIT;
function Pair (A,B,C,D: in INTEGER )
   return BOOLEAN is
begin
return not( (A) or ((A=C)and  B)); end;
function Max (N: inProcLIst ) return
BOOLEAN is
Maximum: INTEGER := INTEGER'MIN; begin
for I in  ProcList'RANGE loop
   if N(I)  Maximum then
     Maximum := N(I);
   end if;
end loop;
return Maximum;
end;
function Permit(I: INTEGER ) return BOOLEAN
is
variable Proceed: BOOLEAN:=TRUE; begin
for J in  ProcList'RANGE loop
   ifChoosing ( J ) /= 0 then
     Proceed := FALSE; end if;
```

```
if (Number    ( J ) /=0 and
   Pair(Number(J),J,Number(I),I)
 then
      Proceed := FALSE; end if;
end loop;
return Proceed;
end;

-- Ith process
process P is
begin
Choosing ( I )  : = 1 ;
Number ( I ) := 1 + Max( Number);
Choosing ( I )  : = 0 ;
wait on Wakeup' TRANSACTION
   until Permit( I );
Critical Section;
Number ( I ) := 0 ;
Wakeup <= ' 1'; Non-Critical Section;
end P;
```

The Ith process is said by Lamport to be "in the doorway" and taking a number while Choosing (I) = 1. It is in the bakery from the time it resets Choosing (I) to 0 until it leaves the critical section. If I entered the bakery before K, Number (I) < Number (K). The function Pair must evaluate to TRUE if process J is in the critical section and I is in the bakery. These two facts lead to the processors entering their critical sections in a first-come, first-served basis, preventing starvation. A complete proof is in Lamport's paper.

One difficulty with Lamport's algorithm is that the value assigned to Number (I) may become arbitrarily large and cause an overflow. There does not seem to be a solution to this difficulty except to handle such an overflow when it occurs by resetting the values and then proceeding.

Knuth (1966) has given a starvation-free mutual exclusion algorithm, which does not, however, provide first-come, first-served ac-

cess of processes to their critical sections. Here it is, as improved by
de Bruijn (1968):

```vhdl
variable Q: array ( 1 to N) of INTEGER:=0;
variable K: INTEGER:=0;
signal Wakeup: BIT;
function Permit(I: INTEGER ) return BOOLEAN
is
variable Proceed: BOOLEAN:=FALSE;
begin
Q ( I ) := 1;
for J in  K downto 1 loop
   if  I = J then
      Proceed := TRUE;
      exit;
   end  if;
   if Q ( J) = 0 then
      Proceed := FALSE;
      exit;
   end if;
end loop;
if not Proceed then
   for J in  N downto 1 loop
      if  I = J then
         Proceed := TRUE;
         exit;
      end  if;
      if Q ( J) = 0 then
         Proceed := FALSE;
         exit;
      end if;
   end loop;
end if;
if Proceed = FALSE then return  Proceed;
end if;
Q ( I ) := 2;
for J in  ProcList' REVERSE_RANGE loop
```

```
   if J   /= I and Q ( J ) = 2 then
      Proceed := FALSE;
   end if;
end loop;
return Proceed;
end;


-- Ith process
process P is
begin
wait on Wakeup' TRANSACTION
   until Permit(I);
Critical Section;
if Q ( K ) = 0 or K = I then
   if  K  = 1 then
      K := N;
   else
      K := K - 1;
   end if;
end if;
Q ( I ) := 0;
Wakeup <= ' 1' ; Non-Critical Section;
end P;
```

Knuth's method is a modification of an algorithm by Dijkstra (1965), which is a generalization of one by Dekker. de Bruijn reduced the maximum waiting time for a process to enter its critical section over that of Knuth's algorithm. A further improvement is due to Eisenberg and McGuire (1972). In their method, before a process yields the critical section to another, it decides how to fairly pass control on to the next contending process. This is done in a round-robin sequence. For an implementation in Ada of some of these methods and a discussion, see Saeed et al. (1992). Ben-Ari's (1982) book provides a careful development of the method, and Tanenbaum (1992) provides a discussion of mutual exclusion, focusing on Peterson's simplified algorithm.

VHDL Mutual Exclusion

It is natural to use resolution functions to resolve disagreements between processes as to which deserves to enter the critical section. For example:

```
-- process ID Number with permission
signal Proceed: Permit NATURAL:=0;
-- Ith process
process P is
begin
-- Request permission
Proceed <= I;
wait on Proceed until Proceed = I;
Critical Section;
Proceed <= 0; Non-Critical Section;
end P;
function Permit (Requestors :
   array of NATURAL ) return NATURAL is
begin
for I in Requestors' RANGE loop
pick one of the requestors
end loop;
end;
```

Note that after we assign the value I to signal Proceed, the wait will take effect until the next simulation cycle. At that point, the resolution function will have done its job and the value of Proceed will be the resolved value, that is, one of the processes will have been given permission to enter its critical section by having Proceed set to its ID number. (See Chapters 2 and 7 for a discussion of the **wait** statement, if this is unclear to you.) The resolution function acts as a supervisory process that chooses among the contending processes.

Here we could pick the process with the minimum or maximum I, for example, thereby establishing a priority scheme. Such a method would not prevent starvation. For a first-come, first-served (FCFS) method, signal Proceed would have to be a record type including a time stamp. We could then select the processor with the earliest time associated with its request. A FCFS discipline would prevent starvation, for latecomers would not prevent the earliest requester from receiving service indefinitely, as they could not even prevent it from preceding themselves:

```
-- process on First Come, First Served Basis
type Request is record
   IDNumber : NATURAL :=0;
   Priority : TIME; end record;
signal Proceed: Permit Request;
-- Ith process
process P is
begin
-- Request permission
Proceed <= ( I, NOW );
wait on Proceed until Proceed.IDNumber = I;
Critical Section;
Proceed <= ( 0 , NOW ); Non-Critical Sec-
tion;
end P;
-- Resolution function
function Permit (Requesters : array of NATU-
RAL ) return NATURAL is
variable Go: NATURAL; variable Most: TIME;
begin
if Requesters' LENGTH =0 then return (0,NOW) ;
-- otherwise, at least one requester
Most := Requesters.Priority(1); for I in Re-
questers' RANGE loop
   if Requesters( I ) . Priority  Most then
      Most := Requesters ( I) . Priority;
      Go := I;
   end if;
end loop;
return ( Go, Most); end;
```

Obviously, the scheme could be refined with a more complex data record that could, for example, specify different priority classes for different processes. Because the resolution function is passed an array of signal values to be resolved, without information as to which driver is the source of which value, the signal must contain components with any associated information, such as time stamps or priorities.

Because the signal is not of type **register**, the resolution function might be called with an empty array under the circumstance that no process wishes to enter the critical section at the present time. If we had declared the signal to be of type register, then we would have to use only guarded assignments, which is not desirable.

The approach given here should be used for mutual exclusion in VHDL-87 programs, instead of the classic algorithms, as it should be simpler and more natural. The classic algorithms should be used as needed for exclusion outside of the VHDL environment, either in hardware or software. In such cases, the original algorithms as published should be studied, as the translation to microcode would be more direct.

Atomic Instructions

The difficulty in mutual exclusion is maintaining the consistency of shared variables. If process P1 checks the "all clear" flag and finds that it is okay to proceed into its critical section, it is possible that process P2 will do the same before P1 resets the flag to exclude others. One approach to solving this problem is to provide an atomic, that is, indivisible instruction, which both checks the flag and sets it. There are a number of different versions of such hardware solutions.

One example is the exchange instruction, which is available on a number of architectures including EXG instruction in the Motorola 68000 family, the XMEM of the 88100 RISC chip, also from Motorola, the SWAP instruction of the SPARC architecture from

SUN, and the 80386 XCHG and others in the Intel 80x86 family. The XCHG A,B instruction has this effect:

```
TEMP := A; A:=B; B:=TEMP;
```

where these three actions are indivisible. On the 80386, A must be a register variable, but B can be a memory location, so A will be a global but B can be local to each process. If a 0 denotes that it is safe to enter the critical section, consider the effect of a process that sets its local value of B to 1 and does an XCHG A,B. If B is now 0, it is safe for the process to proceed into its critical section. If not, it must wait (or do something else). This method obviously general-izes trivially to any number of processes. However, starvation is not precluded. Other hardware support for mutual exclusion, such as the test and set instruction, behaves similarly.

The i486 added six new instructions to the instruction set of the 80386, three of them atomic exchanges: Exchange and Add, com-pare and Exchange, and Byte Swap. The last is primarily intended for use in changing between big-endian and little-endian data for-mats, while the other two atomic instructions should be of use in a multiprogramming and multiprocessor environment. (The other three instructions were for invalidating cache and translation lookaside buffers.)

Other architectures provide different atomic instructions that may be used in a similar fashion to coordinate concurrent processes. For example, the Intel 80960 family, while not having an exchange instruction, does support two instructions, the atomic add and atomic modify. The latter will alter selected bits of a word, and therefore supports a generalization of our example of exclusion us-ing the exchange instruction, which used only values 0 and 1. It could therefore be used to support a prioritized mutual exclusion algorithm.

Shared Memory, Locks

When multiple processors can access shared memory, they must communicate with control signals to prevent simultaneous access. This includes cases in which a microprocessor and a support chip, such as a DMA (Direct Memory Access) controller, might both wish to access the same memory. Many microprocessors have a LOCK signal that, when active, tells other processors sharing the memory bus not to attempt to access memory. Obviously, such an arrangement works only if one processor is the bus master, with the other processors subordinate to it and obeying its commands in this regard.

Shared memory concerns may arise when a number of data items can be altered separately and must be consistent. For example, if a real-time system is updating the observed X and Y coordinates of a target, it is desirable to prevent inconsistent values of X and Y being read, as might happen if the read occurs after X is updated but before Y is. Concerns may also arise when a single variable can be written to and read from by a number of processes, for which mutual exclusion is required. An example is the semaphore variable, discussed in the next section.

VHDL-92 introduces **shared** variables. It had been proposed to support critical sections which are declared as **protect**-ed blocks, but this feature did not make it into the draft standard. Therefore, the user will have to control access to such variables by means of the techniques discussed here.

Semaphores

Assuming we have a mutual exclusion method, how do we make use of it? One aid to users would be to encapsulate the entry and exit for critical sections. Such a mechanism is called the semaphore. Typically, operating systems provide two functions, called either *wait()* and *signal()*, or *P()* and *V()* (based on the abbreviations for the corresponding Dutch words, as first presented by semaphore inventor Dijkstra). The usage is then of the following form:

wait();
critical section;
signal();
non-critical section;

Most real-time operating systems provide support for semaphores. Semaphores are a relatively low-level form of mutual exclusion, and require all users to behave well. For example, if one process fails to execute its signal() call properly, for any reason, this will cause the entire system to deadlock and fail. Ben-Ari (1982) provides many examples for the use of semaphores. Semaphores may be used for purposes other than mutual exclusion. Synchronizing processes so that they perform actions in a controlled sequence is one such use.

Monitors

A higher-level and therefore safer approach to mutual exclusion is the monitor, a concept due to C. A. R. Hoare (1965). A monitor encapsulates the calls to wait() and signal(), preventing mistakes in user code from abusing these calls.

Each object of possible contention is assigned a monitor, and this monitor is the only allowed form of access to this resource. Thus, a shared variable will have an associated monitor, and all reads of or writes to that variable are through requests of the monitor. In this way, if the system's programmer has done his or her job well and written the monitor correctly, there need be no concern about user mistakes.

Ben-Ari (1982) book devotes a chapter to monitors, showing how semaphores may be implemented with monitors and vice versa. Because of this symmetry, neither has more expressive power than the other.

Readers and Writers

A generalization of the mutual exclusion is the readers/writers problem. This consists of a buffer into which one process writes while, concurrently, another process reads data from the buffer. This problem is more complicated than the usual mutual exclusion problem because of the different nature of the two processes that require access to the data buffer.

In one version of the problem, a reader consumes data. The buffer may contain any number, up to the limit imposed by the buffer's size, of such data packets, and the reader may consume them until they are exhausted. In this version of the problem, a write to the buffer should not prevent one or more intervening reads from taking place as soon as possible.

In another version, the data represents a set of associated readings being continuously updated. Here, the reader should access the most recent, complete data set. This may be implemented with a buffer holding two sets of data; then it becomes a special case of the other version of the problem. The producer or writer process writes alternately to buffers A and B. The consumer or reader will read first from A, assuming it has been filled, then it will wait until B is filled and read from it, alternating and reading from one half of the buffer while the producer is writing to the other.

Tokens and the Token Ring Bus

A bus or network is a shared resource that generally has a mutual exclusion requirement. At most one device must be transmitting on the bus at any time; otherwise, a garble will result and no message will be clearly received. Chapter 16 will cover bus protocols in detail. Here we will briefly discuss the mutual exclusion problem as it applies to busses.

The Token Ring Bus IEEE 802.5 protocol is an example of a solution to the problem. The basic idea is that there is a "token" that gives permission to talk over the bus. This token is passed from node to node on the bus. Obviously, if the token is lost, the bus is deadlocked. Therefore, procedures have to be developed to detect such a circumstance and regenerate the token.

Ricart and Agrawala present a distributed algorithm, based on Lamport's Bakery Algorithm, for first-come, first-served mutual exclusion on a computer network by sending messages between processors. Any process wishing to enter the critical region sends a message declaring its desire to do so to all the other processes. This message is time-stamped. The requester then waits until it has received permission from all other possible contenders. Receiving processes take one of three actions, depending on their status:

(1) If they are not in the critical section and do not wish to contend for entering it, they reply to the sender, stating that they have no objections.

(2) If the receiver is in the critical section, it queues the information until it exits. Then it sends its permission to all of the queued requestors (emptying the queue in the process).

(3) If it is not in the critical section but wishes to enter, it compares its priority to do so with that on the received request. This is done by comparing when it first requested entry to the critical section with the time-stamp on the received request, the earlier requester winning in the first-come, first-served method of Rickart and Agrawala. If the requester has priority, the receiver replies with its permission. Otherwise, the information is queued until the receiver has departed the critical section, at which point it sends permissions and empties the queue.

There are modifications, as discussed in Tanenbaum (1992), to prevent the failure of a processor from causing starvation. One method is to have an acknowledgment always sent upon reception of a request. This permits the sender to determine that a processor is "down," if no acknowledgment is received before a specified timeout period, and that it should not wait for permission from that processor before entering the critical section.

Caveat

Mutual exclusion is a minefield. Many published solutions have been wrong, and it is not impossible that errors have crept into the code in this chapter. Great care must be taken in testing and, if possible, proving correctness.

REFERENCES

The following references provide good coverage of data structures and algorithms. Because VHDL syntax has been based on that of

Ada, books on such topics in Ada are particularly useful to the novice.

Aho, A. V., Hopcroft, J. E., and Ullman, J. D., *Data Structures and Algorithms* (Reading, MA: Addison Wesley, 1983).

Baase, Sara, *Computer Algorithms*, 2nd ed. (Reading, MA: Addison Wesley, 1988).

Booch, Grady, *Software Components with Ada* (Menlo Park, CA: Benjamin/Cummings Publishing Co., 1987).

Feldman, M. B., *Data Structures with Ada* (Reston, VA: Reston Publishing, 1985).

Horowitz, E., and Sahni, S., *Fundamentals of Data Structures in Pascal* (Rockville, MD: Computer Science Press, 1984).

Moret, B. M. E., and Shapiro, H. D., "Algorithms from P to NP" (Menlo Park, CA: Benjamin/Cummings Publishing Co., 1991).

Weiskamp, K., Shammas, N., and Pronk, R., "Turbo Algorithms: A Programmer's Reference" (N. Y.: John Wiley and Sons, 1989).

The following references provide a good start into topics of concurrency.
Axford, T., *Concurrent Programming* (N. Y.: John Wiley & Sons, 1989).

Ben-Ari, M., *Principles of Concurrent Programming* (Englewood Cliffs, N. J.: Prentice Hall, 1982).

de Bruijn, N. G., "Additional Comments on a Problem in Concurrent Programming Control," *Communications of the ACM*, **11**, pp. 55-56, January 1968.

Dijkstra, E. W., "Solution of a Problem in Concurrent Programming Control," *Communications of the ACM*, **8**, pp. 569-570, Sept. 1965.

Eisenberg, M. A., and McGuire, M. R., "Further comments on Dijkstra's Concurrent Programming Control Problem," *Communications of the ACM*, **15**, p. 999, Nov. 1972.

Hoare, C. A. R., "Monitors: An Operating System Structuring Concept," *Communications of the ACM*, **17**, pp. 549-574, Sept. 1974.

Jaeschke, R., *C User's Journal*, Ma, 1992, pp. 20-28.

Knuth, D. E., "Additional Comments on a Problem in Concurrent Programming Control," *Communications of the ACM*, **9**, pp. 321-322, May 1966.

Lamport, L., "A New Solution to Dijkstra's Concurrent Programming Problem," *Communications of the ACM*, **17**, pp. 453-4, Aug. 1974.

Peterson, G. L., "Myths About the Mutual Exclusion Problem," *Information Processing Letters*, **12**, pp. 115-116, 13 June 1981.

Raynal, M., *Algorithms for Mutual Exclusion* (Cambridge, MA: MIT Press, 1986).

Raynal, M., *Distributed Algorithms and Protocols* (N. Y.: John Wiley and Sons, 1988).

Ricart, G. and Agrawala, A. K., "An Optimal Algorithm for Mutual Exclusion in Computer Networks," *Communications of the ACM*, **24**, pp. 9-15, Jan. 1981. Corrigendum *Communications of the ACM*, **24**, p. 578, Sept. 1981.

Saeed, F., George, K. M., Samadzadeh, M. H., "Implementation of Classic Mutual Exclusion Algorithms in Ada," *Ada Letters*, **12**, pp. 74-84, Jan./Feb. 1992.

Tanenbaum, A. S., *Modern Operating Systems* (Englewood Cliffs, N. J.: Prentice Hall, 1992).

Chapter 12

Discrete Event Simulation

PURPOSE

A VHDL simulation is a special case of a discrete event simulation. In the discrete event simulation, time does not advance continuously but from one simulation time to the next. A continuous simulation would typically solve differential equations that describe the evolution of variables with respect to time. Such a simulation might be discretized into a finite-difference problem with finite time steps, giving rise to an approximate simulation that is in some sense a discrete event simulation. The term "discrete event simulation," however, is generally reserved for one in which the underlying process is not continuous. The behavior of a microprocessor, or for digital electronics in general, with a clock causing events to occur at periodic times, is an example of a system suitable for discrete event simulation.

Discrete event simulations are particularly suitable for simulating clocked or synchronous devices. An analog or mixed-signal device is an example of a system that is not suitable for such a simulation, and one that cannot be simulated in VHDL in any straightforward manner. To determine the precise waveform as a function of time requires a continuous simulation, as performed by programs such as

SPICE. In reality, such programs use a discrete timestep, which is, however, small compared with times of interest. Such simulations would be extremely expensive for complex digital devices, so VHDL simplifies the problem by restricting the number of values a signal may take, and by advancing from event to event.

It is necessary to discuss discrete event simulations for three reasons. First, because a VHDL simulation is a special case of such simulations, a better understanding of such simulations would be of use in guiding the VHDL user to more efficient, intelligent use of VHDL. Second, because VHDL is a special case of discrete event simulations, its queuing of transactions on signals with inertial or transport delay may lack the functionality required for a complete simulation of reality. Often, the system to be modeled in VHDL is part of a larger system. That system may have to be modeled with a discrete event simulation. For example, we may have a real-time embedded system to contend with. It may be desirable to model the external universe within VHDL, and we will discuss here how a general functional model can be developed within VHDL by the user managing his own event queue. Alternatively, the user may need to interface to either non-VHDL code, or concurrent simulations. This latter approach will be discussed further in a chapter devoted to this topic. In either event, understanding what you are doing is necessary. The third reason is that not all simulations will be deterministic. Occasionally you might be simulating a microprocessor system running a specific piece of code, but this will usually be the final test case. More often, a number of runs with the statistical properties of characteristic programs will be used. These statistics will include the instruction mix as well as statistical models of external events, response times, and so forth. In such cases, it is necessary to understand the appropriate statistical models to use. If such simulations are being done to evaluate the relative merits of, say, alternative caching strategies, it is necessary to understand how best to extract such results and characterize their significance. Variance reduction techniques are employed in discrete event simulation to make the most efficient use of such simulations, and can be employed in VHDL simulations.

Gelenbe and Mitrani (1980) and Ferrari (1978) discuss the analysis of computer systems performance.

VHDL AS DISCRETE EVENT SIMULATION

There are two approaches to discrete event simulation: event-scheduling and process-interaction. In the former approach, taken by VHDL, the simulation program proceeds from event to event. The process-interaction approach is more suitable for the simulation of queuing systems. It follows a customer through the system as the customer is served. The process-interaction approach is that adopted by the language SIMULA, which originated the "object-oriented" approach to programming. Here, the object is the customer, and the methods are the service queues that interact with the customer object. One might wish to view signals as the objects in such an approach, but the strong interaction between signals makes the process-interaction model unsuitable.

Simulation methods can also be classified as to using the data-driven and applicative state transition (AST) models. The former corresponds to the conventional event-driven method of VHDL. The latter attempts to model the flow of events, so that a process is not activated unless it is genuinely affected by the event. See, for example, the article by van der Hoeven et al. (1990) on AST.

Modeling Considerations

The typical discrete event simulation program maintains a queue of pending events, often called a priority queue because events are ordered in time, with earlier events having higher priority. Because of the importance of this problem, a vast number of data structures have been developed to handle such priority queues, including heaps, leftist heaps, splay tree, pagodas, Fibonacci heaps, and binomial queues.

VHDL poses special problems for simulation. Particularly when the default, inertial delay is assumed for a signal, many deletions of pending transactions may be expected. Each driver must individually maintain a projected waveform. The simulator must therefore maintain several quantities for each signal:

1. The most recent event (time and value pair) must be maintained to enable the current value of the signal to be determined, as well as the S' LAST_EVENT attribute.

2. The next scheduled transaction (time and value pair) are needed. This may be maintained as a separate data element for each signal, or may be determined as the earliest scheduled transaction of any source of the signal, and be maintained as part of the list of projected waveforms for each driver. This enables the simulation kernel to advance to the simulation cycle. During the simulation cycle (see Chapter 2) "the simulation time advances to the next time at which a driver becomes active or a process resumes" (LRM 12.6.3). Recall that an active driver is one that has just had a transaction in the current simulation cycle. The simulation kernel advances to the next transaction and determines whether an event has occurred as a result, assuming no intervening **wait for** reactivations. Consequently, it is the earliest scheduled future transaction that determines how the simulation cycle will advance.

3. When an event occurs on any signal, the value of the signal before the event must be saved so that S' LAST_VALUE may be determined.

4. Any transaction on a signal should update the value that S' LAST_ACTIVE would return, so clearly such a TIME value must be retained for this purpose.

A master priority queue will contain the time of the next scheduled transaction for each signal S as well as any scheduled "wake up" times for processes waiting due to a **wait for** statement. If it is a transaction, the signal will be resolved if necessary to determine the resultant value, and it will be determined if an event has occurred. The S' ACTIVE attribute for the signal will be set TRUE, S' LAST_ACTIVE will be set to NOW, and if the signal value has changed, S' LAST_EVENT will be set to NOW and the old value saved in S' LAST_VALUE. (But all signal values S will be updated before any of the implicit signals are.) Then the processes sensitive to signals that have had events are executed until suspension, at explicit or implicit **wait** statements. If the execution of these processes has resulted in any transactions, that is, any active drivers, a simulation cycle must be done with the time variable NOW unchanged, that is, with a delta delay advance in time. Otherwise, the time advances to the next scheduled process resumption or the next scheduled transaction on any signal, whichever is earlier.

Note that the past histories of signals are not maintained by or accessible to the simulation, although such values may have been saved in a time history file for later analysis. Access to the past is only through implicit signals, such as, S′ DELAYED(T), S′ STABLE(T), S′ QUIET(T), and the information inherent in S′ LAST_EVENT S′ LAST_ACTIVE, and S′ LAST_VALUE. The information content of S′ LAST_EVENT exceeds that of S′ STABLE, since S′ STABLE will merely tell us whether the signal has been stable for a predefined time, whereas NOW − S′ LAST_EVENT will give us the duration for which the signal has been stable.

The structure of the form of VHDL discrete event simulation has a number of implications for efficient simulation. First, consider the implications of using a finite propagation delay compared with an instantaneous gate delay model relying on delta delays. A simplistic simulation that ignores gate delays may not be of sufficient fidelity to the real world to be of interest. If it is, either in some preliminary phase of design or in a late stage of design at which "logic gremlins" may be presumed to have been exorcised from the design, such simulations should be substantially more economical. Although the same sequence of steps would occur for the latch to switch states, these could all happen in concert with similar changes on other latches, whereas with finite time delays specified, more simulation cycles would be needed. The overhead of these additional cycles would be avoided. (We assume here that not all components have identical delays. If they did, there would be little difference with a zero delay model. It is likely that the cost of a simulation cycle with a delta delay should not generally be much different from that with a finite delay from the previous cycle.)

The use of **inout** ports should be limited to those circumstances in which they are essential. Not only does their usage limit the error checking inherent in port modes, the burden on the simulation kernel for performing signal resolution is increased. Any driver connected through such a port may contribute to determining the effective signal value, so the calculational burden inherent in preparing to call the resolution function is increased. Thus, the behavioral model of the RS_Latch discussed in Chapter 2, which had no feedback, hence no need to read the value of the Q and Qbar signals, and would therefore have worked with a mode **out** port, would have a number of advantages over the structural model.

The *User's Guide* accompanying the Vantage VHDL spreadsheet system recommends that the use of access types and generics be minimized for the sake of efficiency. Access types of course will not be used for any component that will be synthesized. They will most likely be used in functional models employing stacks, queues, and so on. At such high levels of a top-down design, their use will probably bring more efficiency than a less flexible structural model. Weiss remarks in his book (1992, p. 51) that he once sped up a code by a factor of 25 by removing the Deallocation() of nodes. It therefore appears likely that some run-time environments incur large overheads in dealing with storage allocation and deallocation. Pointer arithmetic should not be excessively costly, however, unless the compiler performs many burdensome checks. Therefore, it would seem plausible to interpret this suggestion from Vantage to minimize the allocation and deallocation of access types. Generics are discouraged because of the storage they consume. Their power and value in situations requiring back-annotation, for example, makes them difficult to do without.

Recall from Chapter 3 that the sequence of events in simulating the latch (flip-flop) built from NAND or NOR gates as shown in Figures 1.4 and 1.5 the feedback loops result in the need for a number of simulation cycles to be executed each time the input changes, whether zero delay or finite propagation delay is used. A higher-level model of the latch would not have this feedback, and would result in fewer simulation cycles (deltas). Given the nature of the VHDL simulation cycle, the greater the depth of the feedback, the more cycles will be needed to reach a new stable value. Where possible, models with feedback should be replaced with models without. Such higher-level modeling will generally be more efficient, but with circular signal-flow graphs, the significance is even more pronounced.

Event Queues

Signal assignments, inertial or transport, cause the deletion of any transactions of that signal scheduled at the same or a later time than that of the transaction being posted. This may be a fine model for electrical signals, but such a model does not support enqueueing of events. Thus, one cannot use a VHDL signal to represent a list of external events. To do so, you have to manage your own event queue. Fortunately, VHDL has the expressive power to do this. Unfortunately, you have to do the coding! Such event queues are probably necessary, at least implicitly, in simulating any system that has to deal with an outside world.

As noted previously, there are a great many approaches to simulating event or priority queues. See Moret and Shapiro (1991) and Weiss (1992) for good coverage of these algorithms. They all order data records on the basis of a data item, called the *key*, which we will take to be of type TIME and prioritized so that smaller (earlier) values have higher priority, that is, first-come, first-served ordering. The choice of appropriate data structure (and associated algorithms) is determined by a number of factors: how likely it is that events will be deleted from the queue, whether it is be desirable to meld separate queues into a single queue, and what resource allocations including programming effort and computer time and storage are appropriate.

Some data structures, such as binomial queues, readily support melding, while binary heaps do not. On the other hand, deleting an arbitrary item (with specified key) from the queue typically requires an exhaustive search through all the enqueued elements, as these data structures are "lazy" and do not order the elements until absolutely necessary, and then only as much as required to find the minimum. In some circumstances, such as projected signal driver waveforms, it might be desirable to use a lazy method, as many of the projected transactions would be deleted before they would ever take place. However, the updating rules (LRM 8.3.1 and Chapter 2 of this book) are such as to virtually require ordering of the projected transactions to determine which are to be deleted, particularly for signals of type **transport**. Our purpose here is not to discuss how to implement a VHDL kernel but how to implement event queues for which the kernel implementation does not provide convenient support. We will provide here a simple linked-list implementation. Weiss (1992) and Moret and Shapiro (1991) would make good starting points for more sophisticated algorithms for anticipated large queues.

```
--Singly Linked List, Ordered
type Node;
type NodePtr is access Node;
type KeyType is TIME;
type Node is record
   Key: KeyType;
   Next: NodePtr;
   -- any other data
end record;
type List is NodePtr;

procedureCreateList(L: out List)
begin
List:= new Node;
-- initialize to empty.
List.Next:=null;
end CreateList;


-- return the earliest event from queue,
-- removing it procedure DequeListFirst(Fir-
stEvent: out NodePtr; is
  L:inout List)
First: NodePtr; begin
First:= L.Next; FirstEvent:= First;
L.Next:= First.Next;
```

```
-- for safety:
FirstEvent.Next:=null;
end DequeListFirst;

procedure InsertListN( X:Key; L: List;
    Element:NodePtr) is
variable Position: NodePtr:=L.Next;
variable Previous: NodePtr:=null;
begin
if Position=null then
   L.Next:=Element;
   Element.Next:=null;
   return;
endif;
while Position /= null and X >= Posi-
tion.Key  loop
   Previous:=Position; Position:=Position.Next;
end  loop;
if Position=null then
   -- insert at end of current (nonempty) list
   Previous.Next :=Element;
   Element.Next :=null;
   return;
endif;
if Position /= L.Next then
   -- not first element,
   -- hence there is a previous
   Element.Next:=Previous.Next;
   Previous.Next :=Element;
else
   -- new first element
   Element.Next:=L.Next;
   L.Next:=Element;
endif;
Position.Next:=null;
end;
```

```
-- delete all events later than key
procedure DeleteListAfter ( X:Key; L: List)
    is
 variable Position: NodePtr:=L.Next;
variable Previous: NodePtr:=null;
begin
-- nothing to delete?
if Position = null then return; end if;
while Position /= null and
  Position.Key  >= X loop
  Previous:=Position;
  Position:=Position.Next;
end  loop;
if Previous = null then
  -- delete entire list
  L.Next:=null;
else
  Previous.Next:=null;
end if;
-- CAVEAT:Previous used as temporary below;
it's really next
while Position /= null loop
  Previous:=Position.Next;
  Deallocate(Position);
  Position:=Previous;
end loop;
end;
-- locate element of known key.  --    do
not delete it
function FindListN ( X:Key; L: List)
   return NodePtr is
variable Position: NodePtr;
begin
Position:=L.Next;
while Position /= null and
```

```
      Position.Key /= X loop
    Position:=Position.Next;
end   loop;
-- return null if not found
return Position;
end;
procedure RemoveListN( X:Key; L: List; Ele-
ment: out NodePtr) is
variable Position: NodePtr:=L.Next;
variable Previous: NodePtr:=null;
begin
while Position /= null and
    Position.Key /= X loop
    Previous:=Position;
    Position:=Position.Next;
end   loop;
if Position=null then
    Element:=null;
    -- nothing to delete
    return;
endif;
Element:= Position;
if Position /= L.Next then
    -- not first element,
    -- hence there is a previous
    Previous.Next :=Position.Next;
else
    -- dequeue first element
    L.Next:=Position.Next; endif;
Position.Next:=null;
end;
```

Note that in function FindListN, procedure RemoveListN, and others, the short-circuit property of the **and** function is employed to prevent the illegal access through a null pointer.

A procedure to create a list element has not been included in the preceding code but could easily be written. It would use the **new** operator to access a new node of type Node. The entire code segment could be encapsulated in a package. See Chapter 15 for an example of the use of a user-managed event queue for the simulation of an embedded real-time system responding to external events.

DETERMINISTIC SIMULATION

A deterministic simulation contains no stochastic or random elements. For example, we might be simulating an embedded microprocessor that has a very rigid task to perform. Or, we might be simulating a processor running a specific program, such as a boot-up sequence. For sufficiently simple systems, we might be exhaustively testing all possible input vectors (for combinatorial logic with no memory), or all sequences of interest for sequential logic.

In subsequent chapters we will discuss simulation of microprocessors and bus interfaces, covering deterministic simulation and test input generation as appropriate.

One popular form of simulation is *trace-driven* simulation. For a trace-driven simulation, data that has been collected from a bus monitor which has recorded the sequence of addresses used during a run of some program is used. Detailed information as to the instruction sequence is not retained. The sequence of memory references is typically used to help in the design of caches. The cache hit ratio can then be determined for various strategies and trade-offs evaluated.

Often, the luxury of deterministic simulation is not available. We generally do not know beforehand precisely what computer code will be run on a microprocessor under development. If the hardware is under development, there may not be any tested code for it. An exception to this is the development of a new member of a family of devices. The development of the Intel i486 included simulating the running of the MS-DOS startup code. As many microprocessors are now part of a family that evolves, compatibility is an important issue. Deterministic simulations are useful in determining such compatibility as well as correct operation.

Recent microprocessor development history has shown that even rather extensive testing can allow bugs to slip through. An example is the early 386/387 combination. The first version, Step A chips, could not be switched from protected mode to real mode. The next version, Step B, had two major bugs, Erratum #17 and Erratum #21. The former occurred when a coprocessor instruction crossed a page or segment boundary and the second page could not be accessed without triggering a fault. In such cases, instead of signaling the page or segmentation fault, the processor merely locks up. Erratum #21 occurred when a hardware interrupt emptied the prefetch queue during sequential coprocessor instructions, if paging was enabled. If the 80386 prefetch unit requests a memory read at the same time the 80387 requests an operand, the chips can deadlock. The 80486 is not free from bugs either, and had undergone five revisions as of May 1992. The INS instruction, which reads multiple values from a port, would hang early versions of the chip if a double-word boundary were straddled, for example. Simultaneous hardware interrupts and general protection faults on some instructions could lead to errors. Eliminating problems in going from Step B0 to Step B1 required additional space, which resulted in the XBTS (Extract Bit String) and IBTS (Insert Bit String) instructions being eliminated. See the articles by Prosise (1991, 1992) for the history, and Hummel (1992) for a more complete list of errata.

The bottom line is that the earlier a problem is caught, the less severe are the consequences. It is likely that more extensive and elaborate simulations that try to exercise all possible states and transitions of interest will be more common.

STOCASTIC SIMULATIONS

Statistical Considerations

One rarely has the luxury of knowing precisely what code will be running on the system of interest. Design therefore involves attempting to develop a system that is near optimal for cases of special interest while remaining robust so that performance has not become unacceptable in other circumstances. This is an art, not a science. Choices can be guided by simulation. Even this is somewhat subjective. For example, an article on the 80386 design by Crawford (1990) notes that using a four-way associative cache would reduce the miss rate compared with that of a two-way cache by 10%. An article on the i860 design by Perry (1989), quoting other Intel designers, said the cost was only 5%. The 80386 designers chose the four-way cache, the i860 designers the two-way cache. It is likely this difference in the critical statistic was due to different assumptions as to the tasks to be performed, as the i860 was intended primarily as a graphics coprocessor, and not as a general purpose CPU (at least initially). The instruction sets for the two processors are rather different. Nevertheless, it is clear that to a large extent, what you get in terms of answers is controlled by what assumptions are put into the calculation. It is therefore important to start out on the best footing possible.

Assuming you have chosen the simulation test cases and determined the different design choices to be compared, it is important to draw valid conclusions from the results. This entails doing a sufficient amount of simulation to obtain statistically significant differences. A single comparison of simulation results for one set of random numbers is rarely decisive. You must therefore simulate economically, and here is where a number of tricks, called "variance reduction methods," come in handy. These issues will be discussed in turn.

Random and Pseudorandom Numbers

To perform a statistical simulation, you must have random numbers. Truly random numbers may be obtained by various methods such as using electrically-generated "Johnson" noise, from say, avalanche breakdown of a semiconductor junction. Such random numbers are less useful than they might seem. They are inconvenient to use as they require large tables. More useful are pseudorandom numbers, which are generated by simple arithmetic operations and have many of the characteristics of the true random numbers. There is a large (and growing) literature on generating such numbers, with large amounts of effort devoted to testing the resulting number distributions for randomness. See the review article by L'Ecuyer (1990) for an overview of recent work. See Baker (1991, 1992) for extensive amounts of C code for random number generation and the use of these numbers for the generation of random deviates, that is, numbers randomly taken from specified probability distributions. These topics are of course discussed in books on DES, such as Law and Kelton (1982), Kobayashi (1981), Deo (1979), and Bratley et al. (1987).

The following VHDL code is based on the portable 16-bit arithmetic generator given in L'Ecuyer (1988). It will produce pseudorandom numbers U that are uniformly distributed in the interval between 0 and 1. All pseudorandom number generators for computational use seem to obey this convention.

```
procedure RANDOM16(u: out REAL; S16,S26,S36:
inout INTEGER) is

variable Z,K: INTEGER;
-- RECOMMENDED INIT: S16:=12,S26:=23,S36:=34;

begin
k:= S16/206;
S16:=157*(S16-K*206)-K*21;
if S16 0 then S16:= S16+32263; end if;
K:=S26/217;
S26:=146*(S26-K*217)-K*45;
if S26 0 then S26:= S26+31727; end if;
K:= s36/222;
S36:=142*(S36-k*222)-K*133;
if s36 then S36:=S36+31657; end if;
Z:=S16-S26;
if z706 then Z:=Z-32362; end if;
Z:=Z+S36;
if z then Z:=Z+32362; end if;
```

```
U:=REAL(Z) * 3.0899e-5;
end RANDOM16;
```

Note the use of the conversion of the `INTEGER` variable `Z` to `REAL` at the end of the subprogram. A procedure is used in order to permit modification of the variables `S16,S26,S36`. These maintain the state of the random number generator. This permits the use of one subprogram for computing a number of independent random numbers. The value of this flexibility will be seen when variance reduction techniques are discussed later.

This random number generator is designed for 16-bit arithmetic. The article by L'Ecuyer (1988) gives a suggested generator for 32-bit arithmetic systems. The article by Park and Miller (1988), from the same issue of the *Communications of the ACM*, suggests a portable "minimal" pseudorandom number generator for arbitrary systems.

Statistical Event Distributions

A. K. Erlang began the study of the statistics of telephone traffic around 1918. He studied the pattern of call arrival rates, durations, the number of subscribers waiting for service, and so forth. This work has become the foundation of a great deal of network analysis and queuing theory.

Assume that arrivals are completely random and independent. Then the probability of an arrival in any time interval is a constant (proportional to the duration of the interval for small intervals). Then it is easy to show the probability of an interval of duration t is given by the exponential distribution, that is, $P(t) = \exp\left(-\frac{t}{T}\right)$, where T is a constant. The probability of n arrivals in any interval t is given by the Poisson distribution, $P(n,t) = \left(\frac{t}{T}\right)^n \frac{1}{n!} \exp\left(-\frac{t}{T}\right)$.

This function has a maximum at finite t, reflecting the fact that as time increases, the likely number of arrivals increases, then passes by the value n as it becomes more likely that more than n arrivals have occurred. The Poisson distribution is a discrete distribution, i. e., it gives the probability of the distribution of discrete (integer) values. It is probably the most popular distribution used in simulation, due to its simplicity and universality.

If random variables $X, Y, \ldots$ are given by identical exponential distributions, then $X + Y + \ldots$ is described by Erlang's eponymous distribution, called the n-Erlang distribution where n exponential variables are summed. Alternatively, if we have a Poisson arrival process, and select every nth arrival, then new arrival process defined has an n-Erlang distribution of intervals between arrivals. The popularity of the Erlang distribution is probably more because of its flexibility and ability to fit observed data rather than the theoretical applicability of the model of a sequence of n identical servers.

Similarly, the Weibull distribution is often used in statistical analysis of component failure due to the facility with which it may be manipulated. The shape of the Weibull distribution is similar to that of the gamma distribution, of which the n-Erlang distribution is a special case (namely, for integer values of the shape parameter α).

The gamma distribution is given by: $\beta^{-\alpha} x^{\alpha-1} \exp\left(-\frac{x}{\beta}\right) \frac{1}{\Gamma(\alpha)}$,

the Weibull distribution is given by: $\alpha \beta^{-\alpha} x^{\alpha-1} \exp\left(-\left(\frac{x}{\beta}\right)^{\alpha}\right)$.

These distributions are typically fit to observed data and then used in the analysis, making them empirical distributions. There is no particular theory of failure that implies that the Weibull distribution is the preferred form for the distribution. It is just convenient to use and sufficiently flexible to be fit to typical observed distributions.

The hyperexponential distribution is a sum of exponentials, and is appropriate to a random choice from a number of different exponential distributions. This might correspond to a queue with a number of servers with different characteristics. The extreme value distribution (called the Gumbel distribution in Bratley et al., 1987) is appropriate when the random variable is the maximum of a collection of random variables. Kobayashi (1981) and Bratley et al. (1987) have good coverage of distributions.

When the random quantity is the sum of a large number of other random quantities, then the normal distribution is appropriate. When it is the product of such random variates, then the lognormal distribution is appropriate. When a random fraction is needed, such as the fraction of defective parts in a shipment, a distribution such as the beta distribution is used.

Finally, there are empirical distributions. If these are used literally as observed, we have a trace-driven simulation, which is deterministic. We may still want to check the representativeness of such distributions by comparing them statistically.

The subject of generating random numbers from these distributions is fully covered in Kobayashi (1981), Deo (1979), Law and Kelton (1982), and Bratley et al. (1987). A variety of programs, written in C, will be found in Baker, *More C Tools for Scientists and Engineers* (1991), and Baker, *C Mathematical Function Handbook* (1992). The latter book has additional distributions.

For example, to obtain an INTEGER drawn from a Poisson distribution, the following code could be used:

```
procedure PoissonRD ( Lambda: REAL;
Answer: out INTEGER; S16,S26,S36:
inout INTEGER) is
variable A, Sum, F: REAL;
variable X: INTEGER;
begin
-- Exponential function Exp ()
--   assumed in a library.
F := Exp ( - Lambda) ;
Sum := F;
RANDOM16( A, S16,S26,S36);
for X in 0 to INTEGER' RIGHT loop
   if Real(X) < Sum then exit endif;
   F:= F * Lambda/(1.+REAL(X)); Sum:= Sum+F;
end loop;
Answer :=IntegerX;
end PoissonRD;
```

To generate random deviates from an exponential distribution you could use this code:

```
procedure ExponRD ( Mean: REAL;
Answer: out REAL; S16,S26,S36:
   inout INTEGER) is
begin
-- Log (base e) function Log()
--   assumed in a library.
Answer := -Mean * Log( RANDOM16
   ( A, S16,S26,S36) ) ;
end ExponRD;
```

There is a slight possibility RANDOM16 would return zero, in which case an error would result. This is not trapped, as it corresponds to the slight possibility that an infinite waiting time would result.

Queueing Theory

Queues are lines of "customers" waiting for "service," be they packets in a network, I/O requests, etc. Many of the simplest queues models are soluble. These results can therefore be used as a check on simulation models, that is, in code validation, or as a functional model of a portion of a system, such as an external bus.

Kleinrock (1976) is the standard reference on the subject, with the second volume devoted to computer applications. Queue models are often described with the shorthand notation A/S/N, where N is the number of servers, A specifies the arrival distribution, and S the service time distribution. Common values for A and S are the following:

M   Markovian, or Memoryless. Arrivals are random and independent. The result is an exponential distribution, that is, Poisson statistics for the arrivals.

E_r Erlang-r, that is, r identical exponential queues in sequence, adding waiting times.

H_r Hyperexponential-r, a sum of exponential terms. This corresponds to a queue with r servers in parallel.

D Deterministic

G General

The simplest system is M/M/1. Its behavior is generally qualitatively similar to most queues. If the arrival rate is λ, the average service time $x = \dfrac{1}{\mu}$, the utilization factor is defined as $\rho = x\lambda$. Then the average number of customers waiting is

$$\overline{N} = \frac{\rho}{1 - \rho},$$

the average time spent waiting for service is

$$\overline{W} = \frac{\rho}{\mu(1 - \rho)},$$

with the average total time spent in the system being

$$\overline{T} = \frac{1}{\mu(1 - \rho)}.$$

Clearly $\overline{T}$ goes from x for zero utilization factor to infinite values as the utilization goes to 1. The distributions of waiting times, service times, and so on, are exponential (Kleinrock, 1976).

The next simplest case is the generalization to m servers. It was studied by Erlang himself. The degradation in service is postponed to greater values of utilization, as would be expected. Detailed results will be found in Kleinrock (1976) and Kobayashi (1981).

Variance Reduction Techniques

For a sequence of random variables $x_1, x_2, \ldots$, the mean value is $\overline{x} = (x_1 + x_2 + \ldots) / N$, where N variables are being averaged. The variance is σ^2, where σ is the standard deviation, and is given by $\sigma^2 = \sum_{i=1}^{N}(x - \overline{x})^2$. The standard deviation and the variance are measures of the spread of the variables. The greater this spread, the larger differences have to be to be significant. It may be expected from the form of this formula that as the number of simulation runs

N increases, the variance will decrease as N, that is, the standard deviation will decrease as $\sqrt{N}$. It is desirable, in the interests of economy, to do better. Here are some of the standard approaches to do just that.

Common Random Numbers

Perhaps the simplest and easiest of the variance reduction methods is to use the same random numbers for the same random variables for each design to be compared. The effect is to insure that differences in performance between such tests is not due to one simulation being done with a particularly fortunate choice of random numbers. This technique is also called correlated sampling. The effective decrease in variance is due to the fact that the two simulations are now correlated, that is, if the two design choices were equally effective, their behavior would be expected to correlate well with one another.

Suppose unrelated random numbers were used for the two simulation runs, giving performance measures $P1$ and $P2$. Our figure of merit is $D = P1 - P2$. Its variance is given by $\sigma_D^2 = \sigma_{P1}^2 + \sigma_{P1}^2$. Now suppose that common random numbers are used. Then $\sigma_D^2 = \sigma_{P1}^2 + \sigma_{P1}^2 - 2\,Cov(P1,P2)$. where $Cov(X,Y)$ is the covariance of X and Y. The beauty of this is that the more similar X and Y are, the larger $Cov(X,Y)$ is and hence the more effectively the variance is reduced.

The use of common random numbers is essentially free. There is therefore no excuse for not using this method.

Antithetic Variables

This trick is relatively simple to understand, although it requires a bit more effort to implement. Consider a simulation run in which our pseudorandom number generator has produced the numbers $U1$, $U2, \ldots$, (uniform in the 0-1 interval). Assume we record these by copying them to a file as they are produced. Then perform a simulation run in which the corresponding values used are $1-U1$, $1-U2$, etc. Intuitively, if the sequence $U1$, $U2, \ldots$ were for some reason particularly favorable to design choice 1 compared to design choice 2, it is plausible if not likely that the sequence $1-U1, \ldots$ would be correspondingly biased toward the alternative. For example, if the sequence *U1, U2, . . .* happens to have an average value below the expected value of .5, then the antithetic variables will have a value above .5 by the same amount.

The analysis underlying antithetic variables is similar to that of common random numbers. Suppose we do two simulations, *P1* and *P2*, of nominally identical systems. We wish to obtain the best estimate of the true system behavior, again with minimum variance. That estimate will be $M = {(P1+P2)}/2$, the mean of the results from two simulations. The variance will be given by

$$\sigma_M{}^2 = \frac{1}{2}(\sigma_{P1}{}^2 + \sigma_{P1}{}^2 - 2\,Cov(P1,P2)).$$ To minimize the variance,

the *Cov(P1,P2)* should now be as small as we can make it. Thus, the numbers *P1* and *P2* should be anticorrelated, if possible. It can be shown that if the function *f(x)* is monotonic, i. e., increasing or decreasing, then *f(U)* and *f(1−U)* will be anti-correlated.

This method can be implemented rather economically. All that is needed is a constant flag value that is of type `BIT` and sent to the random number generator. If it is, say, `' 0'`, then the subprogram generates *U1, U2 . . .* If it is set to `' 1'`, then the values returned by the subprogram are *1−U1*, and so on.

Stratified Sampling

The idea behind stratified sampling is to break down the population to be sampled into classes of minimal variance. An obvious example might be studying separately performance on scientific applications that "number crunch," and business applications that are intensive in operations such as sorting, comparing, and moving data with less computational effort.

Importance Sampling

Importance sampling, as applied to variance reduction, means devoting more simulation runs to the classes of greater variance. If, as discussed in stratified sampling, it was decided that scientific programs were all pretty much alike while business programs varied greatly, we would do more sampling of business programs, even if our customer base were primarily scientific users!

For example, circumstances forcing a cache flush, or a pipeline stall, might be very rare, simply because great effort would be devoted to developing compilers to prevent such unfavorable circumstances. When they do occur, however, the impact will be significant. It is therefore important to perform simulations that have been biased to give a sufficient number of such incidents that their impacts are sufficiently well quantified.

Sequential Analysis

Suppose you had to check ten employees for drug use. One possibility would be to take samples from each and test them all. This will cost you ten tests. Now suppose you divide the samples into two groups, mix the five samples in each group, and test those two combined samples. If you are lucky, and there was no drug use, you have determined this at the cost of two tests instead of ten, a fivefold reduction. If one of the samples tests positive, then you might proceed to test the five individuals who contributed to that sample. You have used six tests instead of ten. If we had successively bisected the groups, then we would need four or five tests (depending on whether the offender were in the group of two or three as we did the split).

The basic idea of sequential analysis is to perform the simulations adaptively rather than in a rigid sequence, adjusting the possibilities to be explored as the result of what is learned along the way. Versions of sequential analysis are "Russian roulette," in which situations of no further interest, or otherwise do not need to be followed further as part of the analysis, are dropped.

Initialization

Steady-state behavior may not be identical to average or typical behavior. Initial transients may die away slowly, for example. If steady-state behavior is the desired figure-of-merit to be determined, the effect of initial transients on the simulation must be accounted for and removed. The system should be initialized as close to the steady-state or equilibrium as reasonable. For example, in a queueing system, the system should not be started with an empty queue if this is atypical. In queues, there is often a strong correlation between service times, because the slow service of one customer delays those customers behind in the queue. Analysis techniques called *blocking* or *batching*, and *jackknifing*, exist to reduce the bias in estimates of steady-state behavior from simulations contaminated by initial transients that may persist due to correlations. See, for example, Law and Kelton (1982) for a discussion.

Stress Testing

Is is important in many applications to determine how the system degrades under heavy load or anomalous circumstances, as well as what typical behavior is. The *Microsoft Windows System Development Kit* includes a utility to reduce available system resources to facilitate testing software under such circumstances. Similar tests of prospective hardware should be done in simulation environments. In other words, the test environments should include both typical and atypical real-world environments. As noted previously, hardware bugs are often the result of coincidences (e. g., simultaneous faults, traps or interrupts) that do not occur in typical testing.

Validating Simulations

Before the results of a simulation are used for making major decisions, there should be some assurance that the results are trustworthy, if only to prevent embarrassment when management asks such questions. See Law and Kelton (1982) for a complete discussion.

The usual validation method is to run the model for simplified conditions for which the correct results are known, and compare with known results. For example, queueing theory may be used for a simple input and service time distribution. If a number of observed cases are known, build the model using only some of them, reserving the others for use as test cases for validation purposes. If fits are used, test the validity of the fits by the usual statistical means, for example, chi-square goodness of fit.

Finally, it is useful to vary parameters to determine the sensitivity of conclusions to assumptions. It may be found that small variations in a highly uncertain parameter can vary the optimal solution found substantially. In such cases, it is well to remember Fisher's Law: the more highly optimized a system is for one circumstance, the more poorly it will perform for others. In such cases, the goal should be to develop a robust system that does reasonably well over a range of parameters.

Interpreting Simulation Results

It is important to draw the right conclusions from our simulations. It is also important to do a sufficient number of simulations to permit the correct conclusions to be drawn reliably, that is, with some confidence that we are indeed getting an accurate picture. Law and Kelton (1982, p. 316) give a cautionary example of two queueing systems, one with two servers and one with a single server that is twice as fast as the others. Comparing the average waiting time for one simulation run of 100 customers entering an initially empty queue, they conclude that the correct answer (the M/M/2 queue wins) would be found only 56% of the time. Interestingly, for the steady-state or asymptotic situation, the tables are turned and the M/M/1 queue with the faster server wins; see, for example, Gelenbe and Mitrani (1980, p. 24). This illustrates the care that is necessary in using analytic comparisons for validation or for drawing other conclusions. It might seem counterintuitive that the M/M/2 system give lower average waiting times, as it would seem that a job with a long service time would delay later arrivals in the M/M/1 but not the M/M/2 queue. This is more than counterbalanced, at least for the mean waiting time figure of merit, by the fact that when there is only one customer in the system, the extra server is not used.

Because simulations are statistical, we can never get the correct answer with absolute certainty. Results must be qualified by the confidence level of the conclusion. If we assume that the random errors are normally distributed, we have the whole apparatus of statistics at our disposal; if not, we can still use nonparametric statistics to check some aspects of our simulation. For normally distributed random errors, confidences are related to the Student-t distribution. Thus, if we have used our common random numbers approach in comparing two alternative systems, we may evaluate the mean difference D due as $\bar{D} = \dfrac{\sum\limits_{i=1}^{N}(P1_i - P2_i)}{N}$, and the variance as

$\sigma^2 = \dfrac{\sum\limits_{i=1}^{N}(P1_i - P2_i^2)}{N(N-1)}$. Then we can assume the difference is

$\bar{Z} \pm \sigma \, t_{n-1,1-\alpha/2}$. Here $t_{n-1,1-\alpha}$ is Student's t for n-1 degrees of freedom and a (two-tailed) confidence of $(1 - \alpha)$. Confidence values are typically taken at 90% or 95%. See an elementary statistics book for a discussion of these concepts. *More C Tools for Scientists and Engineers* (Baker, 1991) and *C Mathematical Function Handbook* (Baker, 1992) contain a handy calculator which will compute the *t* values corresponding to a given confidence level and vice versa.

If common random variables had not been used, a less efficient test of the significance of the difference between the two means would have had to be used. Then the Student-t statistic would be based upon:

$$\frac{\bar{P1} - \bar{P2}}{[\sigma_1^2 + \sigma_2^2]^{1/2}}$$

These results can be turned around to determine the required number of runs for a given confidence level, thus:

$$N = (\frac{t\,\sigma}{D})^2$$

Here D is the required precision to be achieved. Note how N scales with the square of the right-hand side, indicating the value of variance reduction methods! One difficulty is that t is a function of N. For large N, an approximately normal distribution may be used. See, for example, Deo (1979). Then for a confidence level of 90%, t would be approximated by 1.65; for 95%, by 1.96; for 99%, by 2.58.

Finally, the sensitivity of the results to assumptions and parameters should be checked, as discussed in validation.

CONCURRENT SIMULATION

Parallelism and concurrency are major topics in computer science today. Concurrency may be desirable due to the capability of the hardware to perform concurrent operations. Or it may be necessary if the VHDL simulation is to be part of another simulation and must interact concurrently with that other simulation. In the first case, parallelizing your program will be the VHDL compiler's problem. It would still help you to understand something about concurrent simulation so that you may get the best performance out of the compiler. In the second case, you will have to understand concurrency well.

Conservative Concurrent Simulation

There are two basic approaches: optimistic and conservative (pessimistic). In a pessimistic approach (Bagrodia et al., 1987, Chandy and Misra, 1981, Bain, 1990), each of the parallel processes (which may or may not correspond to a VHDL process!) proceeds no further than would be "safe." For example, if one process were an interruptable microprocessor, it would finish one instruction, make sure no interrupt was pending for it at this time, and, if possible, process the next instruction. To make sure it was safe to proceed, it would have to ask all other processes that were possible sources of interrupts if they had one for it by the anticipated model time.

Such an approach has a number of possible pitfalls. First, a great deal of overhead can be consumed by exchanging messages. Second, great care must be taken to prevent deadlocks. For example, suppose a number of processors are on a network, and any processor can affect any other (we ignore any initialization during which their interrupts are masked off). We must prevent a situation in which processor A waits for processor B to tell it that it may proceed, while B waits for A to tell it the same thing! Typically, in a pessimistic approach, the ability to look ahead and predict how long processes may proceed without checking for possible interference is very important to performance. Nicol (1992) presents a technique for using priority to "skew" event generation to higher priority events first, improving the predictability of preemption.

Optimistic Concurrent Simulation

The optimistic approach is in some ways a lot simpler. Each process proceeds independently, but periodically "checkpoints" or saves the state at various associated local simulation times. There is a master clock, which represents the time safely simulated by the system. Processes exchange messages, such as interrupt requests, as needed. When a process finds it has received an interrupt request for a time earlier than its current local simulation time, it backs up to the last checkpoint before the request, and recomputes from that point to the time of requested interrupt, and then proceeds appropriately given the interrupt. Obviously, this approach has the advantage of making the processes approximately independent. It clearly produces great dividends if interrupts are rare. It has an overhead burden in the checkpointing process. The frequency of checkpointing must be tuned carefully to avoid wasting storage and time in excessive checkpointing, versus having to step back too much due to infrequent checkpointing.

Often, the option of optimistic simulation is not available, because the checkpointing and restarting is for some reason impractical or not supported. In such a case, the conservative approach must be followed, with some care devoted to maximizing lookahead.

One popular approach to optimistic simulations is called "Virtual Time." A popular version of Virtual Time is called "Time Warp"; see the paper by Jefferson (1985) and the review by Fujimoto (1990). Briner (1990) has applied the method to simulation of digital electronics. Time Warp involves sending *anti-messages* canceling messages that reflect outdated situations that no longer apply. A paper by Yin and Lazowska (1992) reviews versions of the Time Warp strategy. For example, there are aggressive and lazy cancellation strategies; the former will have a process that is rolled-back immediately cancel messages it sent for times following the rollback point; the latter only cancels anachronistic messages if they are found to be different from the messages that result from the rollback. Different preemption strategies are also possible. Yin & Lazowska conclude that these variations in strategy can have significant effects on performance.

As concurrent simulation is an area of very active research, you should attempt to keep up with current developments. This section was intended as an introduction to the field so that you could easily do so. Due to the current interest in parallel computational architectures, it is likely that these developments will have a marked effect on simulation methods such as VHDL.

WAVEFORM RELAXATION

A discussion of numerical simulation would not be complete without mention of the increasingly popular method of waveform relaxation, as introduced by Lelarasmee et al. (1982). Instead of proceeding in time increments, a "chunk" consisting of a number of such increments is simulated, with the system iterating until convergence. This nonlinear iteration presupposes that the process can be solved by a Newton-Raphson iteration, that is, that the process can be approximately linearized and a Jacobian matrix formed as part of the relaxation process. This assumption may be quite reasonable for analog circuit calculations, but is unlikely to be true in the digital event environment of VHDL. However, the field is one of great activity and other techniques may be developed that might make its application to discrete-event simulations such as VHDL fruitful.

REFERENCES

Ahrens, J. H. and Dieter, U., "Efficient Table-Free Sampling Methods for the Exponential, Cauchy, and Normal Distributions, *Communications of the ACM*, **31**, pp. 1330-1337, Nov. 1988.

Bagrodia, R. L., Chandy, K. M., Misra, J., "A Message-Based Approach to Discrete-Event Simulation," *IEEE Trans. Software Eng.*, SE-13, pp. 654-665, June 1987.

Bain, W. L., "Parallel Discrete Event Simulation Using Synchronized Event Schedulers," in *5th Distributed Memory Computing Conference*, April 8-20, 1990, Charleston, S. C., pp. 90-94.

Baker, L., *More C Tools for Scientists and Engineers* (N. Y: McGraw-Hill, 1991).

Baker, L., *C Mathematical Function Handbook* (N. Y: McGraw-Hill, 1992).

Bratley, P. Fox, B. L., Scrage, L. E., *A Guide to Simulation* (N. Y.: Springer, 1987).

Briner, Jr., J. V., *Parallel Mixed-Level Simulation of Digital Circuits Using Virtual Time*, TR90-38, Center for Microelectronics, Research Triangle Park, N. C., 1990.

Chandy, K. M., and Misra, J., "Asynchronous Distributed Simulation via a Sequence of Parallel Computations," *Communications of the ACM*, **24**, pp. 198-206, 1981.

Crawford, J. H., "The i486 CPU: Executing Instructions in One Clock Cycle," *IEEE Micro*, pp. 27-37, Feb. 1990.

Deo, N., *System Simulation with Digital Computer* (Englewood Cliffs, N. J.: Prentice Hall, 1979).

Ferrari, D., *Computer Systems Performance Evaluation* (Englewood Cliffs, N. J.: Prentice Hall, 1978).

Fujimoto, R. M., "Parallel Discrete-Event Simulation," *Communications of the ACM*, **33**, pp. 30-53, Oct. 1990.

Gelenbe, E., Mitrani, I., *Analysis and Synthesis of Computer Systems* (N. Y.: Academic Press, 1980).

Hummel, R. L., *Programmer's Technical Reference: The Processor and Coprocessor*, (N. Y.: Ziff-Davis Press, 1992).

Jefferson, D. R., "Virtual Time," *ACM Trans. Program. Lang. Systems*, **7**, pp. 404-425, 1985.

Kleinrock, L., *Queueing Systems* (N. Y.: John Wiley & Sons, 1976).

Kobayashi, H., *Modeling and Analysis* (Reading, MA.: Addison Wesley, 1981).

Law, A. M. and Kelton, W. D., *Simulation Modeling and Analysis* (N. Y.: McGraw-Hill, 1982).

L'Ecuyer, P., "Efficient and Portable Combined Random Number Generators, *Communications of the ACM*, **31**, pp. 742-749 & 774, Oct. 1988.

L'Ecuyer, P., "Random Numbers for Simulation," *Communications of the ACM*, **33**, pp. 85-97, Oct. 1990.

Lelarasmee, E., Ruehli, A. E., Sangiovanni-Vincentelli, A., L., "The Waveform Relaxation Method for Time-Domain analysis of Large Scale Integrated Circuits," *IEEE Trans. Computer-Aided Design of ICAS*, **CAD-1**, pp. 131-145, 1982.

Misra, J. "Distributed Discrete-Event Simulation," *Computing Surveys*, **18**, pp. 39-65, March 1986.

Moret, B. M. E., and Shapiro, H. D., *Algorithms from P to NP* (Redwood City, CA: Benjamin/Cummings Publishing Co., 1991).

Nichol, D., "Conservative Parallel Simulation of Priority Class Queueing Networks," *IEEE Trans. on Parallel and Distrib. Systems*, **3**, pp. 294-303, May 1992.

Park, S. K., and Miller, K. W., "Random Number Generators: Good Ones are Hard to Find, *Communications of the ACM*, **31**, pp. 1192-1201, Oct. 1988.

Perry, T. S., "Intel's Secret is Out," *IEEE Spectrum*, pp. 22-28, April 1989.

Prosise, J., "Tutor," *PC Magazine*, pp. 435-437, Oct. 15, 1991.

Prosise, J., "Tutor," *PC Magazine*, pp. 317-19, Feb. 11, 1992.

Prosise, J., "Tutor," *PC Magazine*, pp. 341-2, May 26, 1992.

Righter, R., Walrand, J. C., "Distributed Simulation of Discrete Event Systems," *Proc. IEEE*, **77**, pp. 99-113, Jan. 1989.

Ross, S. M., *A Course in Simulation* (N. Y.: Macmillan, 1990).

Weiss, M. A., *Data Structures and Algorithm Analysis* (Redwood City, CA: Benjamin/Cummings Publishing Co., 1992).

Yin, Y.-B. and Lazowska, E. D., "A Study of Time Warp Rollback Mechanisms," *ACM Trans. Modeling and Computer Simulations*, **1**, pp. 51-72, Jan. 1991.

Van der Hoeven, A. J., de Lange A. A. J., Deorettere, E. F., Dewilde, P. M., "Model for the High-Level Description and Simulation of VLSI Networks," *IEEE MICRO,* pp. 41-49, August 1990.

Chapter 13

Finite State Machines

PURPOSE

Finite State Machines (FSMs) are of great value at all levels of VHDL simulations. High-level or functional simulation of bus protocols, for example, often make use of FSMs. At the other end of the spectrum, FSMs are the most complex processing elements that can be embodied with a known, fixed amount of silicon. They can be used to model regular grammars, and are sufficiently powerful to model the control section of many CPUs and various special purpose chips, such as those used for error detection and correction, and peripheral interface control. FSMs are therefore a useful tool for both the hardware designer and VHDL user.

This chapter cannot hope to present a full treatment of this important topic. Books have been written on various aspects of FSMs, as you will see by consulting the references at the end of this chapter. This chapter is intended instead to provide sufficient foundation for for you to use FSMs and understand the literature on the subject. Dewdney's *The Turing Omnibus* (1989) provides good discussions of regular grammars, circuit minimization, nondeterministic automata, and sequential circuits, among many other topics. Savitzky (1985) covers real-time applications. Comer (1990) examines the design of combinatorial logic and state machines for both synchronous and asynchronous applications. Carmely (1992) gives a good tutorial on the design of FSMs.

Shift registers play an important role in the Boundary-Scan test architecture (IEEE-Std-1149.1), and are a special form of FSM. In an interesting article, Eschermann and Wunderlich (1992) discuss the design of FSMs incorporating a testable structure by construction. Boundary Scan will be discussed in Chapter 14.

MOORE, MEALY, HYBRID MACHINES

The sequential machine or FSM was discussed by Huffman, and is shown in his generic diagram in Figure 13.1. We might say

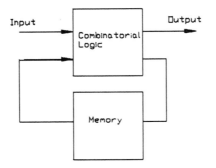

Fig. 13.1 Generic Sequential (State) Machine

FSM=logic+memory. This diagram is sufficiently general and abstract to be almost useless, and more concrete models are needed. Two different models were developed shortly thereafter, by Moore and Mealy.

For a Moore machine, we specify an acceptable set of inputs and outputs, the initial state, and the transitions, that is, the next state that occurs as a function of the current state and the input. The output is a function of the present state alone, and we may therefore identify the present state with the output of the machine. An input will cause the machine to change to a (possibly different) state. The machine may be defined by a table specifying, as a function of current state and input, the output and next state. Consider the state table (Table 13.1) for a toggling or T-type flip-flop:

Table 13.1 T flip-flop as Moore machine			
State	New State for Input		Output
	0	1	
Reset	Reset	Set	o
Set	Set	Reset	1

A type D flip-flop would have been too boring, as the 0 input would cause the next state to become Reset whatever the current state, and similarly a 1 input would set the flip-flop.

Such machines can be readily diagrammed, if the number of states is not too large.   The states and the associated outputs are nodes in a directed graph, the transitions directed edges of the graph. Figure 13.2 is a state diagram for the T flip-flop.

A Mealy machine is different from a Moore machine in that the

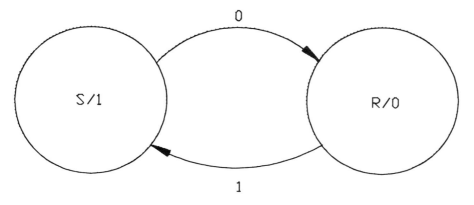

Fig. 13.2 T flip-flop as a Moore machine

output is not a function of the current state. Instead, it is a function of the transition that was last taken. This may be rephrased by say-ing that the output is a function not only of the current state but of the last input, since together these determine the state transition. In this case, the transitions must be labeled with the outputs as well as the inputs. See Table 13.2.

Table 13.2 T flip-flop as Mealy machine		
State	New State/Output for Input	
	0	1
Reset	Reset/0	Set/1
Set	Set/1	Reset/0

The corresponding diagram is given in Figure 13.3.

In the case of a D- or T- type flip-flop, the Moore machine seems a more natural description, as the output is directly related to the state. Consider, however, a device designed to detect rising edges. Such a transition-driven system is more naturally specified

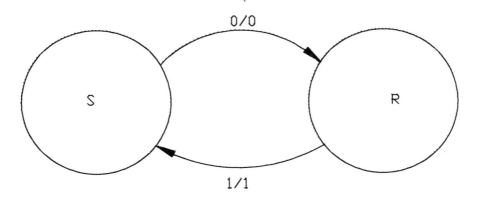

Fig. 13.3 T flip-flop as a Mealy machine

by a Mealy machine (Table 13.3):

Table 13.3 Rising Edge detector as Mealy Machine		
State	New State/Output for Input	
	0	1
High	Low/0	High/0
Low	Low/0	High/1

The corresponding Moore machine is specified in Table 13.4:

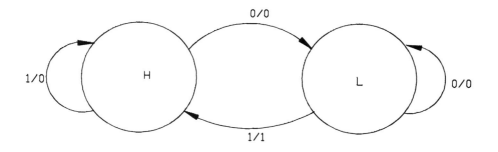

Fig. 13.4 Mealy machine edge detector

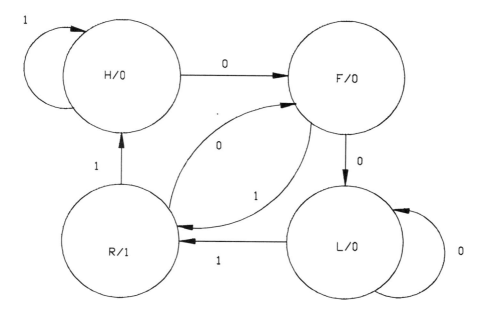

Fig. 13.5 Moore machine edge detector

Table 13.4 Rising Edge detector as Moore machine			
State	New State for Input		Output
	0	1	
High	Falling	High	0
Low	Low	Rising	0
Rising	Falling	High	1
Falling	Low	Rising	0

In this case, the Moore machine has twice as many states as the Mealy machine. This is the maximum it could have, given our algorithm for translating from Mealy to Moore machines. Figures 13.4 and 13.5 give the state diagrams for these two machines.

A Mealy machine can give transient, erroneous output where a Moore machine wouldn't. This is because the output will be that due to the current input and an erroneous state.

In general, a Mealy machine can be found for a given Moore machine and vice versa. A Moore machine equivalent to a given Mealy machine may require more states than the latter. Friedman and Menon (1975) and Hopcroft and Ullman (1979) both give algorithms for such conversions. A Mealy machine with N states and M possible outputs may give rise to a Moore machine with as many as MN states. Some of the MN states may not be reachable, and may be deleted. A Mealy machine can easily be found that will be equivalent to a given Moore machine, by merely defining the output for each transition to be that of state transitioned to for each state of the Moore machine. The states and transitions do not change. As a practical matter, Moore and Mealy machine implementations are not all that different, and often, a hybrid is used. The output in general must be latched or held, making the distinction between Moore and Mealy machines somewhat academic, at least in synchronous systems.

An FSM may be constructed with flip-flops as the memory elements. Typically, D flip-flops are used, although this is not necessary. As each flip-flop can save one bit, N flip-flops can represent an N bit binary number, and consequently, 2^N states.

There is no algorithm for designing an FSM to perform a general, specified task. As will be noted later in this chapter, there are algorithms for constructing an FSM for recognizing a given grammar based on regular expressions, for example.

The first step in FSM design is the determination of the appropriate states and transition conditions. The usual intent is to minimize the number of required states, which will probably approximate minimizing the total number of gates and silicon real estate required. There are various algorithms, such as the Mealy-Huffman algorithm, to perform such a minimization in special cases (see the section on regular grammars later in the chapter). Minimizing combinatorial logic is well studied and addressed by the Quine-McCluskey method, among others. See, for example, Mendelson (1970). Optimization and minimization are not identical, as other considerations, such as speed, can be important. Once an FSM has been designed and the number of states determined, the state assignment must be determined, that is, the representation of each state in terms of the states of the memory elements. The state assignment problem is one of those problems with a combinatorial explosion;NP-hard that is, a problem that is known to be NP-hard (see Hopcroft and Ullman, 1979) and that rapidly becomes intractable as the number of states increases. If there are N_S states being represented by

N_{ff} flip-flops, with $N_S \leq 2^{N_{ff}}$, then there will be $\dfrac{(2^{N_{ff}})!}{(2^{N_{ff}} - N_s)!}$ possible

designs. For $N_s = 10$, we will need $N_{ff} = 4$, which gives 2.91×10^{10}. This, of course, counts numerous designs that are equivalent but simply different orderings of the flip-flops. A more representative estimate of complexity would be the number of unique orderings,

which has an additional factor of $\dfrac{1}{(N_{ff})!}$ to account for the freedom

to reorder the flip-flops, and subtracts one from each of the other factorial arguments to obtain a unique assignment. Still, for our sample case, the number of such unique assignments is over 75 million. Obviously, exhaustive search would not work, and heuristics must be used. One heuristic is to attempt to minimize the number of flip-flop state changes due to state transitions. The use of Gray codes, which change by 1 bit in sequence, is sometimes used. See Comer (1990) and Friedman and Menon (1975) for an introduction to the general topic of FSM design. See, for example, Yang et al. (1991) for a discussion of typical heuristic approaches to state assignment.

When Not to Use FSMs

The FSM is a general construct for modeling anything than can be built with a specific, finite silicon real estate allotment. There are obvious special cases that need not be modeled with this full generality. Shift registers are one obvious example; sequencers that go from one state to another in a fixed sequence without branching are another.

Any sequential machine that only has a finite-duration memory can be represented as a sequence of delay elements. A digital finite-impulse response filter, that is, a digital filter without feedback, would be an example of a system that can be represented as a sequence of delay elements, although not strictly an FSM. A shift-register is another example that is an FSM. Obviously, systems that have a well-defined sequence do not require the full flexibility of an FSM, and might be more simply implemented in other ways.

FSMs, along with combinatorial logic, are often called "random" logic by designers, to distinguish them from regular structures such as memory caches, and so forth. FSMs by their nature have an irregular structure that makes them difficult to modify or verify. It is therefore often desirable to use more structured logic when appropriate.

Hackett and Leach (1992) discuss the use of linear feedback shift registers for a variety of applications. These devices have often been simulated in software for generating cyclic redundancy check (CRC) codes, and in hardware for generating pseudorandom sequences for use in spread-spectrum and other sequences.

Shift registers play an important role in the Boundary-Scan test architecture (IEEE-Std-1149.1), and are a special form of FSM. In an interesting article, Eschermann and Wunderlich (1992) discuss the design of FSMs incorporating a testable structure by construction.

VHDL MODELING

There are numerous ways to model FSMs. Three approaches will be mentioned here.

One conventional method for implementing a state machine employs blocks and guards and is of the following form:

```
type State_Values is (State1, State2,
State3);
type State_Vector is array
    (NATURAL range < > ) of State_Values;
type Out_Values is (Out1, Out2, Out3);
type In_Values is BIT;
signal State: Sresolve State_Values
    register :=State1;


function Sresolve ( State : in State_Vec-
tor) return State_Values is
begin
    assert ( State' LENGTH = 1)
      report
        " FSM not in unique state "
        severity ERROR;
      return State(1);
    end Sresolve;


block (State = 0 and Input = 1 )
begin
   -- assign next state
     State <= guarded 1;
end block;
block (State = 1 and Input = 1 )
begin
     State <= guarded 1;
```

```
end block;
block (State = 0 and  Input = 0 )
begin
     State <= guarded 0;
end block;
-- process to  output appropriate for each
state
Out: process (State)
begin
   case State
     when State1 =>
        Output <=1;--Moore machine Output
        case In
          when ' 1' =>
             Output<= 1;-- Mealy machine Output
          when ' 0' =>
        end case;
     -- other State values similarly handled
     end case;
end process
 Out;
ResetFSM: block (Reset' EVENT and Reset =' 1' )
State <= guarded State1;
 -- or whatever initial state is appropriate
end block;
```

Any valid FSM must be in a unique state at any time. The case statement exploits this by choosing only one case and skipping the others. An **if ... then ... elsif ... endif** construct would accomplish the same thing. However, there are no similar constructs for blocks and processes. Therefore, each guard will be evaluated, and each block entered. If each guard is of the form (State=State_n and . . .), and if the compiler is smart enough to use short-circuited evaluation of these logical expressions, then the cost will be minimal. In any event, the signal State will have to be a resolved signal, because it has a number of drivers. The resolution function will therefore have to be called.

This is wasteful, because all but one of the drivers should be **null**, that driver corresponding to the actual state of the FSM. An alternative FSM, which is much less elegant but probably more efficient, would take advantage of the unique state of the FSM by using variables to avoid multiple assignments to a signal:

```
type State_Values is (State1, State2,
State3);
B? type Out_Values is (Out1, Out2, Out3);
type In_Values is BIT;
signal State: State_Values :=State1;
Out: process (Input)
   variable Next_State: State_Values;
   variable Out: Out_Values;
   begin
   case State
     when State1 =>
       case In
         when ' 1' =>
           Next_State := ; --next state
           Out := ;
         when ' 0' =>
           -- other inputs similar
       end case;
     -- other State values similarly handled
   end case;
   State <= Next_State after ...;
   -- no need to resolve
   Output <= Out;
end process;
```

Note that for this implementation, State need not be a resolved signal and no resolution function need be called. This is because there is only one driver for State, in one process. Note also that if a nonzero disconnect delay is specified, there will be multiple drivers active at any time and a resolution function will be required. However, it is unlikely that this will be useful for most FSM simulations.

Although variables are employed in the above implementation, they are not used as memory; their values at previous simulation times are immaterial. Nonetheless, their use might inhibit synthesis. It is also possible that some synthesizes might need to see that signals are of type **register** to synthesize the required memory elements. In VHDL, declaring a signal to be of type **register** merely affects the calling of the resolution function (see Chapter 2), so is of no interest for unresolved signals.

In this case, the nesting of case statements was with State as the outer variable, and for each input. This can be reversed, of course, depending on which is simpler. There may be situations in which the processing is more dependent on the input than the state, or vice versa. Also, while case statements have been used, if . . . then . . . elsif . . . endif constructs might be used if better suited to the structure of the data.

There is another methodology, in which each state is represented by a process. This approach has been advocated in a paper by Spillane and Navabi (1990). Obviously, we must arrange that only one process is active at any time. This requires a global signal or variable to maintain this information and allow all the processes to determine whether they should be active or not. Normally, such a variable needs protection, such as semaphores, to prevent simultaneous access that might cause an invalid state. In this case, as only one of the processes can be active at any given time, this is not a problem. A sketch of code that uses this approach is shown here:

```
type States is ( State_1, State_2, ... );
  type Outputs is ( Output_1, Output_2, ...
);
  type Inputs is ( Input_1, Input_2, ... );
signal Current_State: Sresolve States;

   State_n : process
  variable Next_State: States;
  begin
```

```
if Current_State = State_n then
   -- this is the current state

   -- Set output here for Moore Machine

   -- Set next state, based upon Input:
   case Input  is
     when Input_1 =>
       Next_State := ...
         -- Set Output here if Mealy machine
       ... -- more when clause for other inputs.
   end case;

   -- assign Next_State to Current_State.
   -- Again, assign here Current_State

   -- Suspend until there is new input
   wait on Input;
   -- Make sure process does not execute unless
   -- it is the current state.
   wait until Current_State = State_n ;
 end if;
 end process;
```

This process is sensitive to the signals Current_State and In-put. We use two **wait** statements to make sure that the process suspends correctly. Note that, if they were placed in the other order, the **wait until** would not cause any waiting because the effect of the assignment to Current_State would not take place at the point this wait statement would be encountered. We do not want the state to change with each delta time increment unless the input has changed. So the "**wait on** Input;" statement has been included first to insure that there is a new input value. At that time, Current_State will be the new, correct current state.

Many vendors provide tools to synthesize FSMs from user specifications. Typically, they will write VHDL code from user specifications of the FSM, often minimizing the state table or performing other optimizations. If hand-coded VHDL is to be input, be sure it is in the format required for the tools to be used.

Finally, we discuss the state table approach. Generally, a state table must be constructed when designing an FSM. This state table leads to a number of representations for FSMs that lead rather directly to software simulation and hardware implementation. The approaches discussed above are attractive for quick implementation of relatively simple FSMs. The software simulation approach we now discuss is the analog of the hardware implementation using a state latch and ROM. In systems with extensive state tables, the state table approach may be the most effective and straightforward. There are a number of options for table structure. As the state table controls the structure of this FSM representation, and Moore and Mealy machines have different state table structures, the type of machine will alter the data structure needed. There are also design options as to whether an *associative memory* approach is used, that is, one in which the input and state are formed into an address and used to access the next state and output. Such an approach is clearly rapid in hardware but requires substantial real estate, unless appropriate combinatorial logic is used to map allowed inputs into a small set of address inputs. Similarly, huge tables will be needed in software unless some effort is directed to prevent such an occurrence.

Consider a relatively simple implementation:

```
type MooreOut is array (range States' RANGE);
type MealyOut is array (range States' RANGE,
range Inputs' RANGE);
type Transitions is array (range
States' RANGE, range Inputs' RANGE);

process (Input)
constant Output_Table: MooreOut:= (... );
  --or constant Output_Table: MealyOut:= (
(...), (...),... );
constant   Transition_Table: Transitions:= (
(...), (...),... );
begin
```

```
Output <= Output_Table
   (Current_State,Input));
-- above for Mealy machine
Output <= Output_Table
   ( Current_State);
-- above for Moore Machine
Current_State <= Transition_Table(Cur-
rent_State, Input);
end process;
```

This tabular approach is similar to microprogramming in approach. We can view the table as a ROM containing actions in the form of output, with the next state information more general than the typical microprogrammed implementation, which sequences through the microcode until an end of sequence sentinel is encountered. Microcoded instructions sometimes have the next instruction specified as part of the current instruction, such implementations resembling state machines to a greater degree. This will be examined in Chapter 15, when microprogramming is discussed.

Races

Because of the feedback inherent in the state machine implementation, critical races are possible. See Chapter 16 for a more complete discussion. This should be evident from the Mealy machine, whose output depends upon the transition, or equivalently, the current state and the input. If we implement this carelessly, making the output a function of the input and the state, when the current state changes, we cannot allow the output to change. Similar difficulties arise in hardware. One solution is to use a two-phase clock (see Chapter 16), with inputs changing and the new state and output being determined on the first phase, and the advance to the new state on the second phase clock pulse.

APPLICATIONS

FSMs are of great value in hardware, firmware, and software implementations. We review the most useful here. We mention some software applications as it may be desirable to model these as part of an effort to model embedded, real-time systems or other applications as part of a VHDL hardware modeling effort. Details on applications to microprocessors will be deferred to Chapter 15, and applications to bus protocols and interfaces will be discussed in Chapter 16. Nelson (1992) discusses the writing device drivers as FSMs.

Microprocessor Control Unit

There are numerous examples of FSMs embedded in various hardware. Typical examples are CPUs and bus controllers. A typical microprocessor will have both, and may therefore harbor a number of FSMs operating concurrently and independently.

The Motorola 68040, discussed by Edenfield et al. (1990), has a six-stage integer pipelined architecture. The instruction execution is managed by three independent controllers. The first two pipelined stages, the instruction prefetching and the program counter arithmetic, is controlled by the program-counter or PC controller, which is an FSM. The effective-address or EA controller handles the operand address calculation and fetch, as well as the write-back of the results, and the date-execution or DE controller handles the actual execution of the instruction. These other two controllers are not FSMs. Instead, the EA and DE controllers sequence through microcode. The FSM-based PC controller takes as input the instruction length and whether a branch or jump is taken to correctly alter the program counter, fetch whatever is necessary, control the instruction cache, and so forth. Note that while the various controllers each maintain some state memory by sequencing through microcode, only the PC controller needs the generality of an FSM. This is an example of the principle discussed at the beginning of this chapter that not everything that could be an FSM should be one.

The MIPS R4000 RISC machine uses a number of FSMs to control the pipeline and cache (Mirapuri et al., 1992). Three state machines (run, slip, and restart) are each pipelined and control the sequence of operations during stall and slip conditions. Another FSM, the *zipper*, controls the write-back of dirty lines from the primary cache to memory. Cache coherency is ensured with a five-state protocol that is a modification of the four-state MESI protocol used, for example, by the Motorola 88110 RISC chip (see Diefendorff and Allen and Chapter 15 of this book).

Marino (1986) gives an FSM specification for the Motorola 6800, which will be discussed in Chapter 15. Such a specification for a microprocessor might be useful for a functional model of a microprocessor, whatever the actual implementation details are.

Memory Control Units

Interfacing many microprocessors with memory requires a variety of support chips to control the bus. One example is the need for inserting one or more wait states if memory is slow. This is a relatively simple FSM implemented with a few D flip-flops.

A number of manuals discuss the implementation of memory control units, using ASICs, for use of various forms of memory such as static-column RAM, in conjunction with the manufacturer's CPU.

Bus Interface Unit and Protocols

The bus interface unit of many microprocessors, as well as various peripheral interface units, are naturally implemented with one or more interacting FSMs. One function is to insert a predetermined number of wait states. Another is to "loop" or hold a level until an appropriate acknowledgment is received. Still another is to control the sequence of a burst-mode transfer, which will occupy a number of bus cycles.

Details on bus protocols, such as the TCP/IP protocol, which is implemented in software and a PI bus controller, implemented in hardware, will be covered in Chapter 16.

Run-Length Limited Encoding

Self-clocking data, such as serial data read from disk drives and compact disks, must provide synchronizing information so the significance of bits read can be interpreted properly. Run-length limited (RLL) encoding enables this to be accomplished without the full overhead of separate clock and data pulses. This is implemented by FSMs. See the tutorial by Immink (1990) for a good overview. RLL codes are variable length, which is why the flexibility of an FSM is needed. See the articles by Shafer (1987), Patel (1975), and Franaszek (1970) for more details.

Real-Time Operating System Kernel

Task management in a multitasking operating system involves, in effect, running an FSM for each task, the status of which is retained in a memory block called the task control block (TCB). Each task has an associated TCB. Bigerstaff (1986) discusses a typical multitasking operating systems kernel. He defines a process as having four possible states: ready, running, suspended, and terminating.

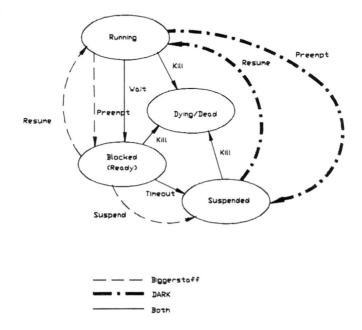

Fig. 13.6 Real-time kernel FSM

The Software Engineering Institutes Distributed Ada Real-Time Kernel (DARK) has a similar task state diagram, also with four states, as will almost all real-time operating systems. This is sketched in Figure 13.6. Each task is either running, blocked, suspended, or dead. The Ready state of Biggerstaff corresponds approximately to the blocked state of DARK, the principal difference being that in Biggerstaff's model, there are no direct transitions between Running and suspended. Instead, the Blocked/Ready state is an intermediate. As the system kernel initiates and controls the preempt, resume, and restart transitions, there is little practical difference in these models. A running task can commit suicide and request to die, or it may be killed by another task, such as its creator. It may be suspended if it has reached the maximum time allotted to it in a particular time slice. It may be blocked while waiting for a resource, or at the equivalent of a rendezvous request (DARK does not support Ada tasking as such). State transitions are controlled by the operating system, and may be triggered by interrupts (such as a time tick indicating the end of a time slice allotment) or by software transactions.

The analogous diagram for UNIX System V (Bach, 1986, p. 148) is even more complex, with nine states, due principally to the distinction between the system kernel and user processes.

LINKED STATE MACHINES AND PETRI NETS

It is natural to model concurrently executing processes and hardware as a number of FSMs that interact. If each machine has N states, and there are M similar machines, then the system may be in N^M possible states. This clearly makes modeling the system as a single FSM intractable for even moderate values of M and N, but modeling the system as a number of interacting FSMs is practical because the individual machines do not care about the details of the state of the other machines. These considerations lead to the model of linked state machines (LSMs). The many internal states of an individual machine may be collected into equivalence classes, that is, sets of states that, from the point of view of the other machines, are equivalent, simplifying the interaction bookkeeping. To describe such machines, an extension of the Petri net formalism is used.

Petri Nets and LSMs

Petri nets were developed to describe concurrent processes that interact and synchronize, that is, wait for one another to perform certain tasks. They are directed graphs in which vertices are called *places* and edges are called *transitions*. In a *marked Petri net*, one or more symbols called *tokens* exist, which occupy places and move along transitions that are said to *fire*. The marking defines the state of the system. Each place represents a condition to be fulfilled for

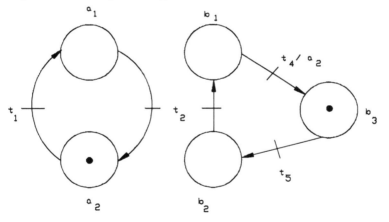

Fig. 13.7 Linked Finite State Machine

the transitions, with the transitions representing events such as the change of machine state.

Transitions may have a number of preconditions that have to be fulfilled to enable the firing of a transition. This is indicated by labeling the transitions as to the conditions required for their enabling. The transition will be enabled if all of its *input places* have at least one token. For LSMs, an extension to conventional Petri net notation is to draw transitions for multiple FSMs that make up the LSM through the same transition marker when these machines synchronously make that transition.

Figure 13.7 illustrates a Petri net as extended for describing LSMs. Johnsonbaugh (1984) includes a discussion of Petri nets (but not as adapted to deal with LSMs). Petri nets can be used as an analysis aid for determining whether deadlocks are possible. Agarwal (1990) has discussed modeling Petri Nets in VHDL. Because real-time systems may usefully be defined in terms of LSMs, this analysis is of interest.

Obviously, the modeling of such LSMs may be effected by modeling each component FSM. There will be additional preconditions for state changes that depend on the states of the other component FSMs. This will require global communication, which must be effected in VHDL-87 by resolved signals, although in VHDL-92 global (shared) variables may be used. With such variables, protected critical sections must be used to insure data integrity. Semaphores are one construct for synchronizing the linked FSMs as required.

FINITE STATE AUTOMATA, LANGUAGES

FSMs may be used to recognize certain simple languages. This is important to many programs, such as UNIX utilities including GREP and AWK. The use of such FSMs in hardware to recognize and process input and event sequences that can be specified in terms of regular expressions makes the following introduction to the topic useful. Greater detail will be found in Hopcroft and Ullman (1979), Friedman and Menon (1975), and Revesz (1983).

Formal Language Theory

The formal theory of language has a long history, the idea of phrase-structure grammars going back to linguist Leonard Bloomfield, with the idea of defining such languages formally by means of productions due to logical Emil Post. Noam Chomsky's influence cannot be overemphasized. He discussed a hierarchy of phrase-structure grammar constructions from the most complex (context sensitive or Chomsky type 1) to context-free (type 2) and regular (type 3). He popularized the idea of applying these ideas to natural

language, and, while they were not of much success when applied
in that domain, these ideas strongly influenced the development of
artificial languages such as those used by computers. The ideas in
this section are necessary to understand the description of VHDL
syntax in Appendix B of the LRM, and the workings of the UNIX
utilities GREP, AWK, LEX, among other things.

In formal language theory, only syntax is of interest. The concern is whether a string of symbols is syntactically valid in the language specified.

A phrase structure grammar is defined by a set of *terminal symbols*, which correspond to the words of the language, *nonterminal
symbols*, which correspond to categories such as nouns of a language, a start symbol, and rules for forming syntactically allowed
sentences in the language, called *productions*. The actual sentences
of the languages are to be composed of the terminal symbols. The
Backus-Naur form (BNF) is the standard method for writing such
productions, and is used in VHDL LRM Appendix A to define the
language. Denoting nonterminal by uppercase letters and terminal
symbols by lowercase letters, and symbols that might be either by
Greek letters, context-sensitive languages allow any productions of
the general form $\alpha AB::=\alpha\beta\gamma$; context-free allow productions of the
more restrictive form $A::=\alpha$, and regular expressions only the two
forms $A::=a$ or $A::=aB$. As an illustration, consider the following
excerpt from the LRM:

```
binding_indication  ::=
   entity_aspect
   [ generic_map_aspect]
   [ port_map_aspect]

@CODE = entity_aspect  ::=
   entity entity_name
     [ ( architecture_identifier)]
   | configuration configuration_name
   | open
```

A word about the notation here. The vertical bar (|) denotes a choice, an alternative, in the metalanguage just as it does in the language. Thus the entity_aspect has three alternative forms. The elements within the square braces [] are optional, and the italicized numbers represent user identifiers, which behave as terminal symbols, as do the reserved words. The first production rule specifies how to write syntactically correct binding indications. The generic and port maps are optional; either or both may be present. The entity aspect can specify an entity, a configuration, or that the port is unbound through the use of the reserved word **open**. If users specify an entity to be bound, they must give a valid entity name, with an optional architecture specified by its name.

If you understood this discussion, you should have no trouble following Appendix A of the LRM.

Regular Grammars and Finite State Automata

Context-sensitive languages are very difficult to recognize or parse. They require a computer of the power of a Turing machine, the most general and powerful computer. Context-free languages require simpler machines called Push-Down automata. These have a push-down stack that can remember an infinite amount of information, but can only retrieve information from the top of the stack, in a last-in, first-out manner. Regular grammars can be recognized by finite-state automata (FSA). FSA are special cases of FSMs. They only have two outputs, 1 and 0, the former being output by an *accepting state*, which is the result for a syntactically valid input. Such automata recognize a language.

Regular grammars would include allowed syntax such as $b^n a b^m$, meaning any number of b's, followed by a single a, followed by any number of b's. A language such as $a^n b^n c^n$ in which the a sequence of n a's must be followed by the same number of b's and then the same number of c's cannot be recognized by a regular grammar. It demands too much ability to recall the past, basically the ability to count an arbitrary number of a's and then to count the b's and c's and compare. Note that one could easily make an FSM to recognize, say, $a^5b^5c^5$. The difficulty comes because we do not know n a priori. The larger n, the larger the number of states we would need to count, and as n is not bounded by our specification, we cannot build an FSM to handle it; this illustrates the F in FSM.

It is often convenient to describe regular grammars, and so forth, with a generalization of FSA called the nondeterministic FSA (NFSA). In aN NFSA, a state transition is not uniquely defined for a given input. Instead, there are a number of choices. One can view the NFSA as being cloned at this point, with each clone following a different allowed path. This happens as often as needed. If any of the clones reach a nonaccepting state they can be discarded and ignored. If any reaches an accepting state, that path corresponds to the correct parse of the input sentence and the input is accepted as having valid syntax. The NFSA is a convenience. It may be shown that any NFSA may be converted to an FSA. This FSA can have as many states as the number of all possible subsets of the NFSA; if the NFSA has N states, the equivalent FSA may have 2^N. This gives an indication of the savings entailed by writing descriptions in terms of NFSA, even if they have no greater recognizing power than the FSA. Languages described by nondeterministic grammars can include so-called ε-moves (epsilon moves), which are transitions due to no input at all. These transitions can simplify the description of the language, but clearly render the grammar nondeterministic.

To handle the potentially infinite number of states needed to recognize something like a^nb^n, we need a system with potentially infinite memory capacity. This is a push-down automaton, with an infinite push-down stack. It would then be trivial to recognize the example, as we could push a 1 for every a encountered, and pop one for every b. If the stack is empty at the end of the sequence, the sentence is accepted. Push-down automata come in deterministic and nondeterministic forms as well, but in this case, the nondeterministic form is more powerful than the deterministic. Nondeterministic push-down automata can handle context free languages. The language with $a^nb^nc^n$ is not context free, as you might have guessed if you tried to develop a push-down automaton to accept it.

Giving the automaton two push-down stacks makes it powerful enough not only to accept context-sensitive languages (type 1) but to accept unrestricted (type 0) phrase structure grammars. Type 1 languages can be recognized by a linear bounded automaton, which has two push-down stacks whose size is limited by the maximum length of the sentences to be recognized.

Friedman and Menon (1975) provide algorithms for the specification of FSMs (Moore type) that recognize a given regular grammar, as well as for determining a regular grammar corresponding to a given FSA of the Moore type. Algorithms for converting nondeterministic finite automata (NDFA) to deterministic ones (DFA) are discussed in Jones and Crabtree (1988). They also present FORTRAN code for the Mealy-Huffman algorithm for minimizing the number of required states of a DFA.

Utilities like GREP construct an FSM in software to process the regular expressions the programmer develops. C code and discussions of how to write FSAs and FSMs for dealing with specified regular grammars may be found in many books and articles. See, for example, Hollub (1986).

REFERENCES

Agarwal, Shishir, "Thinking Petri Nets Through VHDL", *1990 VHDL Fall User's Group Meeting*, Claremont Resort, Oakland, Ca., Oct. 14-17, 1990, pp. 51-59.

Bach, M. J., *The Design of the UNIX Operating System* (Englewood Cliffs, N. J.: Prentice Hall, 1986).

Biggerstaff, T. J., *Systems Software Tools* (Englewood Cliffs, N. J.: Prentice Hall, 1986).

Carmely, T., "Finite-State Software Design," *Embedded Systems Programming,* pp. 54-69, Feb. 1992.

Comer, D. J., *Digital Logic and State Machine Design* (Philadelphia, PA: Saunders College Publishing (Holt, Rinehart, and Winston, 1990).

Dewdney, A. K., *The Turing Omnibus* (Rockville, M. D.: Computer Science Press, 1989).

Diefendorff, K., and Allen, M., "Organization of the Motorola 88110 Superscalar RISC Microprocessor," *IEEE Micro*, pp. 40-63, April 1992.

Edenfield, R. W., Gallup, M. G., Ledbetter, W. B., Jr., McGarity, R. C., Quintana, E. E., and Reininger, R. A., "The 68040 Processor", *IEEE Micro*, February 1990, pp. 66-77, and June 1990, 22-34.

Eschermann, B. and Wunderlich, H.-J., "Optimized Synthesis Techniques for Testable Sequential Circuits," *IEEE Trans. on Computer-Aided Design*, **11**, pp. 301-312, March 1992.

Franaszek, P., "Sequence-state Methods for Run-length-limited Coding," *IBM J. Res. Development*, pp. 376-383, July 1970.

Friedman, A. D., and Menon, P. R., *Theory and Design of Switching Circuits* (Rockville, M. D: Computer Science Press, 1975).

Hackett, R. and Leach, T., "Build Better Sequential Circuits," *ASIC & EDA*, pp. 43-49, March 1992.

Hollub, A., "GREP.C; A Generalized Regular Expression Parser in C" in *Dr. Dobb's Toolbook of C* (N. Y.: Brady Books, 1986). Also in Oct. 1984 issue #86 of *Dr. Dobb's Journal*.

Hopcroft, J. E., and Ullman, J. D., *Introduction to Automata Theory, Languages, and Computation* (Reading, MA: Addison Wesley, 1979).

Immink, K., "Runlength-Limited Sequences," *Proc. IEEE*, **78**, pp. 1745-1759, Nov. 1990.

Jones, R. K., and Crabtree, J., *Fortran Tools* (N. Y.: John Wiley and Sons, 1988).

Johnsonbaugh, R., *Discrete Mathematics* (N. Y: Macmillan, 1984).

Marino, L., *Principles of Computer Design* (Rockville, M. D.: Computer Science Press, 1986).

Mendelson, E., *Boolean Algebra and Switching Circuits* (N. Y.: McGraw-Hill/Schaum's Outlines, 1970).

Mirapuri, S., Woodacre, M., Vasseghi, N., "The Mips R4000 Processor," *IEEE Micro*, pp. 10-22, April 1992.

Nelson, Thomas, "The Device Driver as State Machine," *The C Users Journal* **10**, #3, pp. 41-59, March 1992.

Patel, A., "Zero-Modulation Encoding in Magnetic Recording," *IBM J. Res. Development*, pp. 366-378, July 1975.

Revesz, G. E., *Introduction to Formal Languages* (N. Y.: Dover, 1983).

Savitzky, S., *Real-Time Microprocessor Systems* (N. Y.: Van Nostrand Reinhold, 1985).

Shafer, T., "Choosing a coding scheme to increase drive density," *Computer Design*, pp. 69-74, Sept. 1987.

Spillane, J. and Navabi, B., "Behavioral State Machine for Synthesis," *1990 VHDL Fall User's Group Meeting*, Claremont Resort, Oakland, CA., Oct. 14-17, 1990.

Yang, J.-J., Shin, H., Chong, J.-W., "New State Assignment Algorithms for Finite State Machines Using Look Ahead," *Proceedings of the IEEE 1991 Custom Integrated Circuits Conference*, Town & Country Hotel, San Diego, CA, May 12-15, 1991, pp. 11.21.-11.2.4.

Chapter 14

Practical Considerations

PURPOSE

This chapter gives practical advice on doing VHDL simulations that take account of real-world considerations such as conformity with standards, synthesis, and the realities of simulating complex devices. The digital approximation of a few logic levels is discussed in terms of real-world signal transmission characteristics. This leads to a discussion of how to model such realities through back-annotation and related methods. One piece of advice is to adhere to standards whenever possible, which necessitates familiarity with standards such as the MVL9 multivalued logic level standard, and the WAVES test bench standard. Familiarity with EDIF 2 0 0 and other netlist standards, may also come in handy. It would be impossible to fully define these standards within the bounds of this chapter. Rather, it is our intent to provide sufficient background and references so that you can readily use these standards as necessary.

SIMULATION LEVELS

VHDL provides the ability to perform simulation at a number of levels, to mix components of different levels, and to mix behavioral and structural descriptions.

The highest level of description consistent with simulation goals should be used. This will permit the most efficient simulations, and allow synthesis tools the maximum latitude to vary design choices to achieve desired goals (fastest, smallest, etc.).

Functional Level

Functional or "behavioral" simulation (see comments in Chapter 1 on this terminology) emulates the stimulus response behavior of the device, with no attempt made to replicate the internal mechanism by which this is achieved. The device is considered a "black box." This is generally the most efficient method of simulation. As a crude rule of thumb, behavioral simulations are twice as fast as comparable structural simulations. Functional simulations are likely to be the least faithful and the least likely to uncover hazards. Therefore, functional modeling is most appropriate at early design stages, or at later design phases for portions of the design that are finalized, while attention is concentrated on other portions.

Register-Transfer Level

Register-transfer level (RTL) refers to simulation with components that handle groups of bits, such as registers, memory blocks and multiplexers. Signals at this level might be integers, or they might be instructions or portions thereof. See Coehlo (1988) for VHDL code for many of these models; it also contains an appendix with utilities to convert from, for example, an array of bits to an integer value. This may be of use in behavioral models. Remember the limitations on representable integers, for example, when this is done; the VHDL standard is almost equivalent to 32 bits, except that the specified minimum of the range (-2147483647) is one more than most 32-bit twos-s complement ranges (-2147483648), and it is likely this special value will be an embarrassment if it is not properly handled.

Gate Level

Gate level refers to synthesis where components are gates, for example, NAND gates and flip-flops. Signals at this level correspond to individual bits or nets. Standard gates will be found in vendor packages. Coehlo (1988), and synthesis libraries; therefore, there is little need to discuss this level of component here.

Switch-Level

Switch-level simulations model individual transistors. This is often the level of analog simulations, such as using SPICE, where phenomena such as ground bounce can be quantified. It is unlikely VHDL will ever be used at this level.

Hardware Simulation

It is possible to concurrently run hardware as part of a VHDL simulation. LMSI (soon to merge with Logic Automation to form LMC) produces a device that can be used to couple many components to a VHDL simulation. The device buffers the inputs and outputs to the hardware so that constraints on hold time, and so forth, are observed and results are available to the VHDL simulator when requested. Such devices, at present, are primarily useful for achieving fidelity of the simulation rather than accelerating it. Hardware accelerators for VHDL and other simulation software is a separate topic.

LOGIC LEVELS

While a digital signal on a wire might adequately be described by the binary logic values ′ 0′ and ′ 1′ , more variety is needed to describe devices, and more still are required for the purposes of debugging and synthesis. Consider a component specification for a TTL tri-state device. We must be able to specify when the device is not driving the bus at all, but is in its high-impedance state. The easiest way to do this is to define a new state, ' Z' , which represents the disconnected state of the device. Consideration of MOS device characteristics lead to the need for *weak* states, which can be overridden by a *forcing* value such as ' 0' or ' 1' . These additional states correspond to electrical conditions.

Additional states of an artificial nature, which do no correspond directly to electrical conditions, are useful in analyzing and synthesizing a design. In analysis, the uninitialized or ' U' state may be used to determine whether any signal values have not properly been set. This practice is similar to that of some FORTRAN compilers initializing variables to infinite values, so that if they are used in a calculation an error will be flagged and the user will realize that he failed to properly initialize a variable. A similar logic level is ' X' , for unknown or indeterminate.

Finally, for an aid to synthesis tools, the ' D' for don't care is used. (The representation '-' is also often used for the don't care state.) It enables the synthesis machine to optimize the design more efficiently by taking the value to be ' 0' or ' 1' , whichever produces a more efficient design.

Signals designed to represent actual electrical signals are typically an enumerated type. The number of allowed levels significantly impacts the complexity and the speed of the simulation. Popular choices include types with four, five, nine, or forty-six different values. The multivalued logic 9 (MVL9) system is IEEE-Std-1164, and is therefore a preferred choice. However, it has been reported to be about 20 to 30% slower to use MVL9 than MVL5 (see the article by Egan (1992) which quotes T.-W. Chien of Silicon Graphics using the Vantage VHDL simulator). The article by Cleaver and Derr (1991) advocates the use of five-valued logic. Consequently, it seems likely that no one system of logic levels will do for all purposes.

The MVL5 standard uses the set (' 0' ,' 1' ,' Z' ,' U' ,' X') while the MVL9 augments this to (' U' ,' X' ,' 0' ,' 1' ,' Z' , ' W' ,' L' ,' H' , ' D').

For synthesis purposes, the only logic levels that matter are ' 0' , ' 1' , and ' D' . The levels ' U' and ' X' are only of interest for debugging purposes. Depending upon technology, the levels ' Z' and the weak levels ' W' , ' L' , ' H' (for "weak 0 or 1," "weak 1 or low," and "weak 0 or high," respectively), may or may not exist. For example, for TTL and CMOS the weak levels will not in general exist. NMOS, however, has a weak logical high and a strong low due to signals being gated to ground. Thus, unless some unusual hybrid technology is in use, a reduction in the number of logic levels from MVL9 would generally be practical, and should speed up simulations measurably.

Ryan (1991) discusses the use of multiple-valued logic, particularly the ' X' state in MVL9. The MVLs constitute modal logics far more complex than those discussed by Aristotle or more recent logicians concerned with artificial intelligence applications. The usual Boolean logic rules are of course forgotten. For example, the law of the excluded middle, a **or not** a = ' 1' , is untrue. Care should be taken to see that such rules are not implicit in some simplification or optimization. Libraries should be available (see Chapter 1) for basic logic gates for MVL9, for example, and vendors will supply others (Vantage, for example, has advocated a forty-six-value logic). As noted in Chapter 1, there will be packages supporting MVL9 for the usual logic gates and comparison operations, so users need not concern themselves with how to **or** ' D' and ' W' . (Generally, the most conservative choice representing the maximum uncertainty possible is made.)

EIA-567 STANDARD

One standardization effort of interest is the EIA-567 Commercial Component VHDL Model specification. This requires components to be described using IEEE 1164 MVL9. Flags control various options, such as whether 'X' states are produced upon timing violations. EIA-567 has not been finalized as this book goes to press.

SYNTHESIS CONSIDERATIONS

VHDL can be a powerful tool when used in conjunction with synthesis tools. As noted in Chapter 1, a number of specialized tools exist for producing VHDL for certain families of PALs. Experience to date has shown that it requires care to successfully combine VHDL simulation and synthesis. In this book, only general guidelines can be given, as compilers and synthesis tools will vary greatly and will continue to evolve.

Rissman (1992) gives an example of a synthesis tool that ignored the sensitivity list given explicitly in the **process** statement declaration. Although this was discussed in the documentation and a warning ("ignoring process-specific sensitivity lists") was printed, these were overlooked and erroneous results were obtained. Once the problem was understood, it was easy to finesse by converting the process to an equivalent one with an explicit **wait on** statement at the end of the process.

The obvious moral of this anecdote is that VHDL coders must be cognizant of the peculiarities of the synthesis tools to be used, and must write VHDL code with those idiosyncrasies in mind.

It is more likely that such errors will occur if the VHDL simulation system and the synthesis software are each from different vendors. It is easy to recommend that the synthesized design be fully tested, but how do you test it before fabrication? One vendor of synthesis tools provides automatic generation of test vector sets, but these are not guaranteed to cover all possibilities, and a salesman claimed that problems of the kind discussed by Rissman (1992) were unheard of with their product.

It is likely, of course, that in an approach employing back-annotation, the simulation of the synthesized component will be a natural part of the design process in any case. If a top-down design approach is followed, initial simulations will be relatively high-level functional simulations, and therefore synthesis considerations will be remote.

The best advice would seem to be to have a fully integrated development environment from only one vendor, with the design planned in a top-down fashion, with the capability for simulation at a number of levels.

Often, when programmable logic is used, a tool called a "fitter" is used to optimize the design for the best fit to the device. See Clark (1992) on such programs.

According to an article by Berman (1992) on the VHDL User's Forum in 1991 in Newport Beach, California, users of VHDL for top-down design "all experienced difficulty in bridging the gap between HDL descriptions used for design and the lower-level descriptions used for final verification, especially in doing timing checks." In short, it will be necessary to plan carefully for the final stages of design and synthesis using non-VHDL tools, to avoid major problems coupling to these from VHDL. At present, VHDL cannot be used for all stages of most projects.

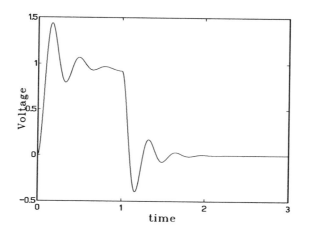

Figure 14.1 Typical distorted pulse

SIGNAL TRANSMISSION

Within the confines of VHDL's representation of signals, the actual waveforms of electrical signal values versus time is approximated by a discrete number of values. Even with the various MVL models, typically only two such physical values, ' 1 ' and ' 0 ', are represented. The actual behavior of voltage as a function of time is not modeled, except through specified delays for the transitions between the times at which the voltage is stabilized within the specified bounds for each logic level.

A rule of thumb is that when (risetime * velocity)/ 8 is roughly equal to or smaller than the path length, transmission line effects are important (see Hailey, 1991). The inductance of traces becomes noticeable, resulting in dispersion and distortion of pulses. In particular, the surge of current as one or more switches change state causes a voltage drop $L\dfrac{di}{dt}$ on the power bus, which can change the level of signals (called *ground bounce*). Decoupling capacitors can mitigate such effects.

For a discussion of transmission-line analysis for digital applications see Deutsch et al. (1990). Ground planes can mitigate such effects; crosstalk will be a problem if traces are closer to one another than to the ground plane over some minimum distance. For long runs, twisted-pair transmission lines are one method to mitigate high frequency effects and reduce noise pickup. Figure 14.1 shows typical waveforms for a square pulse as distorted by a dissipative transmission line.

Just as decoupling capacitors are desirable to keep transients off the power bus, capacitance is the enemy on signal lines. The load capacitance is the principal determiner of signal risetime and delay can be modeled in a lumped-parameter model as related to capacitance through an RC time constant. This fact can be used to compute approximate delays due to total load, called *fan-out dependent* delay. The capacitance must absorb a current of $i = C\dfrac{dv}{dt}$, so for a given ability to drive current, the rate of voltage rise will be inversely proportional to the total load capacitance being driven, this often being the dominant delay term. The power dissipation is then $P = iv = C v^2 f$, where f is the switching frequency for average power dissipation or twice the inverse risetime for the instantaneous power required for a transition.

Capacitance is particularly important for bus transceivers. TTL causes relatively low bus impedances of the order of 10 ohms, and CMOS presents termination problems, making ECL or BTL (bus transceiver logic). BTL uses Schottky diodes to minimize capacitance. See Borrill (1989) on BTL. Finally, impedance matching and line termination are important considerations in long transmission lines. Large reflections can reduce noise margins and lead to long delays before the signal stabilizes due to ringing and overshoot qualitatively similar to the dispersive waveforms seen in Figure 14.1. The characteristic impedance of the line determines the initial current-voltage relationship before the arrival of any reflections, $v = iZ$ and $Z = \sqrt{\frac{L}{C}}$. Load capacitance increases the effective capacitance, resulting in lower impedance and increased current drive required to reach a given voltage change. See United Technical Publications (1976) *Modern Guide to Digital Logic* for examples of semi-analytic reflection analysis. Analog simulation may be used.

BACK-ANNOTATION AND SDF

Back-annotation refers to the process of refining delay models by altering parameter values based on the results of other modeling or synthesis, to make the original, high-level simulations more faithful to the actual device to be constructed. As discussed earlier, delay is a function primarily of the loading, which can in principle be determined from the netlist but in practice is rather difficult to do within VHDL. It is also a function of layout, which must await synthesis for precise determination. See, for example, Turner (1990).

Total delay is generally modeled as the sum of terms, typically due to internal delays and propagation delays. Usually, generic parameters are assigned for each term in the delay.

The paper by Corman (1990) discusses a number of methods for computing fan-out-dependent delay within the VHDL simulation. One approach discussed is to use an artificial, resolved signal carrying the capacitive load of the device. A resolution function sums the values to provide the total load capacitance to be driven by any port. This may then be used with any desired model to determine the delay. The major disadvantage of this method is the overhead. As the capacitive load will not usually change, the resolution function is called only once per port at the beginning of the simulation. As noted in Chapter 12, use of generics incurs an overhead penalty as well.

There is an effort to standardize the importing of delay information for back-annotation. At present, the final format of the Standard Delay Format (SDF) file has not been fixed. When it is, vendors can be expected to provide support to ease the burden of its use. Berman and Ussery (1992) have proposed a format similar to EDIF in its use of parentheses. A triplet such as (5:6:7) is used to specify minimum, nominal, and maximum timings. Delays may be specified in a variety of ways: associated with a path from input to output (IOPATH), associated with a device (DEVICE), due to wiring path between devices (INTERCONNECT), the delay for a complete net (NETDELAY), and the delay associated with a port (without specifying the other end of the connection (PORT). Delays may be ABSOLUTE or INCREMENTAL, being added to other delays if the latter.

WAVES

As mentioned in Chapter 1, WAVES (Waveform and Vector Exchange Specification) is a standard architecture (IEEE-Std 1029.1) for specifying a VHDL simulation of a given entity. It specifies the input waveforms and the expected output as a result. WAVES uses the standard TEXTIO package.

Waveforms are defined as a set of histories of a set of signals (unlike VHDL, in which a waveform refers to a single signal). A waveform is composed of a sequence of *slices*. Slices have a specified *period*, which determines the time until the next slice supplies the signal values associated with the signal set. Each slice associates a *frame* with each signal. A frame is an ordered list of events and their associated times. Frames may contain any number of events (including zero). Events are also somewhat more complex than in

VHDL. In addition to the time, one may specify Boolean logic level and strength independently, direction (an enumerated type):

type DIRECTION_TYPE **is** (STIMULUS,RESPONSE);

and the relevancy to the waveform:

type RELEVANCE_TYPE **is** (OBSERVED,CALCULATED, REQUIRED);

WAVES is consistent with MVL9, MVL5, or other multivalued logic systems, but is potentially more general than any of these.

Each waveform has an associated procedure. The procedure performs APPLY operations, each of which adds one or more slices to the waveform, scheduling events in the slice on the output waveform.

Besides APPLY, WAVES has basic operations TAG and MATCH. The former annotates the waveform. The latter compares response values to expected values, yielding the Boolean values true or false depending on whether the output was as predicted or not. These are all defined through procedures or functions.

A WAVES dataset contains a header file and two or more WAVES files. The former contains the information needed to assemble the other files into the entire WAVES specification. The tabular format is specified in the WAVES standard. Typically, a waveform generator is called by a process of this general form:

```
process
begin
Read_Waveform(signalfile); wait;
end process
```

This is contained in the *test bench* architecture. The file initializes the waveform. Slices are read in and applied to specified input pins.

A detailed example is in Gilman et al. (1990). It is to be expected that WAVES will continue to evolve as more experience with its use is accumulated. Vendors will likely produce packages supporting WAVES, minimizing the amount of code the user will have to develop.

NETLISTS AND EDIF

Netlists

A *net* is defined as a single electrical path in a circuit, which has the same signal values at all of its points. It may be a collection of wires between multiple components.

A complex component or circuit may be viewed as a collection of components and their connections. Each component can be regarded as a black box whose ports are specified. The *netlist* of such a circuit is a representation of it in the form of a listing of each net with its connectivity, that is, what ports of which components are connected to each net. The netlist ignores passive components such as terminals and connectors, which (at least in principle) do not alter in any way the signals passing through them. It ignores the geometry or layout of the components. Therefore, the precise details of propagation delays and possible crosstalk or interference between connections is idealized out of consideration in the netlist description.

There are two conventional ways netlists may be presented: hierarchical and flat. In a hierarchical netlist, a hierarchy of building blocks is interconnected. This is similar to the VHDL structural approach, in which components may be built up of simpler components, with these in turn used to construct more complex components. In a flat file, all of the elements of the hierarchy are elaborated as their smallest component building blocks. This results in a description that is desirable for simulation with a program such as SPICE or VHDL, but is relatively incomprehensible due to its large size and not amenable to analysis. The naming of components in netlists will be hierarchical in such netlists, so it might be possible to reconstruct the hierarchy, at least in principle.

Programs such as OrCAD have the ability to produce both hierarchical and flattened netlists. The ORCAD documentation describes a large number of netlist formats with examples.

EDIF 2 0 0

EDIF is the Electronic Data Interchange Format, and is ANSI/EIA standard RS-548. It is based syntactically on the LISP language, and consequently has a huge number of parentheses enclosing data elements. It is extremely verbose, with EDIF descriptions typically many times the size of other formats for netlist data. On balance, EDIF netlists are a standard, are pure ASCII files, and relatively easily analyzed. See Rubin (1987) for a brief overview.

EDIF has a number of levels:

Level 0 the basic level, with simple constants

Level 1 where variables and expressions are supported

Level 2 which adds looping and conditionals

EDIF files consist of sets of *libraries*, which contain sets of *cells*, each of which contain one or more *views*. Views, like packages, have two portions; the *interface*, which defines the external view of the component (similar to the entity declaration), and the *contents*, similar to the package body or the architecture specification. A generic sort of EDIF file will look something like the following:

```
(edif name
      (status whenwhere)
      (design location)
      (external librariesreferenced)
      (library name
         (technology defaults)
         (cell name
            (viewmap portmapping)
            (view type name
               (interface externals)
               (contents internals)
            )
```

```
        (view...
        )          )
      (cell ...
      )       )
    (library ...
    )

)
```

EDIF specifies a "design-before-use" philosophy that requires any cell to be instantiated to be completely defined before this can happen. Simple cells must be defined before they are used in complex cells. Circular referencing is not permitted. This permits a single-pass compilation of EDIF models. A hierarchical structure is supported.

There are ten types of views allowed, including NETLIST, SCHEMATIC, SYMBOLIC, MASKLAYOUT, PCBLAYOUT, BEHAVIOR, LOGICMODEL, DOCUMENT, GRAPHIC, and STRANGER. The BEHAVIOR view is not fully specified at present. The LOGICMODEL may be used to describe the logical behavior of the cell. The two LAYOUT formats provide physical layout information. They might in principal be used to find delays due to path length or transmission-line effects. The SYMBOLIC view specifies high-level information about a cell. The SCHEMATIC view is used for diagrammatic information about a cell. The user can define the shapes for logic gates, for example, and specify how the circuit should be drawn using these symbols. The NETLIST view provides connectivity between cells as well as the connectivity details for instantiated cells. A view of one type may contain instances of a cell of another view type. The NETLIST view is the one of most interest to us. Nets establish connectivity between ports. Signals are defined in statement of the form

```
(define direction type names)
```

where direction specifies output or input for interfaces, and local or unspecified for the contents of a view. Type may be port for interfaces, signal for contents, or figuregroup for the technology section.

It is possible to define arrays, specified unused signals (similar to linkage in VHDL). The instance statement may be used to instantiate a component within the contents of another, thereby defining a hierarchical model. Technology provides background information, such as timing data.

A netlist specification would specify each device's interface. For example:

```
(cell LS32
     (comment "multiple gate")
     (cellType generic)
     (view NetlistView
        (viewType netlist)
        (interface
           (port InA (direction INPUT))
           (port InB (direction INPUT))
           ...
           (port OutD (direction OUTPUT))
        )
        )
     )
```

along with the connectivity of each net:

```
(net wire1
     (joined
        (portRef InA ))
        ...
     )
```

As in VHDL, nets may carry compound signals. A RIPPER cell has multiple ports and is used to merge nets, for example, to break out signals from a bus carrying a number of signals. Integer values are limited precisely as in VHDL.

GDS II

While EDIF can provide geometrical information as to the layout of the components, it is primarily a netlist format. The most popular format for interchange of geometrical data is the GDS II format (GDS II is a trademark of Calma, a subsidiary of General Electric). Because the VHDL user may encounter this format, it is briefly described here. More details will be found in Rubin (1987).

GDS II is intended primarily for describing the geometry of cells of an integrated circuit. Cells are called *structures*, which contain a number of *elements* specifying boundaries, paths, nodes, boxes, text (for comments), and array and structure references. These latter references define subcells and arrays of subcells, respectively. The GDS II files are designed to be compact, with information encoded in byte fields, and are not easily readable by humans.

JTAG BOUNDARY SCAN

The Joint European Test Action Group became the Joint Test Action Group (JTAG), and developed what is now IEEE-Std-1149.1-1990, the Boundary Scan Test Architecture (1990). A measure of its importance is that the Motorola 68040, MIPS R4000, and Intel 80486 all support this standard. The principal purpose is to support built-in self-test (BIST) on-chip. (See Edenfield et al. in Chapter 13 references for a discussion of the 68040.)

Boundary scan uses a serial I/O methodology to minimize the interface required. Data is shifted into a shift register, which holds one bit for each pin. Data is shifted out simultaneously in the same fashion. The standard mandates four devoted pins, and provides for an optional reset pin. The required four pins are Test Data In (TDI), Test Data Out (TDO), Test Clock (TCK), and Test Mode Select (TMS). These four signals are collectively called the test access port (TAP). The TDI is used to input both data and instructions. The control lines and the state of the on-board controller determines how the input is interpreted.

A number of devices may be connected with the TDI and TDO outputs "daisy-chained," or connected in sequence, in order to make one large Boundary Scan architecture, with the other pins all connected together so that the boundary scan is synchronized for all devices in the chain.

In addition to the shift register, there is a 16-state finite state machine (FSM; see Chapter 13) controlled by the TMS, TCK, and optional reset inputs. If there is no reset provided, the device should reset on power-up. A 1 held on TMS will cycle the controller to reset, and TMS is specified to have a pull-up to achieve this if there is no external reset. A VHDL model (see Chapter 13) might be the following:

```
type TAP_State is
(Reset, RunTestorIdle,
SelectDRscan, CaptureDR, ShiftDr,
Exit1DR, PauseDR, Exit2Dr, UpdateDR,
SelectIRscan, CaptureIR, ShiftIr,
Exit1IR, PauseIR, Exit2Ir, UpdateIR,);
process
variable Next: TAP_State;
begin
-- We assume the optional Reset line --   is
present
-- Change state synchronously on --    clock
rising edge or reset
wait on TCLK, RESET until Reset = 1 or
(TCLK' EVENT and TCLK=1);
if Reset = 1 then
   Next:= Reset;
elsif State= Reset and TMS= 0 then
   Next:=RunTestorIdle;
elsif State= RunTestorIdle and TMS= 0 then
   Next:=SelectDRScan;
elsif State= SelectDRScan and TMS= 1 then
   Next:=SelectIRScan;
<Belsif State= SelectDRScan and TMS= 0 then
```

```
      Next:=CaptureDR;
  elsif State= CaptureDR and TMS= 1 then
      Next:=Exit1DR;
  elsif State= CaptureDR and TMS= 0 then
      Next:=ShiftDR;
  elsif State= ShiftDR and TMS= 1 then
      Next:=Exit1DR;
  elsif State= Exit1DR and TMS= 1 then
      Next:=UpdateDR;
  elsif State= Exit1DR and TMS= 0 then
      Next:=PauseDR;
  elsif State= PauseDR and TMS= 1 then
      Next:=Exit2DR;
  elsif State= Exit2DR and TMS= 1 then
      Next:=UpdateDR;
  elsif State= Exit2DR and TMS= 0 then
      Next:=SelectDRScan;
  elsif State= UpdateDR and TMS= 1 then
      Next:=SelectDRScan;
  elsif State= UpdateDR and TMS= 0 then
      Next:=RunTestorIdle;
  elsif State= SelectIRScan and TMS= 1 then
      Next:=Reset;
  <Belsif State= SelectIRScan and TMS= 0 then
      Next:=CaptureIR;
  elsif State= CaptureIR and TMS= 1 then
      Next:=Exit1IR;
  elsif State= CaptureIR and TMS= 0 then
      Next:=ShiftIR;
  elsif State= ShiftIR and TMS= 1 then
      Next:=Exit1IR;
  elsif State= Exit1IR and TMS= 1 then
      Next:=UpdateIR;
  elsif State= Exit1IR and TMS= 0 then
      Next:=PauseIR;
  elsif State= PauseIR and TMS= 1 then
```

```
    Next:=Exit2IR;
elsif State= Exit2IR and TMS= 1 then
    Next:=UpdateIR;
elsif State= Exit2IR and TMS= 0 then
    Next:=SelectIRScan;
elsif State= UpdateIR and TMS= 1 then
    Next:=SelectIRScan;
elsif State= UpdateIR and TMS= 0 then
    Next:=RunTestorIdle;
end if;
State:=Next; end process;
```

See IEEE-1149 (1990), or the Intel 486DX reference, for a discussion of all of these states.

One may use a number of boundary scan paths, if desired.

The IEEE-1149 standard (1990) document provides a sample layout for a boundary cell, but this design, with two D flip-flops and two T flip-flops is not a mandatory part of the standard. There is one cell for each pin.

The instruction format is not fixed by the standard. The Motorola 68040 uses three bits, while the Intel 80486 uses four. There are three mandatory instructions, and a number of optional instructions. The 68040 supports the three mandatory instructions, EXTEST, BYPASS, and SAMPLE/PRELOAD, and additionally, BYPASS2 and EXTESTZ. The 80486 supports the mandatory codes and RUNBIST and IDCODE. EXTEST is used to test the traces external to the component. It drives the chips pins with the values in the boundary scan registers, and captures the values of the component outputs in the cells. BYPASS is used to bypass the individual component in the daisy-chain, bypassing its test logic. SAMPLE/PRELOAD can be used to sample the pin levels when the TAP controller is in the CaptureDR state. In the UpdateDR state it preloads data to the pins to be used in driving them during the subsequent EXTEST instruction. RUNBIST will run the built-in test function of the chip. For the 486, the controller must be in the RunTest/Idle state for the entire BIST, 1.2 million clock cycles. IDCODE returns a 32-bit ID code identifying the manufacturer (12 bits), the part number (15 bits), and the version number (4 bits); bit zero is fixed at one for the 80486. EXTESTZ disables the output-only pins, and BYPASS2 is an alternate bypass mode without clocking constraints.

See the IEEE-1149 (1990) standard, and the articles by Jarwala (1991) and Maunder and Tulloss (1992) for more details. The updated standard P1149.2 Dervisoglu (1992) is not finalized, but is upward-compatible.

INTERFACING TO OTHER LANGUAGES: AN EXAMPLE

There is no standard at present for interfacing VHDL to other languages. VHDL-92 defines the 'FOREIGN attribute (see Chapter 10), but this feature is implementation dependent. Therefore, in discussing this topic it is necessary to consider a particular implementation. Here, we discuss the Styx interface to the C language as implemented by Vantage. Use of this interface would allow access to all of the file handling and system interface capabilities of C. For example, the use of interprocess communications facilities such as UNIX 4.3BSD's sockets makes it possible to make a VHDL simulation part of a concurrent simulation of a network or other system. Vantage's VHDL compiler generates C code that executes the actual simulation, so the linkage to C is quite natural.

Vantage's STYX Package

Vantage provides a package named STYX that permits interfacing C code with a VHDL simulation. As the Vantage compiler produces C code to perform the VHDL simulation, an interface to C routines is rather natural. A header file, styx.h, is provided to include in any user C files. The user must provide a package declaration in VHDL for the C routines. If the user requires initialization then there should be a use clause for the package `External_Model_Package` in the library system, and this statement in the package:

```
attribute ExternalModel of
  packagename: package is STYX_MODEL;
```

Then the C routine `styxCreate` will be called. The first call in `styxCreate` must be of `STYX_INIT()`.

Finally, the C code must be compiled using the special *styxcompile* command, in which the package name will be specified. No support is currently provided for resolution functions. There are limitations on the permissible run-time library routines that may be called; various math functions (such as log()), string processing (such as strlen()), file handling (such as fscanf() and fopen()), and memory handling (such as malloc() and free()) are allowed. Various data types are available, including signal handles required to read or assign to signals. Due to implementation limitations, this attribute specification should be placed in the package declaration. Users can register their functions to be called upon events on specified signals, and at the end of the simulation, the beginning of the simulation, and at the end of every simulation cycle at the point at which the advance to the next event time is to occur. (At this point, users can schedule transactions if desired.) Processes may be created dynamically, and signals and signal drivers local to the current architecture may be created during initialization. Various routines exist for obtaining information, such as the values of generics, signals, or the 'EVENT attribute of a signal, and transmitting information, such as exporting symbol names. The time of the next event, the value of NOW, and various attributes may be read. A number of utilities for manipulating values of type TIME are provided. This is the initial release, and it is likely that more capability will be added to later versions.

REFERENCES

Berman, V., "VHDL is Coming of Age," *Design Automation*, pp. 42-58, January, 1992.

Berman, V., and Ussery, C., "A Proposed Back Annotation File Format for VHDL," *VIUF Spring 1992 Conference*, Scottsdale, AZ, May 3-6, 1992, pp. 141-149.

Borill, P. B., "The bus-driving problem," *IEEE Spectrum,* p. 37, July 1989.

Clark, T. R., "Fitting Programmable Logic," *IEEE Spectrum*, pp. 36-37, March 1992.

Cleaver, C., and Derr, M., "Design Automation through Synthesis of VHDL," *Design Automation*, pp. 20-24, April, 1991.

Coehlo, D., *VHDL Handbook* (N. Y.: Kluwer, 1988).

Corman, T., "Fanout Dependent Delay Modeling in VHDL," *1990 VHDL Fall User's Group Meeting*, Claremont Resort, Oakland, CA, Oct. 14-17, 1990, Tutorial Sessions.

Dervisoglu, B., "IEEE P1149.2 Decscription and Status Report," *IEEE Design and Test of Computers*, Spet. 1992, pp. 79-82.

Deutsch, A., et al., "High-speed signal propagation on lossy transmission lines," *IBM J. Res. Development*, **34**, pp. 601-609, 1990.

Electronic Industries Association, EDIF Steering Committee, *Introduction to EDIF*, EIA/EDIF-1, EDIF Monograph Series, Vol. I, Sept. 1988.

Electronic Industries Association, *Using EDIF 2 0 0 For Schematic Transfer*, EDIF/AG-1, July 1989.

Electronic Industries Association, *EIA Commercial Component VHDL Model Specification*, EIA-567, Rev. B, Advance Copy, 1992.

Egan, B. T., "ASIC designers turn to VHDL tools despite obstacles," *Computer Design*, pp. 55-64, Feb. 1992.

Gilman, A. S., Wilmot, A. R., "Introduction to WAVES," *1990 VHDL Fall User's Group Meeting*, Claremont Resort, Oakland, CA, Oct. 14-17, 1990, Tutorial Sessions.

Hailey, S., "Digital Logic's Analog Side: When digital is really analog," *Computer Design*, July 1991, pp. 74-75.

IEEE Standard Test Access Port and Boundary-Scan Architecture, IEEE-Std-1149.1990, Approved August 17, 1990.

Intel 486DX Microprocessor Data Book, June 1991.

Jarwala, N., "Boundary Scan Promises Test Alternatives," *Design Automation*, pp. 26-30, April 1991.

Maunder, C. M., and Tulloss, R. E., "Testability on TAP", *IEEE Spectrum*, Feb. 1992, pp. 34-37.

Rissman, P. "What users need to know to be productive with VHDL tools," *Computer Design*, pp. 58-64, Feb. 1992.

Rubin, S. M., *Computer Aids for VLSI Design* (Reading, MA: Addison-Wesley Publishing, 1987).

Ryan, R. "X-State Handling in VHDL," *Design Automation*, pp. 32-35, May 1991.

Turner, S., "Back Annotation for VHDL Structural Models," *1990 VHDL Fall User's Group Meeting*, Claremont Resort, Oakland, CA, Oct. 14-17, 1990, Tutorial Sessions.

United Technical Publications, Inc., *Modern Guide to Digital Logic* (Blue Ridge Summit, PA: Tab Books, 1976).

Chapter 15

Microprocessors

PURPOSE

Table 15.1 shows the transistor count of recently developed microprocessors (Comerford, 1992 and other sources). While many of the transistors are devoted to caches, the table illustrates the increasing complexity of processors. Computational aids to their design are a necessity. VHDL can play a useful role in this process. Chapter 12 discussed the design of the 80386, with reference to a number of bugs that were encountered. Simulation will become increasingly important in getting chips rapidly to market with the minimum of bugs.

This chapter will discuss VHDL code for a few useful components of microprocessor systems, and give general guidance on performing useful simulations. A prototype of a test-bench simulation of a MIL-STD-1750A microprocessor in an embedded system will illustrate the typical processing of interrupts and generation of test statistics. Typical instruction mixes will be discussed. See the article by Kumar and Petrasko (1990) for a tutorial on top-down design of a chip using VHDL.

Table 15.1 Microprocessor complexity	
Microprocessor	Transistor Count (millions)
80386 (Intel)	0.275
80486 (Intel)	1.2
i860 (Intel)	1.0
i860XP (Intel)	2.5
P5 (Intel)	3.0
68040 (Motorola)	1.2
88110 (Motorola)	1.3
Alpha (DEC)	1.68

For an interesting look at the current state of formal verification of VHDL descriptions (for architectures rather than bus protocols), see the paper by Borrione et al. (1992). For the use of VHDL for fault diagnosis, see Pitchumani et al. (1992).

CLOCKS

Consider first the simple task of generating a single-phase clock signal. This presumably should not be a resolved signal, because if we have more than one source for a clock, there can be serious problems. Our clock will look something like this:

```
constant Period: TIME := 20 ns;
constant Duty_Cycle: REAL:= .6;
constant On: TIME:= Period * Duty_Cycle;
constant Off: TIME:= Period - On;
signal Clock: BIT:=' 0' ;
process
begin
Clock <= ' 1' , ' 0' after On ;
wait for Period;
end process;
```

The process will suspend for the Period, and then resume to produce the period of the clock. This is one of many possible designs for such a clock. The signal Clock is initialized to ' 0' so that there will be an event at time 0 ns.

Multiphase clocks are still to be found, but are much less popular. For example, the Intel CPU family up through the 80386 uses an 82284 clock generator to provide a double-frequency clock, that is, an 80386 clocked at a nominal 25 MHz had a crystal with a frequency of 50 MHz supplying clock pulses through the 82284 at the rate of one every 20 ns as the signal CLK. Through two active-low signal lines, S0bar and S1bar, the 80386 fed back to the 82284 information as to the nature of the current bus cycle, for example, memory read or write, I/O read or write, and interrupt acknowledge. This then controls how the 82284 generates the PCLK signal, which is initially at half the frequency of CLK. This complex system has been abandoned with the i486, which uses a single clock signal at the processor frequency, that is, at 50 MHz for a 50 MHz CPU. A crude model for something like the behavior of the 82284 might be implemented in the following way:

```
constant Period: TIME  := 20 ns;
constant Duty_Cycle: REAL:= .5;
constant PhaseLag: TIME  := 5 ns;
constant On: TIME:= Period * Duty_Cycle;
constant Off: TIME:= Period - On;
signal Clk : BIT:=' 0' ;
signal PClk, S0bar, S1bar: BIT:=' 1' ;
process
variable Pcontrol: BIT:=0;
begin
Clk <= ' 1' , ' 0' after On,
    ' 1' after Period , ' 0' after Period +On   ;
-- force PClk High whenever either S0bar or
S1bar active low. -- Strictly speaking,
only if low for last TWO CLK cycles. Pcon-
trol := (S1bar=' 0' and S1bar' STABLE (2* Pe-
```

```
riod )) or      (S2bar=' 0' and S2bar' STABLE
(2* Period ));
-- when S1bar, S2bar both high, PClk oscil-
lates
if Pcontrol = 0 then
   PClk <= ' 0' , ' 1' after Period;
else
   PClk <= ' 1' ; end if;
wait for 2 * Period;
end process;
```

A multiphase clock, such as is used on older Z80 processors with multiple clock signal lines, would resemble the preceding design, but with assignments to different signals:

```
constant Period: TIME  := 20 ns;
constant Duty_Cycle: REAL:= .6;
constant PhaseLag: TIME  := 5 ns;
constant On: TIME:= Period * Duty_Cycle;
constant Off: TIME:= Period - On;
signal Clock1,  Clock2: BIT:=' 0' ;
process
begin
Clock1 <= ' 1' , ' 0' after On ;
Clock2 <= ' 1' after PhaseLag , ' 0' after On
;
wait for Period;
end process;
```

The MIPS R4000 uses a two-phase clock (see Mirapuri et al., in Chapter 13 References). An oscillator produces four times the master clock frequency, which is divided by a number of modules within the chip. The pipeline and most of the logic cycle at twice the master clock frequency, the integer and floating-point multipliers at four times the master. The use of a two-phase clock permits critical races (see the section immediately following) to be avoided with level-controlled logic, without resorting to more expensive edge-triggered circuits.

PRACTICAL CONSIDERATIONS

Hazards and Races

A *race* is defined as a situation in which two or more variables or signals change during a transition (see Friedman and Menon and also Comer, all referenced in Chapter 13). If the final state may depend on the order of the changes, the race is a *critical race*. *Hazards* are situations in which "glitches" or spurious pulses may result from variations in delays. *Static hazards* are situations in which the pulses occur when the output should be constant, while *dynamic hazards* produce a sequence of pulses. Generally, if static hazards are prevented, dynamic hazards will be taken care of (Comer, referenced in Chapter 13). It may be desirable in some circumstances to use additional logic gates to eliminate hazards. Races are of concern primarily for asynchronous sequential circuits, hazards for combinatorial circuits as well. Races and hazards can be due to timing differences between different portions of a logic circuit, due to variations in gate delays, or clock "slews" or variations in timings due to path differences. Synchronous (clocked) circuits are generally used to avoid race and hazard problems. Two-phase clocks are useful in preventing hazards and races in some situations. A master-slave flip-flop is an illustration of this, where the delay between triggering of the master and slave, typically a single gate delay due to the additional inverter in the clock signal path delivered to the slave, enables the slave to be isolated from transients in the behavior of the master, preventing oscillation problems (see Comer for a more complete discussion). Choi and Chung (1992) discuss the use of VHDL simulations to detect races and critical races in asynchronous circuits, and hazards in sequential ones, using multi-valued logic, using a method developed by Eichelberger (1965). They discuss using delta delay models (signals assigned "immediately"), testing for hazards by checking for undefined or $'U'$ states and testing for critical races by comparing expected output with actual output via **assert** statements. Eichelberger's method of hazard detection consists of defining ternary output functions (′ 0′ ,′ 1′ ,′ U′) to gates. A combinatorial (combinational in his 1965 terminology) gate is analyzed for hazards by assigning ′ U′ values to *p* of the inputs and examining the corresponding 2^p out-

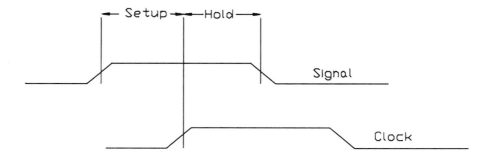

Figure 15.1 Definitions of setup and hold times

puts. If some of the entries are ′ 1′ and some are ′ 0′ , then the corresponding output value is assigned to ′ U′ . For 2-input OR gates, for example, the output is ′ U′ if either of the inputs is ′ U′ and the other is either ′ U′ or ′ 0′ . There is a hazard if and only if the output function f for a transition of input state *A* to input state *B* is ′ U′ and if *f(A)=f(B)* /= ′ U′ . Eichelberger gives an algorithm for critical race detection. The ′ U′ signals are propagated through from the inputs. Eichelberger's method may not terminate (signals may oscillate), and is obviously subject to an exponential complexity explosion, so it will not be practical for large circuits. His paper also discusses methods for eliminating hazards. Due to the computational complexity, synchronous circuits should be used where possible to avoid critical race problems wherever possible.

Edge and Level Triggering

A level-sensitive device can be converted to edge triggering by inserting into its triggering or active control line a combinatorial circuit that would normally never activate the device, but that has had an intentional hazard built in to produce an activating glitch on appropriate input transitions. The duration of the time during which the circuit will then sample its inputs will be the difference in gate delays that determines the hazard duration. Such pulse-narrowing circuits can be found in Comer (reference in Chapter 13), for example, a simple AND gate with an inverter between the signal and one input, with a straight-through path of the signal to the other. The result of this simple circuit is a pulse whose duration is approximately the inverter gate delay.

Edge-sensitive circuits can be modeled by using the 'EVENT attribute on the clock or other appropriate signal.

Setup and Hold Constraints

The two basic timing constraints are minimum setup and hold times. Figure 15.1 illustrates the definition of these two times. Timing constraints are checked by **assert** statements using the appropriate attributes, particularly 'STABLE (see Chapter 6). Chapter 5 has discussed the determination of slack in timing constraints, which would determine the potential increase in clock rate and be more useful than simple go/no-go information. See Lipsett et al. (1989) for a discussion on checking such constraints.

Critical Path Analysis

The critical path is the longest (maximum delay) path a signal can take between specified points. The critical path will determine the maximum permissible clock speed. Critical path timing information may be obtained as follows.

Suppose the critical delay between points A and B is desired. It suffices to send the time of initiation of the event at A through signal propagation paths to B. The resolution function should select the earliest time-stamp of those presented. That time-stamp uniquely identifies the initiating event. At B, it suffices to keep track of the pairs of (time initiated, time arrived), for different values of time initiated, with only the latest arrival time saved for critical path determination. This may be saved to a file and postprocessed. The largest difference gives the longest delay. It will be necessary to have nodes append information to the signal as it passes, if the critical path needs to be determined. As signals must be used in VHDL-87, dynamic structures such as linked lists may not be used, so an array of sufficient size can be passed with each node identifying itself in sequence in that array.

Of course, the usual shortest-path algorithms, such as Dijkstra's (see, e. g., Baase, referenced in Chapter 11), can be modified to produce critical paths, and synthesis tools often provide such information. Such critical paths are more rigorous than simulation results, but can also be overly pessimistic, as they may give a longest path that would not actually occur in practice.

CONTROL UNITS

The control unit typically includes one or more FSMs, generally loosely coupled, with an instruction decoder that can be a simple combinatorial logic system in the case of RISC microprocessors or a complex microcode decoder. For example, the documentation for the PACE1750A microprocessor discusses the use of two *nearly independent* linked FSMs (see Chapter 13 for a discussion of linked FSMs), an execution unit and an external bus unit. If the bus is not used, a typical cycle is three clock periods, while it is four if a bus access is required.

Microprogramming

There are many variations in microprogramming strategies, from RISC chips that employ none to complex hybrid chips that attempt "single clock" operation of simple instructions but provide microcoded interpretation of complex ones. Generally, microprogrammed instructions execute programs in a ROM. The complexity of these implementations varies greatly. Microprogrammed instructions are often classified as "horizontal" (long formats, little encoding, high parallelism possible) versus "vertical" (short, considerable encoding). Typically, horizontal encoding involves one bit per control line, but these definitions are not precise. Often, the (vertical) microcoded instructions are further interpreted, in terms of "nanoinstructions." The 8088, for example (see Tanenbaum, 1990), uses microinstructions 21 bits, storing 504 of them. Of the 21 bits, the leftmost pair of 5 bit fields are used to specify possible register-to-register moves for any instruction. The 11-bit field is vertically-encoded, specifying type of instruction (3 bits), ALU operation type (4 bits), register (3 bits), and a condition code field (1 bit). The microinstructions included two kinds of jumps as well as procedure calls (which are not nested, however). The 68000, by contrast, uses nanoinstructions with 544 17-bit microinstructions and 336 68-bit nanoinstructions.

How best to simulate this? If synthesis is the ultimate goal, obviously, the structure of the VHDL code should reflect the ultimate structure of the microprocessor. However, if this is not the ultimate intent, or if the project is in the early stages of a top-down, functional simulation, there may be better approaches. For example, Marino (1986) gives a (large) state-machine description of the 6800 controller. This may be the best way to model the device, without attempting to model the microinstruction implementation actually used.

Assume the opcode is an integer. If necessary, the opcode may be extracted using the shifts in VHDL-92 and logical operations with masks. Consider first decoding for a microprogrammed CISC processor. The simplest decoding method is to use a jump table, i. e., to use the opcode as the index of an array that specifies the address of the start of the microprogram. Consider, for example, the 1750A processor, which has a byte-sized opcode for 197 different instructions. The jump table would have to contain 256 entries for all possible opcode values (0 to 255), giving an efficiency of 77%.

Coelho (1989) recommends a loop comparing the opcode value to possible values. This has advantages when the opcodes are irregular. He uses a representation of opcodes as bit arrays. This enables the use of bit-by-bit comparisons, which in turn permits comparisons involving "don't care" patterns in the comparisons.

Decoding of RISC instructions is similar to the decoding of horizontal microinstructions. Here, a bit array representation is desirable, as each bit or set of bits correspond to actions.

Conversion between bit arrays and integers is relatively simple, assuming only unsigned integers are of concern and that the default integer size is sufficient:

```
function Int_Bit(BitArray: BIT_VECTOR )
   return INTEGER is
variable Sum : Integer:=0, Index; begin for
Index in BitArray'Length downto 1 loop
   Sum:= Sum+ BitArray(Index);
   Value:=Value*2;
return Value;
end loop;
end Int_Bit;


function Bit_Int(Int, Length: Integer )
   return BitArray is
variable Sum : BIT_VECTOR;
variable Bit: BOOLEAN;
begin for Index in 1 to Length loop
   Bit(Index) = Int and 1; Int:=Int/2;-- or
Int SRA 1 in VHDL-92, or shift up '1'
   if Int = 0 then exit;
end loop;
return Value;
end Bit_Int;
```

CACHES

As mentioned at the start of this chapter, caches have become increasingly prominent in microprocessors. Caches are fast memory that store contiguous pieces of memory, called *lines*, in fast memory. In the fully associative cache, associated with each line is a data field, the *tag*, which corresponds to the high-order portion of the data's memory address; the remainder of the address is determined by the location in the line. To locate data in such a cache, a comparison must be made with each tag. Thus, the overhead of such a cache is high, as a tag must be stored for each line, and circuitry for the simultaneous comparison with each tag and the memory address must be provided. The fully associative cache is also the cache with the highest typical hit rate. At the other extreme is the direct-mapped cache, in which a portion of the address field is used as the line number. The tag for each line is thus reduced in size by the number of bits corresponding to the number of lines. This reduces the area required for the same amount of data stored in the cache, but it means that a memory location can only be stored in one line; if that line is used by another location, one of the datum's will not be cached. The middle ground is a set-associative cache, in which any location can be cached in a small number of lines (typically 2 or 4). Such a cache is usually implemented as a set of direct-mapped caches; if one of the allowed locations for the data is occupied, the others are checked to see if the datum may be cached in them. Caches must also maintain information such as a *dirty bit* for each line. The dirty bit specifies if the cache data has been modified, and needs to be written to memory. Caches may be write-through, in which writes to cached data cause a write to memory, or write-back, in which case the data write to memory is queued for later execution. Most now sport two- or four-way set-associative caches, often separate caches for data and instructions. Choice of cache design depends on application, as the trade-offs for given chip area are not simple. Intel chose a four-way integrated cache for the 486, arguing the four-way had only a 10% lower miss rate for typical applications (see Crawford et al., referenced in Chapter 12); the Intel design group i860 group (Perry et al., referenced in Chapter 12) chose a simpler two-way, split cache, arguing a 5% difference between two- and four-way caches for typical applications for that processor's data cache. The DEC Alpha has 8Kbyte instruction and data caches. For the i860, the data cache (8Kbytes) was twice as large as the instruction cache, whereas for the i860XP, both caches are equally 16Kbytes. Obviously, cache optimization requires extensive trace-driven simulations. The R4000 uses 8Kbyte direct-mapped data and instruction caches on chip, called primary caches, with provision for primary caches up to 32Kbytes, and secondary caches up to 4Mbytes.

RISC processors rely on a cache to make the execution of many simple RISC instructions efficient. CISC processors in effect use a ROM containing microcode for a similar purpose, reducing the necessary access to memory to achieve a given amount of computation.

MEMORY MANAGEMENT

Memory management units have tended to migrate onto the CPU itself, permitting more efficient interaction with the cache. The increasing address space of processors results in the need for hardware support for virtual addressing, which would be prohibitively slow if done in software. The Intel 80x86 family of microprocessors adds further complication to memory management by segmenting memory, which provides sophisticated protection but also caused both programmers and hardware designers grief. On the 80386 and its successors, segments can be up to four gigabytes, making segmentation unnecessary in practice, but it can be used for security purposes in a multitasking environment. The segment selector register contains the address of the global descriptor table (GDT), which contains the offset required to generate the virtual address. To avoid the need for a memory access to the GDT, the associated offset is effectively cached along with the selector.

Virtual memory systems generally divide memory into *pages*, often separately assigned to instructions or to data. The logical address space may represent gigabytes, only a portion of which is in the physical memory at any time. A page table resides in memory and specifies which pages are in physical memory and how they map to the logical address space. The physical address of the needed item is determined by combining in some fashion the address specified in the instruction as well as information in the page table. To keep speed penalties for virtual memory minimal, page table information is also contained in a special cache, usually called the *translation lookaside buffer*. This cache is fully associative on the MIPS R3000 and the Motorola 68040, indicating its importance. If the required page is not in physical memory, an interrupt ("trap" is Motorola terminology for such processor-generated interrupts), called a *page fault*, is generated. This will cause the operating system to do what is necessary. This typically involves purging a page of data currently in memory, reading from mass storage the required data, updating page tables, and so forth, and resuming execution. Cached pages will have a *dirty bit*, which is set when associated data in the cache has been changed and must be written back to the physical location. *Thrashing* occurs when an unfortunate positioning of data or instructions causes frequent page faulting.

Virtual address translation is a multistep process, with the possibility for exceptions at any point. On the Intel 80x86 and 860 architectures (which feature identical memory management), a two-level scheme is used. The CR3 register contains ten bits which point to a page directory table. This selects a page table address using another 10 bits from the virtual address. The remaining 12 bits of the 32-bit virtual address select the physical address within the frame. Thus, two levels of tables are used. In the Motorola 68040, a tree structure with up to five levels (0 to 4 page tables) may be implemented. The 32-bit virtual address may be split into up to five pieces of different sizes, under the control of the translation control (TC) register. A good deal of error checking occurs, even on RISC chips such as the MIPS R4000.

Because of the great variation in architectures, it is difficult to prescribe general methods for modeling memory management. The hardware bugs in the 80386 family mentioned in Chapter 12 often involved situations with simultaneous exceptions (such as the general protection fault or segmentation violation when an operand crossed a 64K boundary) and an interrupt from hardware such as the coprocessor. Obviously, great care needs to be taken to consider all such "unlikely" coincidences. It is likely that a considerable fraction of the total effort will have to be budgeted to modeling the MMU and cache, to insure proper handling of such cases.

PIPELINES AND SUPERSCALAR ARCHITECTURES

Modern processes are capable of concurrently performing a number of operations. Pipelining and superscalar architectures are two approaches that are often combined to achieve high performance through concurrency. In a *pipeline*, different stages of an instruction (such as decoding, operand address calculation, fetching and storing values, and calculation) are organized so that while one instruction is, say, being decoded, other instructions are having their operands fetched, and so forth. Superpipelining refers to long pipelines (many stages) in order to achieve high clock rates and high concurrency with very simple actions performed at each state. *Superscalar* refers to independent units that can perform similar operations concurrently. For example, it may be possible to use the adder and multiply units of an ALU concurrently, or to do floating-point and fixed-point arithmetic simultaneously. The i860 has special instructions to schedule simultaneous operations. Dewar and Smosna (1990) discuss some of the dual operations, combining floating-point adds and multiplies, calling them "extravagantly complex." These instructions have a field to specify sixteen different possible data flow relations. Other RISC machines automatically attempt to queue operations to keep the units busy. Unlike pipelining, for which each instruction in the pipeline is at a different phase of its execution, the actual execution phase of different instructions is occurring simultaneously with superscalar architectures. Vector processors correspond to pipelined machines with instructions to loop within the pipeline, exploiting regularity in the storage of the data. Table 15.2 lists the number of stages in the pipelines of common microprocessors. The trend toward increasingly large numbers of stages is evident. Dewar and Smosna (1990) also note the similarity between superscalar and very-long instruction word (VLIW) machines, that also have instructions that code for multiple simultaneous operations.

Table 15.2 Pipelines	
Microprocessor	Number of Stages
80386	3
68030	3
Sparc	4
88110	4
MIPS R3000	5
80486	5
68040	6
MIPS R4000	8

The 68040, discussed briefly in Chapter 13, has a six-stage pipeline. Note that while it might seem natural to model the pipeline as six processes, one for each stage, the interdependency of these processes is sufficient that the use of three controllers is a better (hardware) implementation. The six stages are: instruction prefetch, program counter calculation and decode, effective-address calculation, operand fetch, execution, and write-back (see Edenfield et al., in Chapter 13 References). One controller, the PC controller, is a finite state machine (FSM) that handles the first two stages. The generality of a FSM to control fetch is required because of the many instruction lengths. The effects of program flow (conditional and unconditional branches and subroutine calls) is accounted for. The other two controllers are microcoded. They operate relatively independently, with one controlling the execution stage and the other the other stages. The MIPS R4000 pipeline will attempt to avoid complete stalls by slipping, that is, only partially stalling. Tanenbaum (1990) considers the 8088 pipelined, having four units for execution, address calculation, decoding instructions, executing instructions, and prefetching. The prefetcher operates completely independently of the rest of the processor. For a pipeline with slippage, multiple, linked FSMs are desirable, with one FSM for each pipeline segment that may slip relative to the others.

If synthesis is the ultimate goal, it will be necessary to have the simulation model reflect the hardware design. It may be desirable, however, to ignore the hardware implementation details in a functional simulation. The pipeline can then be modeled as a simple queue, with instructions flowing from one stage to another in normal operation.

BUS INTERFACE UNITS

Busses can be synchronous or asynchronous. The former permit more throughput, permitting burst mode transfers, while the latter are more flexible. For example, the Intel 80960 has the CA version with a synchronous bus, while the KA and other versions support an asynchronous bus. Arbitration on busses with multiple masters is discussed in this chapter.

Burst Mode Transfers

Some processors, such as the Intel 80960CA and i486, support data transfers in which a number of data units are transferred from contiguous locations. As the bus is not released between each unit, the time spent in arbitrating for the bus is saved. The bus interface unit must have an FSM sufficient to remember the state of the transfer, limiting the size of bursts. The i486, for example, can burst a total of 32 bits on a write, that is, send four bytes of a 32-bit word. The 80960CA allows a maximum of four consecutive data cycles following a single address cycle. The downside of such transfers is that the bus is locked for a longer period, which might delay critical interrupts.

Cache Coherence

Cache coherence refers to the problem of insuring that data in the cache is consistent with data in actual memory. Other microprocessors, or DMA chips, can modify the data in memory, and require any updated values. *Bus snooping*, which is monitoring the address bus for cached values, is typically done with values updated as necessary. Both the MIPS R4000 and Motorola 88110 use variations on the *MESI* (Modified, Exclusive, Shared, Invalid) state-machine system to maintain cache coherence. Exclusive data is data which is not stored in the cache of any other processor. An FSM for the MESI protocol is given in Diefendorff et al., in Chapter 13 References. Data read into a microprocessor which is tagged as exclusive if the other processors, which are engaged in bus-snooping and therefore know if the address is in their cache, do not interfere by reporting this fact. A microprocessor may modify an exclusive data item by writing to it at any time. Write-back caches wait until they must write such data, such as when the cache is flushed due to a context switch. (Write-through caches will write out such items as they are modified, i. e., a write to memory is done whenever the cached value is changed. They greatly simplify the problem of maintaining coherency at the cost of higher required bus bandwidth due to the increased number of writes.) When a line of cache data is written to, it is marked as modified. If the cache that "owns" a line of data notices by snooping that another processor wished to read that data, it intercepts the requited, posts the modified value on the bus from its cache, and marks the memory line as shared in its own cache, as the recipient of the data does as well. To write to a shared line, a processor must broadcast the address to all processors. These will mark their cached value of that data as invalid, if they contain that line. The writing processor will then mark its cached line of data as exclusive, and write the data to the shared memory when appropriate, such as when it flushes its own cache.

If the bus snooper detects that a value that has been Modified is to be read, it copies the modified value's line from the cache to memory, transitions to the Shared state for that line, and then permits the original read transaction to occur. Transitions to Invalid will occur, for example, if a write is detected by the bus snooper. State transitions can result in the need for a cache line file (read) or the copying back to memory of a *dirty* line of data (cache line containing altered data, as indicated by the dirty bit being set). The MIPS R4000 uses a modified MESI protocol with an additional fifth state, the Modified (and, implicitly, exclusive) renamed Dirty exclusive, the Exclusive becoming clean exclusive, and Shared being split into Dirty shared and Shared. This was intended to permit implementing shared data such as semaphores more efficiently (Mi-rapuri et al., in Chapter 13 References).

BEHAVIORAL SIMULATIONS

Trace-Driven Simulations

Trace-driven simulations were discussed in Chapter 12; see also Holliday et al., 1992. Such simulations will rely heavily on the TEXTIO package for data input. Data can be read in as the simula-tion progresses, rather than all at once, thereby economizing on storage. Such a process could become complicated as pipelines pre-fetch data.

Statistical Mix Simulations

Often, only the general statistics of typical code are available. This is less acceptable for machines with caches and pipelines, for exam-ple, for which the precise sequence of instructions matters. Mixes also vary significantly depending on types of application code.

One sample mix is the DAIS (Digital Avionics Instrumentation Specification) mix, used for real-time, embedded MIL-STD-1750A code. This is given in Table 15.3, categorized by general instruction type and memory access type.

Table 15.3 DAIS MIX		
By Memory Access Type	Register	18.5%
	Immediate	11%
	Memory Direct	29%
	Indirect	3.5%
	Relative	38%
By Instruction Type	Load/Store	47%
	Branch	18%
	Arithmetic	25%
	Compare	7%

Other mixes can be found in Stone (1980), and by Ferrari (1982). Typically, load and store operations range from 30 to 42% of the operations, with conditional branches, calls, and jumps comprising 20 to 30% of the instructions. Fixed point adds and subtracts greatly predominate over multiplies, except in some scientific work (due to multidimensional subscript computation). Floating-point operations typically take 10 to 20% of the instructions, with about half as many multiplies as adds/subtracts, and perhaps one-half to one-third as many divides as multiplies.

Example: Prototype Simulation

A sample test-bench prototype architecture is included. This was developed for a project in which the behavior of a complex avionics system is to be simulated (Baker and Turfler, 1991). By using VHDL, a number of advantages could be gained. Different microprocessors in different configurations could be simulated.

The code is a proof-of-principle demonstrator. It runs a simulated system involving a generic MIL-STD-1750A microprocessor in a real-time embedded system, responding to interrupts. The test-bench runs the system for a specified time, then commands the dump of the accumulated statistics. Interrupt handlers are modeled as having a specified mean and average variance of executed instructions, which are selected randomly according to the DAIS mix discussed above. The input data deck, which specifies the timing and type of interrupts, is chosen so that the interrupt handler itself is interrupted once, to test that the stack of interrupted processes is properly handled, and the latency for the interrupted interrupt handler is properly calculated. Because this is a proof-of-principle demo, there are some "hooks" for later features that are not implemented at present.

One virtue of VHDL for such a simulation endeavor is that the use of 1750A processors from different manufacturers can easily be accommodated by changing the architecture selected. For example, the standard specifies a required instruction set, which manufacturers augment with built-in functions. These will have different associated instruction mixes. A hierarchy of models could be developed, for different forms of 1750A processors, for alternative processors such as the R4000 or 80960. Similarly, trace-driven simulations could easily be substituted for the statistical mix by replacing the statistical selection of the next instruction with selection from data read in during the simulation.

There are six file packages. These are reformatted for publication here but are otherwise unaltered from when they were used as part of a demonstration. As a result, some real-world deviations from an ideal package remain. For example, a workaround of a bug present in the compiler at that time (the compiler could not handle more than one access type per package) resulted in a restructuring of the simulation that was not ideal from the structured programming point of view.

SIMULAT.VHD contains the test-bench, entity SIMULATION (lines 6 to 8), its associated architecture SUPERVISE (lines 10 to 106), and the associated configuration SUPERVISE_CON (lines 108 to 125). Process Statistics waits until the end of the scheduled simulation time, then commands the microprocessors (in this case, only one) in the simulation to dump their acquired statistics. An artificial signal, TABULATE (Fini in process Statistics), is used to do this. Each microprocessor has a unique ID number, and when Fini in process Statistics is set to this number on the line connected to them, will terminate and output their individual results.

EVENTQ.VHD contains the package EVENTQ, which was originally intended to model the microprocessor stack, using code very similar to that given in Chapter 11 for such purposes. The code for popping and pushing was moved in-line into PROCESSN.VHD, and this code, which was originally in package USER, was moved into its own pack due to compiler limitations mentioned in comments in the code. The machine stack had to be within a different package. The EVENTQ represents the universe, and maintains a record of scheduled events. As discussed in Chapters 2, 11, and 12, VHDL signals cannot easily be used to record schedule future events. In a system of microprocessors, which may each make requests of others as well as be interrupted, it is necessary to maintain our own queue of events. As noted in the comments, a simple list is used here, as it is not expected that this list would become very long. A variety of packages could be developed, using heaps, sorted lists, and so forth, as desired, and changing algorithms could be as simple as instantiating different packages. Figure 15.2 sketches a

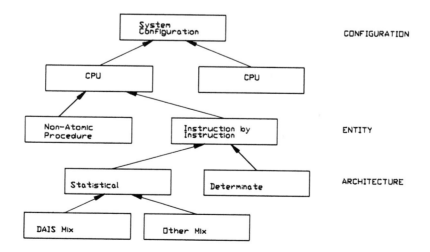

Figure 15.2 VHDL model hierarchy

possible hierarchy of modeling packages that could be mixed in a VHDL simulation of a multiprocessor system. In the example given in this book an instruction-by-instruction simulation is performed. A higher-level simulation, in which procedures are modeled, is labeled "nonatomic procedure" in this diagram.

INSTR.VHD contains a package with the basic routines for the simulation of the instruction sequence. This is a simplified version of the DAIS statistical mix. The random number generator is part of this package. A prototype MMU (memory management unit) is included for later elaboration.

USER.VHD contains various utility routines, including the machine stack and resolution functions.

A1750A.VHD contains the skeleton for the detailed modeling of a MIL-STD-1750A processor. This microprocessor standard mandates 196 different instruction operation codes for 97 instruction types. One has been renamed ABSX instead of ABS, which is a reserved word in VHDL. Data on instruction timings and individual idiosyncrasies of different versions from different manufacturers may be read in. Different functions in the package return a variety of information about the instruction, such as its size, bus participation in the instruction, and the number of clock counts.

File PROCESSN.VHD is the heart of the simulation given here. It records all the statistics and schedules all the events. It performs an instruction-by-instruction simulation of operation. Therefore, with sufficiently detailed data (i. e., a program listing, along with hardware data), it is capable of absolute fidelity. The CPU waits for any of three signals to activate it. TABULATE, asserted at the scheduled end of simulation time by the test bench of SIMULAT, caused the simulation to terminate, the statistics to be printed out, and the process to execute a **wait**; that will suspend the process forever and end the simulation. Local_Events include clock ticks and local events, such as interrupt requests, while Event_Signal includes the end of the executing instruction, interrupts and requests from the bus. Because atomic instructions cannot be interrupted, when an interrupt is sensed, a flag is set. Whenever an instruction terminates, this flag is checked before the next instruction is scheduled, and the interrupt handler is invoked if necessary. The handler pushes the state onto the machine stack and proceeds. When it terminates, the state is popped from the stack and resumed.

The entity definition (lines 8 to 72) defines the ports. These correspond closely to those of the Fairchild 9450/9451 1750A CPU, and would be used in a more detailed model of the CPU. Various signals are not used in this prototype simulation, such as those defining the privilege level and memory access key. The architecture BehaviorCPU is most of the rest of the file (lines 74 to 696), with the configuration (lines 698 to 702) at the very end. Procedure ENTEREVENT (lines 102 to 145) places a new event in the event queue at the head. Function OpIndex (lines 147 to 153) uses the 'POS attribute to find the position in the opcode list for the given instruction opcode. It would be used to determine the properties of the instruction, such as cycle count, by looking these up in arrays of that information. Function Operation (lines 161-175) is a skeletal function for determining the opcode of an instruction. RUNCPU is the key process. The initialization is handled between lines 302-419. This involves reading the statistics of the interrupt handler (average and variance of its instruction count). followed by the sequence of events to be simulated. (If you are interested in the mechanics of using TEXTIO then you should study this code.) These events are presumed to be given in time sequence in the data file, and are assigned to the LocalEvent signal, using transport delay. Rather than use ' TRANSACTION to convert transactions to events, a subsequent assignment of none was used to insure a change in signal value occurred. The last step is to begin the simulation by scheduling the end Instruct transaction on the EventSignal, indicating that the initialization BIST has finished, specified at the arbitrary 4 ns time. Line 421 is a **wait** statement defining the sensitivity of the process. The statistics dump is from lines 430 to 464. Upon sensing an interrupt (Local_Event or Clock_Tick) the PendingInt flag is set and the statistics updated. When an instruction ends, this results in EventSignal being equal to Instruct. If an interrupt is pending, the interrupt flag is cleared (line 517), the current status is pushed onto the stack via ENTEREVENT, and the statistics for the interrupt handler are computed (ToGo, the number of instructions this run through the handler should take). Otherwise (line 551), we check to see if we have hit the end of the handler (line 572). If so (lines 572 to 679), the statistics are updated and a diagnostic printout occurs. Otherwise, we drop through to the code (lines 682 to 692), which generates the next instruction. (This same code would generate the first instruction of the handler if an interrupt had been handled.)

REFERENCES

Baker, L., and Turfler, R. F., *Phase One Final Report: VHDL Simulation for Ada Systems*, Mission Research Corp. report MRC/ABQ-R-1409 to Naval Avionics Center, Code 643, Indianapolis, IN, March 1991.

Borrione, D. D., Pierre, L. V., and Salem, A. M., "Formal Verification of VHDL Descriptions in the Prevail Environment," *IEEE Design and Test of Computers*, June 1992, pp. 42-55.

Choi, S. H., and Chung, M. J., "Methodology of System Design using VHDL," *VIUF Spring 1992 Conference*, May 3-6, 1992, Scottsdale, AZ, pp. 17-18.

Coelho, D., *The VHDL Handbook* (Boston, MA: Kluwer Academic Publishers, 1989).

Comerford, R., "How DEC developed Alpha," *IEEE Spectrum*, **29**, pp. 26-31, July 1992.

Dewar, R., and Smosna, M., *Microprocessors*, (N. Y.: McGraw-Hill, 1990).

Eichelberger, E. B., "Hazard Detection in Combinational and Sequential Switching Circuits," *IBM J. Research & Development*, **6**, pp. 90-99, March 1965.

Ferrari, D., *Computer Systems Performance Evaluation* (Englewood Cliffs, N. J.: Prentice Hall, 1982).

Holliday, M. A., "Accuracy of Memory Reference Traces of Parallel Computations in Trace-Driven Simulations," *IEEE Trans. on Parallel Distributed Systems*, 3, pp. 97-109, Jan. 1992.

Kumar, K. A., and Petrasko, B., "Designing a Custom DSP Circuit Using VHDL," *IEEE MICRO*, pp. 46-53, October 1990.

Lipsett, R., Schaefer, C., and Ussery, C., *VHDL: Hardware Description and Design* (Boston, MA: Kluwer, 1989).

Marino, L. R., *Principles of Computer Design* (Rockville, MD: Computer Science Press, 1986).

Pitchumani, V., Mayor, P., and Radia, N., "A VHDL Fault Diagnosis Tool Using Functional Fault Models," *IEEE Design and Test of Computers*, June 1992, pp. 33-41.

Stone, H. S., *Introduction to Computer Architecture* (Chicago, Il: Science Research Associates, 1980).

Tanenbaum, A. S., *Structured Computer Organization,* 3rd. edition, (Englewood Cliffs, N. J.: Prentice Hall, 1990).

Sixteen-Bit Computer Instruction Set Architecture, MIL-STD-1750A, July 2, 1980. (Draft 1750B was completed 30 June 1989 and recommended on 4 April 1990, but was disapproved on cost-benefit grounds. It contained significant floating-point enhancements.)

```
1    use std.textio.all;
2    use work.A1750a.all;
3    use work.USER.all;
4    use work.EVENTQ.all;
5
6    entity SIMULATION is
7
8    end SIMULATION;
9
10   architecture SUPERVISE of SIMULATION
11   is
12
13   -- no signals or constants at present
14   component CPU
15      port
16         (
17   --       Addressbus: inout integerR;
18
19   --       Databus: inout integerR;
20   --       BUSY: inout IntegerR;
21   --       READWRITE: inout BITR;
22   --       Ack: inout BITR;
23   --       BUSIN: in  BIT;-- this and
24   --next signal part of daisy chain
25   --       BUSOUT: out BIT;
26   --       IACKin: in BIT;-- this and
27   --next signal part of daisy chain
28   --       IACKout: out BIT;
29   --       IRQ: inout integerR;
30          Tabulate: in integer -- signal
31   --to dump results
32          );
33   end component;
34
35   -- components for Arbitration, sensors
36   possible here
37
38   signal Ab, Db, INTR, BusBusy : integerR;
39
40   signal BusAck, BusRW: BITR;
```

```
41
42    signal BLink1,ALink1,ALink2: BIT;
43    signal LinkH: BIT:=' 1' ;
44    signal LinkL: BIT:=' 0' ;
45    signal Fini: integer;
46
47  begin
48
49  Statistics: process
50
51      constant STOPTIME: TIME:=100 us;
52
53      constant NodeCount: INTEGER:=1;
54      variable DELAY: TIME;
55      variable Id: INTEGER;
56      variable M: MESSAGEIO;
57      variable L: LINE;
58
59      begin
60      wait for STOPTIME;
61          DELAY:= 0 ns;
62          for Id in 1 to NodeCount   loop
63
64              M:="          SIMULATE ID = " ;
65    WRITE(L,M);
66              WRITE(L,ID); WRITELINE(OUTF,L);
67
68              Fini <= transport Id after DELAY;
69
70              DELAY := DELAY + 1 ps;
71              -- signal each node to do
72              -- statistics dump
73          end loop;
74      wait;
75  end process; -- Statistics;
76
77  Proc1: CPU
78                  port map
79          (
```

```
 80   --          Addressbus => Ab,
 81   --          Databus => Db,
 82   --          BUSY => BusBusy,
 83   --          READWRITE => BusRW,
 84   --          DATAVALID: out integerR;
 85   --          DATAREADY: in integerR;
 86   --          InstData: out integerR;-- is
 87   -- fetch instruction or data
 88   --          IntReq: in integerR;-- interrupt
 89   --includes pwr down, user, iol, ext
 90   --request,timer clk,reset
 91   --      Fault: in integerR;
 92   --        Error: out integerR;
 93         --DMA
 94   --        DMARequest: in integerR;
 95   --        DMAAck: out integerR;
 96   --        DMAEnable: out integerR;
 97   -- multiproc. interface of f9450
 98   --        BusReq: out integerR;
 99   --        BusLock: out integerR;
100   --        BusGrant: in integerR;
101
102           Tabulate => Fini -- signal to
103           --dump results
104           );
105
106   end SUPERVISE;
107
108   configuration SUPERVISE_con of SIMULATION
109   is
110
111     for SUPERVISE
112         for Proc1: CPU
113             use configuration work.Behavior_c
114   on
115         generic map (ID => 1 );
116         end for;
117
118     end for;
119
```

```
120    end SUPERVISE_con;
121
122
123    -- CPU SUBSTITUTED HERE FOR PROCESSNODE
124    BY BAKER 12/22/90
125    -- TO KEEP ALL NAMES UNIQUE.
```

```
1
2    use std.textio.all;
3    use work.A1750a.all;
4
5    package EVENTQ is
6
7
8    type Event is
9       (Clock_Tick, Local_Event, Bus_IntReq, Instruct,
10   Start_Handler, None);
11
12   type Request is
13      ( None, Bus_IntSend, Bus_Read, Bus_Write
14   );
15
16   type REGarray is array ( 1 to 8) of
17   integer;
18
19   type BusRequest is   ( Want, Take, Free
20   );
21
22
23   -- Event Queue:
24   -- manage  as a simple list for the
25   -- time being
26   -- not even sorted or stacked, just
27   -- a linear search
28   type EQueueEl;
29   type EQueuePtr is access EQueueEl;
30
31   type EQueueEl is record
32         Eventtype: Event;
33         -- CHANGED TO INTEGER FROM TIME
34   FOR INSTRUCTION PER INSTRUCTION SIM.
35         Resumed, Accumulated, Delay : INTEGER;
36
37         Initiated:TIME;
38         --Additional Delay initially 0,
39         --increases due to interrupt(ions)
40
41         Previous: EQueueptr;
```

```
42        end record;
43
44   end EVENTQ;
```

```
 1   -- INSTR
 2
 3   use std.textio.all;
 4   use work.USER.all;
 5   use work.EVENTQ.all;
 6
 7   package INSTR is
 8
 9   procedure RANDOM16(u: out REAL; S16,S26,S36:
10   inout INTEGER);
11
12   procedure INST_TIME(SoFar: Integer;
13     Handler: Event;
14     S16,S26,S36: inout INTEGER;
15     total: out time);
16
17   end INSTR;
18
19
20   package body INSTR is
21
22   procedure RANDOM16(u: out REAL; S16,S26,S36:
23   inout INTEGER) is
24
25   variable Z,K: INTEGER;
26   -- RECOMMENDED INIT: S16:=12,S26:=23
27   ,S36:=34;
28   begin
29   k:= S16/206;
30   S16:=157*(S16-K*206)-K*21;
31   if S16< 0 then S16:= S16+32263;
32   end if;
33   K:=S26/217;
34   S26:=146*(S26-K*217)-K*45;
35   if S26< 0 then S26:= S26+31727;
36   end if;
37   K:= S36/222;
38   S36:=142*(S36-K*222)-K*133;
39   if S36<0 then S36:=S36+31657;end if;
40
41   Z:=S16-S26;
```

```
42   if z>706 then Z:=Z-32362;end if;
43   Z:=Z+S36;
44   if z<1 then Z:=Z+32362;end if;
45
46   U:=real(Z) * 3.0899e-5;
47
48   end RANDOM16;
49
50   -- Local routines, hidden from direct
51   -- access:
52
53   function MMU( U: in real ) return TIME
54   is
55
56   constant PCHIT: real :=0.0;
57   -- CACHE HIT PROBABILITY=0 IF NO CACHE
58   begin-- U IS 0-1 URV
59   -- CACHE HIT (IF CACHE)
60   if U < PCHIT then
61      return   50 ns;-- never happens if
62   no cache to hit!
63   else
64      return 100 ns;
65   end if;
66
67   end MMU;
68
69   procedure DAIS( Handler: Event; S16,S26,S36:
70   inout INTEGER;
71      DURATION :out time) is
72
73      variable U: real;
74      begin
75            -- generate uniform random
76   number (0. to 1.)
77            RANDOM16( U, S16, S26, S36);
78
79               --APPROX DAIS mix
```

```
 80              if   U  < 0.474 then ;
 81                 -- load/store
 82                   Duration:= MMU( U / 0.474)
 83  ;
 84              elsif   U < 0.474 + 0.124
 85  then -- add/subtract
 86                   DURATION := 50 ns;
 87              elsif   U < 0.474 + 0.124
 88  + 0.083 then -- multiply
 89                   DURATION := 75 ns;
 90              elsif   U < 0.474 + 0.124
 91  + 0.083 + 0.011 then -- divide
 92                   DURATION := 80 ns;
 93              else
 94  -- compare and branch= 6.8 % + 18.
 95  % rest shifts,logical,bit=2%ea
 96                   DURATION := 90 ns;
 97              end if;
 98  return;
 99  end DAIS;
100
101
102  procedure STATMIX( Handler: Event;
103  S16,S26,S36: inout INTEGER;
104      DURATION : out time) is
105
106  begin
107  --choose appropriate statistical mix
108  based upon Handler type
109  -- at present, only 1 choice
110
111     DAIS(Handler, S16,S26,S36, duration);
112
113
114  return;
115  end STATMIX;
116
117  -- user-visible routine:
118
119  procedure INST_TIME(SoFar: Integer;
120   Handler: Event;
```

```
 1   -- A1750A
 2   -- SIGNALS ARE ASSUME LOGICAL
 3   HIGH, E.G. BUSY IS BUSY WHEN '1'
 4   NOT '0'
 5
 6   use std.textio.all;
 7
 8   package A1750A is
 9
10   type Opcode is
11       ( XIO,VIO,   -- i/o
12       SBR,SB,SBI,RBR,RB,RBI,TBR,TB,TBI,
13       TSB,SVBR,RVBR,TVBR,-- bit ops
14       SLL,SRL,SRA,SLC,-- shifts
15       DSLL,DSRL,DSRA,DSLC,SLR,SAR,SCR,
16       DSLR,DSAR,DSCR,
17       JC,JCI,JS,SOJ,BR,BEZ,BLT,BEX,BLE,
18       BGT,BNZ,BGE,--BRANCHES
19       LST,LSTI,  --EXIT FROM INTERRUPT
20                  -- ROUTINE (LOAD STATUS)
21       SJS,URS,-- SUBROUTINE JMP,RETURN
22       LR,LB,LBX,LISP,LISN,L,LIM,LI,DLR,
23       DLB,DLBX,DL,DLI,LM,EFL,LUB,
24       LUBI,--LOADS
25       LLB,LLBI,POPM,STB,STBX,ST,STI,
26       STC,STCI,MOV,DSTB,DSTX,DST,DSTI,
27       --STORES
28       SRM,STM,EFST,STUB,SUBI,STLB,SLBI,
29       PSHM,
30       -- ABS IS A RESERVED WORD:
31       -- RENAMED ABSX
32       AR,AB,ABX,AISP,A,AIM,INCM,ABSX,
33       DABS,DAR,DA,FAR,FAB,FABX,FA,
34       EFAR,EFA,--MATH
35       FABS,SR,SBB,SBBX,SISP,S,SIM,DECM,
36       NEG,DNEG,DSR,DS,FSR,FSB,FSBX,
37       FS,
38       EFSR,EFS,FNEG,MSR,MISP,MISN,MS,
39       MISM,MR,MB,MBX,M,MIM,DMR,DM,
```

```
40        FMR, FMB, FMBX, FM,
41        EFMR, EFM, DVR, DISP, DISN, DV, DVIM,
42        DR, DB, DBX, D, DIM, DDR, DD, FDR, FDB,
43        FDBX, FD,
44        EFDR, EFD,
45        ORR, ORB, ORBX, ORX, ORIM, ANDR, ANDB,
46        ANDX, ANDZ, ANDM, XORR, XORZ, XORM,
47        NR, N, NIM, --LOGICALS
48        FIX, FLT, EFIX, EFLT, -- CONVERT
49        XBR, XWR, --EXCHANGE
50        CR, CB, CBX, CISP, CISN, C, CIM, CBLD,
51        CR, DC, FCR, FCB, FCBX, FC, EFCR, EFC,
52        --COMPARES
53        NOP, BPT--NOP, BREAKPOINT(HALT/NOP)
54
55        );
56
57    -- FOR EACH INSTRUCTION CODE:
58    -- NUMBER OF CLOCK CYCLES/TIME
59    -- SIZE 16/32 BITS
60    -- MEMORY OPERATIONS: REG. ONLY,
61    -- IMMEDIATE, 16 BIT , 32 BIT, SPECIAL
62    -- UNUSED: type AdrMode is
63    -- (R, D, DX, I, IX, IM, MX, ISP, ISN, ICR, BX, S);
64
65    type OpParam is array ( 1 to 196 )
66    )of INTEGER;
67    type Pages is array (1 to 256)
68     of INTEGER;
69
70    end A1750A;
71
72    package body A1750A is
73
74    function OpSize(Op:Opcode) return
75    INTEGER is
76    -- OPCODE SIZE IN WORDS 1 OR 2
77    constant SIZE: OpParam:=(1,1,--i/o
78        0,1,1,0,1,1,0,1,1,1,0,0,0,--biT
79
```

```
80      0,0,0,0,0,0,0,0,0,0,0,0,0,0,
81      -- shift
82      1,1,1,1,0,0,0,0,0,0,0,0,1,1,1,0,
83      --xfer
84      0,0,0,0,0,1,1,1,0,0,0,1,1,1,1,
85      1,1,1,1,--load
86      0,--pop
87      0,0,1,1,1,1,0,0,0,1,1,1,1,1,1,
88      1,1,1,0,--store,push
89      0,0,0,0,1,1,1,0,0,0,1,0,0,0,1,
90      0,1,0,0,0,0,0,1,1,1,
91      -- Math. to decrement
92      0,0,0,1,0,0,0,1,0,1,0,0,0,0,1,
93      1,0,0,0,1,1,0,1,0,0,0,1,0,1,
94      -- Math. to ext mult
95      0,0,0,1,1,0,0,0,1,1,0,1,0,0,0,
96      1,0,1,--divides
97      0,0,0,1,1,0,0,0,1,1,0,1,1,0,1,1,
98      --logical
99      0,0,0,0,0,0,0,0,0,0,0,1,1,1,0,
100     1,0,0,0,1,0,1,--convert,exch,compare
101     0,0);--nop,break
102
103 begin
104     return  SIZE(Opcode' Pos(Op));
105
106 end OpSize;
107
108
109 function OpMEM(Op:Opcode) return
110 INTEGER is
111 -- OPCODE  WORDS FOR MEMORY ACCESS:
112 --0 NONE 1 READ 1, ETC. -1 WRITE
113 -- 1, ETC
114 -- if >100 read and write n-100
115 -- >1000 SPECIAL
116 constant MSIZE: OpParam:=(0,1018,--i/o
117     0,101,101,0,101,101,0,1,1,1010
118  ,0,0,0,--bit
```

```
119        0,0,0,0,0,0,0,0,0,0,0,0,0,0,
120        --shifts
121        1,1,1,1,0,0,0,0,0,0,0,0,
122        --branch
123        1,1,  --ld status
124        0,1,  --misc xfer stack/call
125        -- unstack/return
126        1,1,1,1,1,1,1,2,--load,single
127        2,2,2,2,3,1015,3,1,2,1,2,--loads
128
129        1014,--popmultiple
130        -1,-1,-1,-2,-1,-2,-1013,--store
131        -- move mult to memory
132        -2,-2,-2,-3,-1,-1016,-3,1,2,1,
133        2,-1014,--store,push mult
134        0,1,1,0,1,0,101,--adds, increment
135        memory
136        0,0,0,2,0,2,2,2,3,3,0,--flt
137
138        0,1,1,0,1,1,--subtract
139        101,--decrement mem
140        0,0,0,1,0,2,2,2,0,3,0,--flt pt
141
142        0,0,0,1,0,0,1,1,1,0,0,2,0,2,2,
143        2,0,3,--mult
144        0,0,0,1,0,0,1,1,1,0,0,2,0,2,2,
145        2,0,3,--divides
146        0,1,1,1,0,0,1,1,1,0,0,1,0,0,1,
147  0,--logical
148        0,0,0,0,0,0,--convert,exchange
149
150        0,1,1,0,0,1,0,1019,  --compare,
151        --compare btwn limits
152        0,2,0,2,2,2,0,3,--compares
153        0,0 );-- noop,break
154
155  begin
156        return   MSIZE(Opcode' Pos(Op));
157
158
159  end OpMEM;
```

```
160
161    function OpClocks(Op:Opcode) return
162    INTEGER is
163    -- OPCODE clockcount
164    variable CLKCOUNT: OpParam;
165    variable FIRST: INTEGER:=1;
166    --file INF: TEXT is in "C750A";
167    --
168
169    variable L : line;
170    begin
171       if FIRST=1 then
172          for FIRST in 1 to 196 loop
173          --read clockcount from appropriate
174          -- data file
175    --          READLINE(INF,L);
176    --          READ( L, CLKCOUNT(FIRST));
177    -- ONE PER LINE
178    -- FOR THE SIMPLE STATISTICAL SIMULATION,
179    -- SET EACH OP. TO 5 CLKS
180             CLKCOUNT( FIRST ) := 5;
181
182          end loop;
183          FIRST:=0;
184       end if;
185       return   CLKCOUNT(Opcode' Pos(Op));
186
187    end OpClocks;
188
189    end A1750A;
```

```
 1    --PROCESSN
 2    use std.textio.all;
 3    use work.USER.all;
 4    use work.EVENTQ.all;
 5    use work.A1750a.all;
 6    use work.INSTR.all;
 7
 8    entity ProcessNode is
 9
10      generic
11         (Id: in integer --;
12    --        BOARDTYPE: in integer
13         );
14    -- port is signals from 1750A CPU/MMU
15    -- COMBINATION
16    -- ALL POSSIBLE VARIABLES NEEDED FOR
17    -- ANY SIMULATION OF 1750A
18    -- WILL COMMENT OUT THOSE NOT NEEDED
19    -- FOR STATISTICAL SIM
20    port
21       (
22    --        Addressbus: inout integerR
23    -- := -1;
24    --        Databus: inout integerR :=
25    -- -1;
26    --        BUSY:    inout integerR :=0;
27    --asserts when in control of bus
28    --        READWRITE: inout BITR :='0';
29    --   (direction)
30    -- set '1' by Node doing read,
31    -- thus requesting slave to put
32    -- data on bus
33    -- set '0'  for write, requesting
34    -- addressed node to accept data
35    --        DATAVALID: out integerR;
36    --        DATAREADY: in integerR;
37    --        InstData: out integerR;-- is
38    -- fetch instruction or data
39    --        IntReq: in integerR;-- interrupt
40    --includes pwr down, user, iol,
41    --ext request,timer clk,reset
```

```
42
43    --          Fault: in integerR;
44    --          Error: out integerR;
45    --DMA:
46    --          DMARequest: in integerR;
47    --          DMAAck: out integerR;
48    --          DMAEnable: out integerR;
49
50    -- multiproc. interface of f9450
51    --          BusReq: out integerR;
52    --          BusLock: out integerR;
53    --          BusGrant: in integerR;
54
55    --   AS/PS 4 LINES FOR PROCESSOR
56    -- AND ADDRESS STATE OF STATUS WD
57    -- AS DEFINES PAGE REGISTER
58    -- SET WHEN IMPLEMENTED
59    -- PS=0 FOR PRIV. INSTRUCT. ALSO,PS
60    -- MEMORY ACCESS KEY WHEN IMPLEMENTED
61    -- these might be implemented as signals
62    -- between CPU and MMU if required
63    -- in any event, no external
64    -- signals are needed
65
66    -- f 9450 has SYNC MEMORY BUS
67    -- OUTPUT line. purpose?
68
69    Tabulate: in integer   -- signal
70        --to dump result
71          );
72    end ProcessNode;
73
74    architecture BehaviorCPU of ProcessNode
75    is
76        -- EVENT QUEUES
77        signal EventSignal: Event;--next
78    instruction(SCHEDULED)
79        signal LocalEvent: Event := none;
80
```

```
81   --interrupt generated by node locally,
82   --    i.e by a sensor
83
84   -- FOR STATISTICS: DATA latency
85
86   -- defined by total
87   -- time to service interrupts (not
88   --just to get to service routine)
89   -- also average, maximum.
90   -- ENTEREVENT:
91   -- enter scheduled event into MY event
92   -- queue, so that when
93   -- the signal occurs, we can figure
94   -- out what to do.
95   -- this is needed, for example, if
96   -- the next scheduled instruction
97   -- has been preempted by an interrupt
98   -- and the delay must be
99   -- recalculated.
100  -- used by Local_Event
101
102  procedure ENTEREVENT(EventType: in
103      Event ;
104      TopEvent,EventQueue: inout EQueueptr;
105
106      SoFar,ToGo: in INTEGER;
107      -- INSTRUCTIONS SO FAR.
108      --DIFFERENT FROM PROCESS NODE!
109      StartTime: in TIME
110      ) is
111  -- no event signal assignment required
112  -- put it into local event queue
113
114  variable MSG:MESSAGEIO;
115  variable L: LINE;
116  begin
117      MSG:=" IN ENTEREVENT   AT ";
118      WRITE(L,MSG);WRITE(L,NOW);
119      WRITELINE(OUTF,L);
120      EventQueue := TopEvent;
121      TopEvent := new EQueueEl;
```

```
122        if TopEvent=NULL then
123            MSG:=" null pointer  AT    ";
124            WRITE(L,MSG);WRITE(L,NOW);
125            WRITELINE(OUTF,L);
126        end if;
127        TopEvent.EventType := EventType;
128
129        TopEvent.Previous := EventQueue;
130
131        TopEvent.Initiated := StartTime;
132
133        TopEvent.Resumed := 0;
134        TopEvent.Delay := ToGo;
135        TopEvent.Accumulated := SoFar ;
136        MSG:=" DEPART ENTVNT   AT ";
137        WRITE(L,MSG);WRITE(L,NOW);
138        WRITELINE(OUTF,L);
139        -- note that required Count will
140        -- not change,
141        -- so Accumulated,Resumed not really
142        -- needed! Unlike a time delay,
143        -- which will change if subsequent
144        -- interrupts!
145    end ENTEREVENT;
146
147    function OpIndex( Op: Opcode) return
148        integer is
149 -- find the index in OPDELAY array
150 -- corresponding to Opcode
151 begin
152        return Opcode' Pos(Op);
153 end OpIndex;
154
155 -- used to read in the ASCII instruction
156 -- name in a 1-for-1
157 -- simulation with full code listed
158 -- in file.  returns Opcode
159 -- not used for statistical instruction
160 -- mix simulation
```

```
161    function Operation(Op: OpName) return
162    Opcode is
163    variable L:LINE;
164    variable RESULT: Opcode;
165    variable MESSG: MESSAGEIO;
166    begin
167        case Op is
168            when OTHERS =>
169                MESSG:=" bad OPcode:          ";
170
171                WRITE(L,MESSG);
172                WRITELINE(OUTF,L);
173                null;
174        end case;
175    end Operation;
176
177
178    begin   -- behaviorCPU
179
180
181
182    RUNCPU: process
183
184    -- ONLY ONE PROCESS IS USED FOR CPU/MMU
185    -- COMBINATION
186    -- THIS WILL EASE PORTING TO PROCEDURAL,
187    -- SEQUENTIAL LANGUAGE SUCH AS C
188    -- IF LATER DESIRED TO DO SO TO INTERFACE
189    -- TO BUS MODEL!
190
191    -- wakes up for: initialization, Local_Event,
192
193    -- EventSignal Instruct(ion)
194    -- Tabulate(end of processing),
195
196    -- ALL POSSIBLE VARIABLES NEEDED FOR
197    -- ANY SIMULATION OF 1750A
198    -- WILL COMMENT OUT THOSE NOT NEEDED
199    -- FOR STATISTICAL SIM
200
201    --    variable  ONBOARDmemory: RAM (1 to 512) ;
```

```
202
203  --     variable   MEM: ROM (1 to 512) ;
204
205  --     variable   REG: REGISTRcpu (1 to 16);
206
207  --     variable   IC: integer:=100;--
208  --      instruction COUNTER
209  --     variable   SP: integer:=255;--stackpointer
210  variable   INITIAL: integer:=1;
211  --     variable   DATA,ADDRESS: integer;
212
213  --     variable   Queue,TopQueue: Queueptr
214  -- :=null;
215  constant   HOLD: TIME:= 100 ns;--
216  -- arbritrary value
217  constant   SETUPTIME: TIME:=100 ns;
218  --arbritrary value
219  -- below are addresses of various
220  -- service routines, etc.
221  --     constant   LEventService: INTEGER:= 100;
222
223  --     constant   BusService: INTEGER:=200;
224
225  --     constant   ClockService: INTEGER:=300;
226
227  --     constant   Startup: INTEGER:= 1;
228  --     caveat:addesses are naturals
229  variable PendingInt: INTEGER :=0;
230  --BITS FOR EACH INTERRUPT PENDING
231  variable StatusWord: INTEGER;
232  variable FaultReg: INTEGER;
233  variable IntMask: INTEGER;
234  variable MemFaultStatReg: INTEGER;
235  --optional:
236  variable IOI1,IOI2: INTEGER;
237  --OPTIONAL I/O INTERRUPT CODE REG
238  variable MEMLOC: INTEGER ;
239  --memory contents
240  variable INSTR: Instruction;--instruction
```

```
241    -- decode
242    variable OP: Opcode;
243    variable DELAY: INTEGER;
244    -- CHANGED FROM TIME FOR INSTRU/INSTRUC
245    -- 1750A
246    --   variable ADDR: INTEGER ; --address
247    -- of instruction
248    --   variable MEMADDR,REGADDR: integer;
249
250
251    variable L: line;
252    variable Oper: OpName;
253    variable MESSG: MESSAGEIO;
254
255    variable EventQueue,TopEvent: EQueueptr
256        :=null;
257    variable E,P: EQueueptr;
258
259    variable Duration: TIME:=0 NS;
260    -- DURATION OF INSTRUCTION
261
262    variable U : real;
263    -- UNIFORM 0-1 RANDOM VARIABLE
264    variable S16 : integer := 12;
265    variable S26 : integer := 23;
266    variable S36 : integer := 34;
267
268    variable PendingEvent,CurrentEvent:
269        Event;
270    variable Average: INTEGER :=0;
271    --interrupt handler statistics:
272    variable Variance: INTEGER :=0;--
273    --interrupt handler statistics:
274    variable SoFar: INTEGER :=0;
275    --how much of handler done so far.
276    variable ToGo: INTEGER :=65000;
277    --how much of handler we have to go.
278    variable StartHandler, NewEvent :
279        TIME := 0 ns;
280        --   variable LASTE: TIME := 0 ns;
281
```

```
282    variable LOCALEST,LOCALETOTAL,LOCALEMAX,
283        LOCALEAV: TIME:=0 ns;
284    variable LOCALEKT: INTEGER:=0;
285
286    file INF: TEXT is in "IN";
287    --HOW DO WE MAKE THIS DIFFERENT FOR
288    -- EACH CPU, E.G. DEPENDENT UPON
289    -- ID? COULD USE & CONCATENATION
290    -- IF WE COULD STRING-IZE ID
291
292    -- alternatively, kludge this by
293    -- passing in file name thru the
294    -- generic statement
295
296    begin
297
298    --initialization is here to set
299    --up variables in RUNCPU as well as
300    -- local events.
301
302    if INITIAL=1 then
303    -- read in generic parameters
304    -- which can vary between process
305    -- nodes and bus architectures,
306    -- such as neighbors in
307    -- daisy chain, etc.
308    -- read in timing into OPDELAY
309    -- data
310
311    -- read the program into ROM
312    -- could also read until blanck
313    -- line?
314    -- for this calc., assume one
315    -- kind of interrupt and
316    -- associated handler
317    -- we could define a number of
318    -- different local interrupts, each
319    -- with associated statistical
320    -- parameters.
```

```
321                READLINE(INF,L);READ(L,AVERAGE);
322                READ(L,VARIANCE);
323
324                MESSG :="              ID=        ";
325
326                WRITE(L,MESSG); WRITE(L,Id);
327                WRITELINE(OUTF,L);
328
329                MESSG :="              AVERAGE = ";
330
331                WRITE(L,MESSG); WRITE(L,AVERAGE);
332
333                WRITELINE(OUTF,L);
334
335                MESSG :="              VARIANCE = ";
336
337                WRITE(L,MESSG);
338                WRITE(L,VARIANCE);
339                WRITELINE(OUTF,L);
340
341                --        READLINE(INF,L);
342                -- READ(L,INITIAL);
343                --          NUMBER OF INSTRUCTIONS IN
344                --CODE
345                --  for ADDR in 1 to INITIAL loop
346                --    READLINE(INF,L);
347                --         READ(L,Oper);
348                -- MEM(ADDR).Op :=Operation(Oper);
349                --cannot set fieldsize, justification
350                -- on read-only write!
351                -- will it read in until whitespace
352                -- (as in C) or entire line?
353                --
354                -- if L' LENGTH = 0 then
355                -- READLINE(INF,L);end if;
356                -- READ(L,MEMADDR);
357                -- READ(L,REGADDR);
358                --   MEM(ADDR).Op:=Op;
359                --   MEM(ADDR).mAddress :=MEMADDR;
360                -- MEM(ADDR).rAddress :=REGADDR;
361
```

```
362                 --end loop;
363
364                 -- read in events
365                 -- and queue them in local event
366                 -- queue:
367                 while not ENDFILE( INF ) loop
368                 READLINE( INF , L );
369                 if not (L' length=0) then
370                     READ( L , INITIAL );
371                     -- INTEGER INITIAL = 0 FOR CLOCK
372                     -- TICK, 1 FOR LOCAL EVENT
373                     READ( L , DELAY );--READ
374                     --UNTIL EXECEPTION FOR NO DATA
375                     MESSG :="            Initial = ";
376
377                     WRITE(L,MESSG);
378                     WRITE(L,INITIAL);
379                     WRITELINE(OUTF,L);
380                     MESSG :="            Delay = ";
381                     WRITE(L,MESSG);  WRITE(L,DELAY);
382                     WRITELINE(OUTF,L);
383                     if INITIAL = 0 then
384                         -- ENTEREVENT(Clock_Tick,
385                         -- TopEvent,EventQueue,DELAY,
386                         -- LocalEvent);
387                     LocalEvent <= transport
388                     Clock_Tick after DELAY *1 us;
389                     -- next may not be
390                     -- necessary if
391                     -- scheduled event
392                     -- triggers
393                     -- even if no change
394                     -- of signal value
395                     LocalEvent <= transport
396                     none after DELAY * 1 us +1 ns;
397                     -- Not initial:
398                     else
399                     -- ENTEREVENT(Local_event,Top
400                     -- Event,EventQueue,
```

```
401                    -- DELAY,LocalEvent);
402
403                    LocalEvent <= transport
404                    Local_Event after DELAY *1 us;
405                    LocalEvent <= transport
406                    none after DELAY * 1 us +1 ns;
407                end if;
408           end if;
409           end loop;
410           --HANDLE EXCEPTION TO PREVENT ABORT
411
412           -- end of initialization code.
413           INITIAL := 0;
414           -- START THE PROCESSOR
415           --        IP:=Startup;
416           EVENTSIGNAL <= INSTRUCT after 4 NS;
417
418           -- NO: START WITH FIRST LOCAL EVENT!
419     end if;
420
421     wait on LocalEvent,EventSignal,Tabulate;
422
423     --     until (not (LASTE=NOW));
424
425     --        LASTE := NOW;
426
427     if Tabulate= Id then
428     -- output/send the statistics data
429
430         MESSG :="            ID=          ";
431         WRITE(L,MESSG); WRITE(L,Id);
432         WRITELINE(OUTF,L);
433         MESSG:=" TOTAL T MASKED OFF ";
434         WRITE(L,MESSG);
435         -- WRITE(L,MOFFTOTAL);
436         WRITELINE(OUTF,L);
437         MESSG :=" TOTAL INTERRUPTS   ";
438         WRITE(L,MESSG);
439         -- WRITE(L,INTERTOTAL);
440         WRITELINE(OUTF,L);
441         MESSG :=" TOTAL WTG FOR BUS  ";
```

```
442          WRITE(L,MESSG);
443          --          WRITE(L,BUSWTOTAL);
444          WRITELINE(OUTF,L);
445          MESSG :=" TOTAL  LOCAL  EVENTS ";
446          WRITE(L,MESSG);
447          WRITE(L,LOCALETOTAL);
448          WRITELINE(OUTF,L);
449          MESSG :=" count LOCAL  EVENTS ";
450          WRITE(L,MESSG);
451          WRITE(L,LOCALEKT);
452          WRITELINE(OUTF,L);
453          MESSG :="aver.   LOCAL  EVENTS ";
454          WRITE(L,MESSG);
455          LOCALEAV := LOCALETOTAL / REAL(
456               LOCALEKT) ;
457          WRITE(L,LOCALEAV);
458          WRITELINE(OUTF,L);
459          MESSG :="max.   LOCAL  EVENTS ";
460          WRITE(L,MESSG);
461          WRITE(L,LOCALEMAX);
462          WRITELINE(OUTF,L);
463      wait;-- stop
464  end if;
465
466  if LocalEvent = Local_Event then
467          --interrupt request sensed
468          --LocalEvent <= none;-- reset
469          -- OOPS- THE ABOVE WOULD CLEAR
470          -- THE LOCAL EVENT QUEUE!!!!!!
471          MESSG:=" LOCALEVENT     AT    ";
472          WRITE(L,MESSG);WRITE(L,NOW);
473          WRITELINE(OUTF,L);
474          NewEvent := NOW;
475          -- when first requested!
476          PendingInt := 1;
477          PendingEvent := Local_Event;
478          LOCALEKT := LOCALEKT +1;
479          -- do not actually interrupt
480          -- an atomic instruction
```

```
481          -- wait until end
482          -- this is different from the
483          -- generic process node mode, in
484          -- which processes are multiple
485          -- instructions and interruptable
486      elsif Local_Event = Clock_Tick then
487          MESSG:=" clocktick      AT      ";
488          WRITE(L,MESSG);WRITE(L,NOW);
489          WRITELINE(OUTF,L);
490          NewEvent := NOW;
491          -- when first requested!
492          PendingInt := 1;
493          PendingEvent:=Clock_Tick;
494          -- LocalEvent <= none;-- reset
495          --for next instruction
496          -- for this simulation, will
497          -- not treat clock ticks as different
498          -- class of occurences but as
499          --  another type of local event
500          -- code for a clock tick will
501          -- be identical to the above except
502          -- for different statistics of
503          -- different handler
504          -- would have to remember type of
505          -- handler
506      end if;-- local event
507
508      if EventSignal = Instruct then --
509          --schedule next instruction
510          EventSignal <= none after 2 ns;
511
512          -- is an interrupt pending?
513          if ( PendingInt = 1 ) then
514          -- yes, handle pending interrupt
515          -- push interrupted event on
516          -- my stack
517          PendingInt := 0;
518          ENTEREVENT(CurrentEvent,TopEvent,
519              EventQueue,SoFar,
520              ToGo,StartHandler);
521              StartHandler := NewEvent;
```

```
522              RANDOM16( U,  S16,  S26,  S36);
523
524              MESSG:="                 U=           ";
525
526              WRITE(L,MESSG);  WRITE(L,U);
527
528              WRITELINE(OUTF,L);
529              MESSG:="               Average = ";
530
531              WRITE(L,MESSG);WRITE(L,Average);
532
533              WRITELINE(OUTF,L);
534              MESSG:="             Variance = ";
535
536              WRITE(L,MESSG);WRITE(L,Variance);
537
538              WRITELINE(OUTF,L);
539              -- VERY simple model for handler
540              -- duration:
541              ToGo:= Average+integer( (U
542                  - 0.5) * real( Variance) );
543              MESSG:="             ToGo        ";
544              WRITE(L,MESSG);WRITE(L,ToGo);
545              WRITELINE(OUTF,L);
546              SoFar:=0;
547              -- handler
548              -- EventSignal <= transport
549              -- Instruct after 3 ns;
550
551      else -- nothing pending. schedule
552              --   next instruction
553
554
555              MESSG:=" EVENTsignal(instr) ";
556              WRITE(L,MESSG);WRITE(L,NOW);
557              WRITELINE(OUTF,L);
558              -- GENERATE INSTRUCTION, INCLUDING
559              -- TIMING DELAY TO NEXT
560              -- INSTRUCTION AND MEMORY ACCESS
```

```
561             --USAGE
562             --PROBABILISTIC
563             -- IF PIPELINED, DO REQUIRED
564             -- PREFETCH OF INSTRUCTIONS
565             -- REQUEST MEMORY ACCESS IF NECESSARY
566
567             --(IF PIPELINED, MAY BE OF PRIOR
568             -- INSTRUCTION)
569             -- if branch TAKEN, and pipelined,
570             -- clear pipe
571             SoFar:=SoFar+1;
572             if SoFar > ToGo then
573                 -- reached end of handler DO
574                 --ITS STATISTICS,
575                 -- THEN POP DOWN TO PREVIOUS
576                 -- AND DO STATISTICS
577                 DURATION:= NOW - StartHandler;
578
579                 LOCALETOTAL:=LOCALETOTAL+DURATION;
580
581                 if LOCALEMAX < DURATION then
582                     LOCALEMAX := DURATION;
583                 end if;
584                 MESSG := "      start handler = ";
585                 WRITE(L,MESSG);
586                 WRITE(L,StartHandler);
587                 WRITELINE(OUTF,L);
588                 MESSG := "           DURATION = ";
589                 WRITE(L,MESSG);
590                 WRITE(L,Duration);
591                 WRITELINE(OUTF,L);
592                 MESSG := "          LocalEMAX = ";
593                 WRITE(L,MESSG);
594                 WRITE(L,Localemax);
595                 WRITELINE(OUTF,L);
596                 MESSG := "        LocalEtotal  = ";
597                 WRITE(L,MESSG);
598                 WRITE(L,Localetotal);
599                 WRITELINE(OUTF,L);
600             -- POP DOWN TO PREVIOUS, INTERRUPTED
601             -- (IF ANY) HANDLER
```

```
602            EventQueue:=TopEvent;
603            if not (EventQueue=NULL) then
604
605            -- was loop for Process
606            -- node simulation,
607            --   where can't be sure
608            -- will be on top of queue!
609            -- Here, can be sure,
610            --   no need to search
611            -- therefore, EventQueue
612            -- and TopEvent are
613            -- somewhat redundant
614                if EventQueue.Eventtype=
615                    Local_Event
616                    or EventQueue.Eventtype=
617                    Clock_Tick then
618                    ToGo := EventQueue.Delay;
619
620                    SoFar := EventQueue.
621                    Accumulated;
622                    StartHandler:=EventQueue.
623                    Initiated;
624                    MESSG:=
625                    "        ToGo Popped = ";
626
627                    WRITE(L,MESSG);
628                    WRITE(L,ToGo);
629                    WRITELINE(OUTF,L);
630
631                    MESSG:=
632                    "        SoFar Popped = ";
633
634                    WRITE(L,MESSG);
635                    WRITE(L,SoFar);
636                    WRITELINE(OUTF,L);
637                    MESSG:=
638                    "        StartHandler = ";
639                    WRITE(L,MESSG);
640                    WRITE(
```

```
641                      L,StartHandler);
642                      WRITELINE(OUTF,L);
643
644                  end if;--localevent/clocktick
645                  -- POP (REMOVE TOP EVENT
646                  -- from queue)
647                  if (EventQueue= TopEvent)
648                      then
649                      TopEvent:=TopEvent.Previous;
650
651                      MESSG:=
652                      " pop TopEvent          ";
653                      WRITE(L,MESSG);
654                      WRITE(L,NOW);
655                      WRITELINE(OUTF,L);
656                      --              else
657                      -- P.Previous:=
658                      -- EventQueue.Previous;
659                  end if;-- eventqueue==top event
660
661                  deallocate(EventQueue);
662                  EventQueue := TopEvent;
663                  --P:=EventQueue;
664              else
665                  -- nothing in Queue-nothing
666                  -- interrrupted.
667                  -- processor idle or doing
668                  -- busy work.
669                  StartHandler:=NOW;
670                  MESSG:=" NOthing queued      ";
671                  WRITE(L,MESSG);
672                  WRITE(L,NOW);
673                  WRITELINE(OUTF,L);
674                  -- continue to do nothing
675                  -- until next local/interrupt
676                  -- or clock tick
677              end if;-- not null
678                  -- else-- SoFar<ToGo
679          end if;-- if(SoFar) end of handler
680          --test
681      end if;-- if interrupt pending
```

```
682   -- go on to next instruction
683   -- schedule next instruction
684   -- (nothing pending)
685   INST_TIME(SoFar,CurrentEvent,S16,S26,S36
686   , DURATION);
687   MESSG:="          Duration  = ";
688   WRITE(L,MESSG);
689   WRITE(L,DURATION);
690   WRITELINE(OUTF,L);
691   EventSignal <= transport Instruct
692        after Duration;
693   end if;-- if EventSignal= Instruction
694   end process;   -- CPUMMU;
695
696   end BehaviorCPU;
697
698   configuration Behavior_con of ProcessNode
699   is
700        for BehaviorCPU
701        end for;
702   end Behavior_con;
```

```
30  6
1   5
1  25
1  27
1  50
1  75
1  90
```

```
                ID=              1
              AVERAGE  =  30
            VARIANCE  =  6
             Initial  =  1
                Delay  =  5
             Initial  =  1
                Delay  =  25
             Initial  =  1
                Delay  =  27
             Initial  =  1
                Delay  =  50
             Initial  =  1
                Delay  =  75
             Initial  =  1
                Delay  =  90
   EVENTsignal(instr)  4 NS
          Duration   =  200 NS
   EVENTsignal(instr)  204 NS
          Duration   =  190 NS
   EVENTsignal(instr)  394 NS
          Duration   =  200 NS
   EVENTsignal(instr)  594 NS
          Duration   =  200 NS
 . . . . .
   EVENTsignal(instr)  4944 NS
          Duration   =  190 NS
   LOCALEVENT      AT     5000 NS
   IN  ENTEREVENT    AT  5134 NS
   DEPART  ENTVNT    AT  5134 NS
                U=            6.36117713E-1
             Average  =  30
             Variance  =  6
               ToGo        31
           Duration   =  200 NS
   EVENTsignal(instr)  5334 NS
          Duration   =  180 NS
 . . . . .
   EVENTsignal(instr)  10979 NS
          Duration   =  175 NS
```

```
EVENTsignal(instr) 11154 NS
    start handler = 5000 NS
            DURATION = 6154 NS
           LocalEMAX = 6154 NS
      LocalEtotal  = 6154 NS
       ToGo Popped = 65000
      SoFar Popped = 27
      StartHandler = 0 NS
pop TopEvent         11154 NS
           Duration  = 150 NS
EVENTsignal(instr) 11304 NS
           Duration  = 200 NS
.....
 EVENTsignal(instr) 24749 NS
           Duration  = 200 NS
 EVENTsignal(instr) 24949 NS
           Duration  = 200 NS
LOCALEVENT      AT    25000 NS
IN ENTEREVENT     AT 25149 NS
DEPART ENTVNT     AT 25149 NS
            U=         3.122343949999999E-1
           Average = 30
           Variance = 6
             ToGo        29
           Duration  = 190 NS
 EVENTsignal(instr) 25339 NS
           Duration  = 190 NS
.....
.....
 EVENTsignal(instr) 26904 NS
           Duration  = 200 NS
LOCALEVENT      AT    27000 NS
IN ENTEREVENT     AT 27104 NS
DEPART ENTVNT     AT 27104 NS
            U=         8.858125319999999E-1
           Average = 30
           Variance = 6
             ToGo        32
           Duration  = 200 NS
 EVENTsignal(instr) 27304 NS
           Duration  = 200 NS
```

```
. . . . .
. . . . .
  EVENTsignal(instr) 33159 NS
          Duration  = 200 NS
  EVENTsignal(instr) 33359 NS
      start handler = 27000 NS
             DURATION = 6359 NS
           LocalEMAX = 6359 NS
        LocalEtotal  = 12513 NS
         ToGo Popped = 29
         SoFar Popped = 9
         StartHandler = 25000 NS
  pop TopEvent         33359 NS
          Duration  = 150 NS
  EVENTsignal(instr) 33509 NS
          Duration  = 200 NS
. . . . .
. . . . .
  EVENTsignal(instr) 37164 NS
          Duration  = 200 NS
  EVENTsignal(instr) 37364 NS
      start handler = 25000 NS
             DURATION = 12364 NS
           LocalEMAX = 12364 NS
        LocalEtotal  = 24877 NS
         ToGo Popped = 65000
         SoFar Popped = 100
         StartHandler = 0 NS
  pop TopEvent         37364 NS
          Duration  = 190 NS
  EVENTsignal(instr) 37554 NS
          Duration  = 175 NS
. . . . .
. . . . .
  EVENTsignal(instr) 49794 NS
          Duration  = 200 NS
  EVENTsignal(instr) 49994 NS
          Duration  = 190 NS
  LOCALEVENT      AT    50000 NS
```

```
IN ENTEREVENT     AT 50184 NS
DEPART ENTVNT     AT 50184 NS
              U=           7.137360009999999E-1
          Average = 30
          Variance = 6
          ToGo        31
          Duration  = 190 NS
EVENTsignal(instr) 50374 NS
          Duration  = 200 NS
. . . . .
. . . . .
 EVENTsignal(instr) 55994 NS
          Duration  = 180 NS
 EVENTsignal(instr) 56174 NS
     start handler = 50000 NS
          DURATION = 6174 NS
          LocalEMAX = 12364 NS
     LocalEtotal   = 31051 NS
      ToGo Popped  = 65000
      SoFar Popped = 166
      StartHandler = 0 NS
pop TopEvent         56174 NS
          Duration  = 200 NS
 EVENTsignal(instr) 56374 NS
          Duration  = 200 NS
. . . . .
. . . . .
 EVENTsignal(instr) 74709 NS
          Duration  = 190 NS
 EVENTsignal(instr) 74899 NS
          Duration  = 200 NS
 LOCALEVENT      AT   75000 NS
 IN ENTEREVENT     AT 75099 NS
 DEPART ENTVNT     AT 75099 NS
              U=           6.016653279999999E-1
          Average = 30
          Variance = 6
          ToGo        31
          Duration  = 190 NS
 EVENTsignal(instr) 75289 NS
          Duration  = 150 NS
```

```
. . . . .
. . . . .
  EVENTsignal(instr) 80604 NS
         Duration   = 200 NS
  EVENTsignal(instr) 80804 NS
         Duration   = 175 NS
  EVENTsignal(instr) 80979 NS
     start handler = 75000 NS
          DURATION = 5979 NS
          LocalEMAX = 12364 NS
      LocalEtotal   = 37030 NS
       ToGo Popped = 65000
       SoFar Popped = 265
       StartHandler = 0 NS
pop TopEvent        80979 NS
         Duration   = 200 NS
  EVENTsignal(instr) 81179 NS
         Duration   = 190 NS
. . . . .
. . . . .
  EVENTsignal(instr) 89939 NS
         Duration   = 200 NS
  LOCALEVENT      AT    90000 NS
  IN ENTEREVENT   AT 90139 NS
  DEPART ENTVNT   AT 90139 NS
             U=         6.315755599999999E-2
         Average = 30
         Variance = 6
         ToGo        27
         Duration   = 200 NS
  EVENTsignal(instr) 90339 NS
         Duration   = 200 NS
  EVENTsignal(instr) 90539 NS
         Duration   = 175 NS
  EVENTsignal(instr) 90714 NS
         Duration   = 175 NS
  EVENTsignal(instr) 90889 NS
         Duration   = 200 NS
  EVENTsignal(instr) 91089 NS
```

```
                   Duration   = 200 NS
   EVENTsignal(instr)  91289 NS
                   Duration   = 200 NS
   EVENTsignal(instr)  91489 NS
                   Duration   = 150 NS
   EVENTsignal(instr)  91639 NS
                   Duration   = 200 NS
   EVENTsignal(instr)  91839 NS
                   Duration   = 200 NS
   EVENTsignal(instr)  92039 NS
                   Duration   = 150 NS
   EVENTsignal(instr)  92189 NS
                   Duration   = 200 NS
   EVENTsignal(instr)  92389 NS
                   Duration   = 150 NS
   EVENTsignal(instr)  92539 NS
                   Duration   = 175 NS
   EVENTsignal(instr)  92714 NS
                   Duration   = 190 NS
   EVENTsignal(instr)  92904 NS
                   Duration   = 190 NS
   EVENTsignal(instr)  93094 NS
                   Duration   = 200 NS
   EVENTsignal(instr)  93294 NS
                   Duration   = 200 NS
   EVENTsignal(instr)  93494 NS
                   Duration   = 190 NS
   EVENTsignal(instr)  93684 NS
                   Duration   = 150 NS
   EVENTsignal(instr)  93834 NS
                   Duration   = 200 NS
   EVENTsignal(instr)  94034 NS
                   Duration   = 190 NS
   EVENTsignal(instr)  94224 NS
                   Duration   = 200 NS
   EVENTsignal(instr)  94424 NS
                   Duration   = 150 NS
   EVENTsignal(instr)  94574 NS
                   Duration   = 175 NS
   EVENTsignal(instr)  94749 NS
                   Duration   = 200 NS
```

```
EVENTsignal(instr)  94949 NS
          Duration  = 200 NS
EVENTsignal(instr)  95149 NS
          Duration  = 150 NS
EVENTsignal(instr)  95299 NS
      start handler = 90000 NS
           DURATION = 5299 NS
          LocalEMAX = 12364 NS
        LocalEtotal = 42329 NS
        ToGo Popped = 65000
       SoFar Popped = 312
       StartHandler = 0 NS
pop TopEvent          95299 NS
          Duration  = 150 NS
EVENTsignal(instr)  95449 NS
          Duration  = 190 NS
EVENTsignal(instr)  95639 NS
          Duration  = 190 NS
EVENTsignal(instr)  95829 NS
          Duration  = 190 NS
EVENTsignal(instr)  96019 NS
          Duration  = 200 NS
EVENTsignal(instr)  96219 NS
          Duration  = 190 NS
EVENTsignal(instr)  96409 NS
          Duration  = 190 NS
EVENTsignal(instr)  96599 NS
          Duration  = 200 NS
EVENTsignal(instr)  96799 NS
          Duration  = 200 NS
EVENTsignal(instr)  96999 NS
          Duration  = 150 NS
EVENTsignal(instr)  97149 NS
          Duration  = 175 NS
EVENTsignal(instr)  97324 NS
          Duration  = 190 NS
EVENTsignal(instr)  97514 NS
          Duration  = 150 NS
EVENTsignal(instr)  97664 NS
```

```
            Duration   = 190 NS
  EVENTsignal(instr)  97854 NS
            Duration   = 200 NS
  EVENTsignal(instr)  98054 NS
            Duration   = 200 NS
  EVENTsignal(instr)  98254 NS
            Duration   = 150 NS
  EVENTsignal(instr)  98404 NS
            Duration   = 190 NS
  EVENTsignal(instr)  98594 NS
            Duration   = 190 NS
  EVENTsignal(instr)  98784 NS          Duration   = 190
NS
  EVENTsignal(instr)  98974 NS          Duration   =
175 NS
  EVENTsignal(instr)  99339 NS          Duration   = 190
NS
  EVENTsignal(instr)  99529 NS          Duration   = 150
NS
  EVENTsignal(instr)  99679 NS          Duration   = 200
NS
  EVENTsignal(instr)  99879 NS          Duration   = 200
NS
         SIMULATE ID = 1
              ID=          1
  TOTAL  T MASKED OFF
  TOTAL  INTERRUPTS
  TOTAL  WTG FOR BUS
  TOTAL  LOCAL  EVENTS  42329 NS
  count  LOCAL  EVENTS  6
aver.    LOCAL  EVENTS  7054.833333 NS
max.     LOCAL  EVENTS  12364 NS
```

Chapter 16

Busses and Protocols

PURPOSE

This chapter is devoted to the simulation of busses. It should be no surprise that finite-state machines will play a significant role in implementing bus protocols. This is because modern busses must maintain state information, such as position in a burst transfer. FSMs are often sufficient, as the protocols must be simple for maximum efficiency, and are often implemented in hardware (e.g., the Intel M82553 Protocol Management Unit for the MIL-STD-1553 bus and the M82916 for the PI bus). Verifying the proper operation of such hardware implementations is important, and will be discussed here. VHDL simulations of busses may also be used to determine anticipated performance of contemplated system configurations. Fortier and Desrochers (1990) consider the general problem of analyzing networks.

There is a wide range of bus topologies and protocols. The early busses were common signal paths between modules. All stations on the bus were connected to each other, in effect wired in parallel. A transmitting station would be received all along the bus. Busses such as Ethernet and the various microprocessor busses were of this form. Modern busses can be more complex. The SAE High-Speed

Ring bus, discussed in this chapter, is significantly different. The bus is wired point-to-point through each station, with that station controlling what is passed on to the next station. Two rings compose the bus, one for clockwise transmission and the other passing messages in a counterclockwise direction. Fiber-optic busses naturally lend themselves to pairs of uni-directional busses with each station on the bus controlling transceivers for each of the component rings (see Limb, 1992).

TYPICAL BUS PROTOCOLS

Synchronous and Asynchronous Busses

Synchronous busses assume a single clock that controls the system, with *masters* sending requests and *slaves* complying with those requests. Wait states may be needed to permit slow slaves to operate, but it is assumed on a synchronous bus that data is present and stable when it should be. If some peripherals are too slow to respond in a clock period, the number of wait states is generally fixed, with slow peripherals slowing the entire bus by requiring fixed, hardware-generated wait states. On the other hand, synchronous busses are generally simpler and faster. Burst mode data transfers can be implemented relatively simply. The (Sun) SBus and the Intel 80960CA bus are examples of synchronous busses. The SAE (Society for Automotive Electronics) High-Speed Ring Bus is a serial bus that synchronizes clocks from point-to-point, while the IEEE 802 token ring bus assigns one station the role of clock master, with the station downstream synchronizing to its signal. Data frames are decoded based upon this synchronized clock.

By contrast, *asynchronous* busses make no assumptions as to slave response times as do synchronous busses. Instead, handshaking signals are used to ensure that slaves are warned that a request is being made of them (and that the requisite data and address lines are valid), with the master then waiting until an appropriate acknowledgment is signaled before attempting to read the data. All this complicates the implementation and can reduce the maximum data rate, but makes the system much more flexible. Problems due to *bus slew*, the fact that signal propagation on some lines may be faster than on others, are minimized compared with a synchronous bus. Most members of the 80960 family, Futurebus+, and the VME-bus, are examples of asynchronous busses.

Obviously, one can attempt a VHDL implementation of a bus controller by writing straightforward blocks of code, for example, assigning the address signal, waiting for the setup period before assigning the memory request signal, and waiting until the acknowledge signal is received. Such code is inflexible and easily broken (and hardware similarly designed would also be fragile). Instead, it is recommended here that bus controllers be developed as FSMs (see Chapter 13). Thus, after the appropriate memory request signal assignment has been made, it is easy to implement a range of responses to situations, such as timeouts and interrupts, in addition to the "expected" acknowledgment. A BUSIDLE state can connect to various semiautonomous machines that perform reads and writes. Examples of state diagrams for typical busses will be given later in this chapter.

Comer and Stevens (1991) give complete state machines for the (software) TCP/IP protocols, implementing them with C code. Such state diagrams are fairly similar to the diagrams for hardware protocols, due to the similar nature of the tasks to be accomplished. If anything, the hardware protocols will be simpler. See the References at the end of this chapter for additional sources on typical bus protocols, and Tanenbaum's book (in Chapter 15 References) for a good overview of microprocessor busses as well as the VMEbus.

Bus Arbitration

Many busses have a single controller that arbitrates between devices requesting to become bus masters. Arbitration can be fixed by the hardware, as in daisy-chaining priority schemes that are typically hard-wired, or software controlled. Daisy-chaining is illustrated in the next section. The controller informs the next master of its selection and "retires." Sometimes, for reliability or other reasons, arbitration is distributed. The PI bus is an example of a complex distributed arbitration scheme, and is discussed later in this chapter. The SAE High-Speed bus is an example of distributed arbitration, using a token ring. A token is passed from node to node along the logical ring, possession of the token giving permission to control the bus. Such protocols must monitor bus activity to check for lost tokens, and prevent multiple tokens from appearing.

Bus arbitration can be modeled in VHDL in a general fashion using a finite-state machine. The resolution function for the bussed request signal will typically be a WIRED-OR type of resolution. The output of this signal is the input for the bus arbiter, which needs to know the current state of the bus as well as the status of request signal. If the bus is idle, the grant sequence can begin. The resolution function should be kept free from side effects, so the arbiter subprogram should be kept separate.

Typical Busses

Many busses have similar protocol features, and have detailed specifications, although busses are rarely defined as rigorously as the VHSIC busses.

Futurebus+ (IEEE 896.1 for the logical layer, 896.2 for the physical layer, and 896.3 for guidelines) is discussed in the article by Sha et al. (1991). Like the PI-bus family, it is also intended for real-time systems and has been adopted by the U. S. Navy. It supports 31 modules (similar to the PI-bus family, which supports up to 32). It supports a distributed arbitration scheme very similar to that of the PI-bus, and a centralized scheme in which a controller resolves contention. Hardware, as the Texas Instruments TFB2010 Arbitration controller, exists to implement the bus protocols Futurebus+ differs from the PI-bus in that the distributed arbitration takes place on eight dedicated lines in parallel with data transfer. Centralized arbitration is handled by three signals: bus request, grant, and preempt. Modules may request the bus with the first, and are granted use of the bus with the second. The preemption line is used by the central arbiter to tell the current owner of the bus that a higher-priority request has been received and it should give up control as soon as possible. Thus, the ability to suspend a block transfer exists, similar to the PI-bus. Messages on Futurebus+ are composed of a header and a body of data, similar to the PI-bus. Shared-memory access can also be used, and can coexist with message-passing protocols.

One form of arbitration, mentioned previously, is *daisy-chaining* (see Figure 16.1). The bus grant line is not bussed to each processor

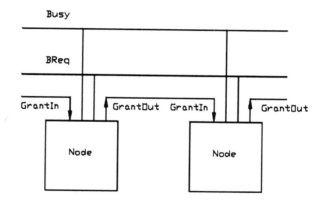

Figure 16.1 Daisy-chain distributed arbitration

(as are the request and busy lines), but routed through each processor, which receives an in value from one processor and passes on a possible value to the next processor in the chain. The leftmost processor in the chain has its bus grant input connected to the arbiter's output, or, in a decentralized system, tied to a level signaling the granting of the bus. In a centralized arbitration scheme, the controller activates the bus grant line, such as the DATAIN/DATAOUT lines of the ETM bus of PI bus family (discussed later in this chapter). The first requesting module that sees the signal does not pass it along the chain, but instead takes control of the bus. The priority of each processor is determined by its position in the chain, which is hardwired and consequently inflexible. The daisy chain is susceptible to point failures, but is often used on microprocessor busses. Its simulation in VHDL is simple and corresponds to the hardware implementation, with a simple gate passing the grant signal along or not depending on whether the module is requesting the bus, and interrupting or otherwise informing the CPU when the incoming grant is asserted. The bus request can be handled by the CPU or a separate unit. Multibus offers a form of daisy-chained arbitration, without a central arbiter. The first module in the daisy chain is effectively always granted permission. Thus, the module nearest this one requesting the bus will have the highest effective priority and receive the bus mastership. (Multibus offers centralized arbitration as well.) Daisy-chaining may be used with multiple priority levels by daisy-chaining each level, the arbiter determining the highest level requesting the bus and granting access to that level. Within each level, the priority is still hardwired and fixed. In the decentralized architecture, there is no arbiter and each module decides for itself whether to pass along the grant signal level if it is present at its input, or whether it wishes to take control of the bus by passing along a not-granted signal along the chain. It must then clear its own assertion of the bus request line and wait until other contenders do so.

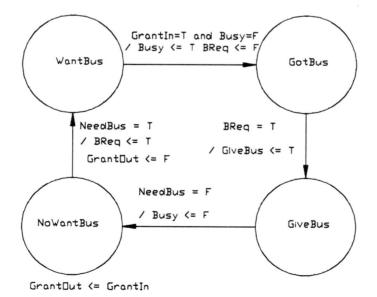

Figure 16.2 FSM for daisy-chain arbitration

The arbitration can be handled by the FSM shown in Figure 16.2. All signals are of type Boolean, with NeedBus and GiveBus local signals between the bus interface unit and the main processor of the node. The former signals the interface unit that the bus is desired, the latter is an optional signal informing the processor that the bus is desired by another node. Depending on the protocol, the processor may suspend its use of the bus. Initially, all nodes should be in the NoWantBus state. In state NoWantBus, the GrantOut signal is set to whatever the GrantIn signal is. Otherwise, GrantOut is set to False to prevent interference from lower-priority nodes in the chain. The Busy signal is necessary to prevent higher-priority users from trying to use the bus while a lower-priority user (to the right in the chain) still has possession. The BReq (bus request) signal informs the "arbiter," which in this distributed daisy-chain scheme is whoever has the bus at the moment, that it is desired by some other node. This signal could indicate the priority of the requester, and the current bus master could use this information to decide what to do. The required FSM is very simple, as no branching occurs.

A bussed data read will generally have the following sequence:
Node arbitrates and takes control of the bus (becomes master).
Data address is placed on bus.
Wait for setup time.
Assert Busread and Data signals to signal the addressed Slave what to do. Wait for acknowledgment (or timeout).
Slave posts data on bus, waits for setup time, and signals via the Acknowledge line that valid data is on the bus.
If acknowledged before timeout, read in data. Then, deassert the Busread and Data signals. Go on to next task, relinquishing bus if desired. Otherwise, handle the error (retry a fixed number of times, signal error).
Slave will remove acknowledge and posted data when the Busread signal is no longer sensed.
A data write is similar:
Node arbitrates and takes control of the bus (becomes master).
Data address and data are placed on bus by the Master.

Master waits for setup time, Assert BusWrite to signal the addressed Slave valid data is on the bus. Wait for acknowledgment (or timeout).

If acknowledged before timeout, deassert the Busread and Data signals. Go on to next task, relinquishing bus if desired. Otherwise, handle the error (retry a fixed number of times, signal error).

Slave will remove acknowledge when the BusWrite signal is no longer sensed.

These sequences of actions for bus reads and writes is based on that for the MultiBus, but is generic.

The VMEbus (IEEE-Std-1014), like the Multibus and the PI bus family, is actually a set of busses, having a serial VMS bus, and a local memory VMB bus in addition to the main VMEbus. It is asynchronous. Reads and writes of 1, 2, and 4 bytes, with 16-, 24-, or 32-bit addressing, is supported. Indivisible read-modify-write cycles are used to support modifying semaphores or other shared memory. Interrupt acknowledge bus cycles exist, as well as address-only cycles to warn slow devices that an address will soon be requested. Preemption of the current bus master is possible. Like Multibus, interrupt requests can be sent along lines for such purposes.

Multibus (IEEE-Std-796) is another family of busses, including a system bus, a multichannel bus for input/Output, and a local memory bus (iLBX bus). Interrupts can be either bus-vectored or non-bus-vectored. The latter are handled by the bus master, and may use the eight interrupt lines. The former method has the master assert the interrupt acknowledge line to freeze the state of the system. The master then polls the slaves that may have posted the interrupt request, putting their addresses on the address bus and signaling via the interrupt acknowledge line for the slave to acknowledge via the data lines. When the slave in question has posted its data, it activates the acknowledge signal indicating the data is valid, and the controller reads the data. Radial lines are for bus request and bus grant. Up to 16 modules with the potential for bus mastership can be present. This parallel arbitration is faster, but uses more signal lines.

Data transfers on Multibus, VMEbus, and microprocessor busses are generally similar. The address and control lines are asserted and after a suitable setup time the request valid signal is asserted. After the slave unit, such as memory, posts the data response on the bus, it asserts the data valid signal, and the data is read. The request lines are then dropped, and in response the slave can drop its data and data valid lines. Consider, for example, a memory unit acting as a slave. Then it may be modeled as an FSM with code (sketched as follows- see Chapter 13):

```
type Mem_State is (IDLE, ADDRESSED, POSTING);
signal MemoryState: Mem_State:=IDLE;
...
when (MemoryState = IDLE)
and
    (AddressValid=TRUE) and Address >=
        MemAddressLow
    and Address <= MemAddressHigh =>
        NextState <= ADDRESSED;
        Data <= RAMContent(Address) after
            Delaytime;
        DataValid <= TRUE after
            Delaytime+DataSetuptime;
when (MemoryState = ADDRESSED) and
    (AddressValid =FALSE) =>
        NextState <= IDLE;
        DataValid <= FALSE after Delaytime;
...
```

This simple code fragment will wait until an event occurs on its sensitivity list, such as on the AddressValid line changing. Additional **when** clauses can be added to handle anomalous conditions, such as changes in the Address value during the ADDRESSED state while AddressValid is true (presumably, an error will be asserted), violation of setup/hold criteria, and so on. The precise choice depends on the behavior of the hardware to be modeled. If the memory element latches the address, it will behave differently from memory that does not and is subjected to a transient on the address line.

The CPU or reader may use different FSMs for data and I/O reads and writes, or the same FSM with different signals set to specify the operation. The latter is of course more economical if the operations are otherwise identical.

PI and Related Busses

The Parallel Intermodule (PI) bus was developed by IBM and Honeywell for the Department of Defense. It plays an integral role in the Joint Integrated Avionics Working Group (JIAWG) standard, which is intended for the Air Force F-22 fighter program, the Army Commanche helicopter program, and others. It is documented in Rickard, Anderson, and McIver (1988), and its simulation via FSMs using VHDL in Crossland and Adams (1992). A number of manufacturers have developed support chips, such as the Intel M82916 PI bus controller. The paper by Rickard, Anderson, and McIver describes three busses, the TM (Test and Maintenance) bus, the ETM (Element Test and Maintenance) bus, and the PI bus, and provides state diagrams for each. These are included, in abbreviated form, as Figure 16.3 for the PI bus, Figure 16.4 for the TM bus, and Figure 16.5 for the ETM bus. The bus protocols, particularly the PI bus, are quite complex. Messages can be interrupted, bus masters have absolute tenure limits, and a complicated VIE sequence exists to arbitrate bus request, in addition to the option of tenure being passed by means of a token sent from the current bus master to its designated successor.

The PI bus is a synchronous bus with 32 bits of parallel data, and up to 32 modules. With all error correction lines, it has 58 signal lines. Data is transferred in words (16 bits) or double words (32 bits). It is a linear bus, not a ring or start architecture but a simple bus line with a number of modules connected to it. Devices on the bus each have a 32-bit virtual address space, as well as 256 data registers that behave as a separate address space and are the

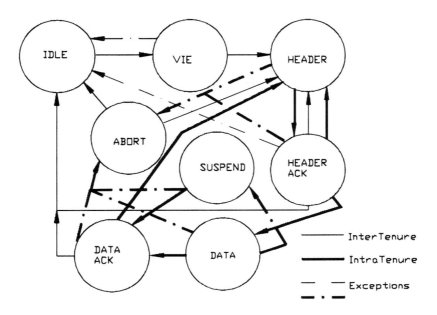

Figure 16.3 PI bus state machine

control registers of the bus interface unit. Each module has a physical address ranging from 0 to 31.

There are five major signal classes: Data, Cycle Type, Acknowledge, Wait, and Bus Request. The data lines are used to transfer data, with error correction in a number of possible schemes. The current cycle type is posted on the cycle type lines. The Acknowledge lines are used by slaves, or contenders during a Vie, to indicate errors. Permissible signals are acknowledge, negative acknowledge, not selected, or recognize. Wait lines are used to introduce wait states, and bus request lines are used to request the bus from the current master.

The PI bus state diagram has eight states shown. The state of the bus is specified by Cycle Type signal lines, which would carry the state of the bus to all processors. Each of the states lasts either a fixed number of cycles, such as eight bus cycles for the Vie state, or for a specified number of cycles, such as in block messages. Therefore, additional linked FSMs within each of the eight states are not needed. The states shown behave as follows:

Idle: In this state, there is no valid bus master. The only valid state that can follow Idle is Vie, in which a bus master is selected.

Vie: This is actually a sequence of eight bus cycles, divided into four steps of two cycles each. During these cycles, the contending processors post their priorities on the wired-OR data signal lines, as well as monitoring those lines and saving the state of the data in the appropriate register. If a module determines that a more significant bit has been asserted than its priority code possesses, that means that a higher priority module is contending for the bus, and the module drops out of contention. Three bits of the Vie priority code are resolved at each step. The distributed contention scheme of Futurebus+ (IEEE 896) uses an arbitration mechanism similar to the PI bus Vie. Vie shall be followed by Idle if no bus master is selected, or by Header if one is selected.

Header: The state starts a bus master's tenure. It is entered after a Vie, or after the Header Acknowledge state when tenure is transferred directly by the Tenure Pass message mechanism. The header state may also be entered during the continuing tenure of the current bus master, from an Abort state or from a Header Acknowledge state after a parameter write sequence. During the header state, information is transmitted by the bus master specifying the type of message to be transmitted, the identity of the slaves participating, and the number of bus cycles required for that transmission. Consequently, the header state may be implemented with an FSM.

Header Acknowledge: This state is used for slaves to respond to the bus master. For the parameter write sequence, possible successor states are Header, Idle, and Abort. The first of these initiates a new message and continues the current bus master's tenure. Idle terminates the current master's tenure, while Abort may terminate the parameter write message sequence. For block and bus interface message sequences, either Abort or with Data states are possible successors, Data continuing the current master's tenure. For a tenure pass sequence, the successor states may be Header or Abort or, when the intended new bus master fails to obtain mastership of the bus, Idle.

mix chips from different manufacturers on the same bus (Knudsen, 1992)! Obviously, the specification did not sufficiently constrain behavior, with different manufacturers interpreting the standard somewhat differently. VHDL can be used for testing conformance of hardware to bus protocol specifications. In so doing, it may find problems with the bus specification, although there are better approaches to protocol validation than simulation. The method is similar to that used for hardware testing (Adams et al., 1992), ignoring the mechanical and electrical standards. The bus specifications of interest are the low-level timing and logical behavior, and the higher-level logical behavior of the complex transfers and arbitration. A test-bench may be used and various rules checked while monitoring the bus. Adams et al. (1992), for example, discuss in detail how hardware is checked for compliance with Rule 13.5.1.2 of the Multibus II specification, sending a buffer request to the device under test, ensuring that it is of the necessary form to evoke the expected response (not able to receive the message, in this case, due to insufficient memory). If no appropriate reply is received in the specified time, an error report is generated. An **assert** statement could be used in such a case. For many such tests, a WAVES specification would be a very natural approach.

Protocol testing naturally requires the generation of appropriate test inputs. The paper by Dahbura et al. (1990) reviews four approaches to generating such sequences, with specific application to Open Systems Interconnect (OSI) specifications, and references papers on obtaining FSM models from protocol specifications.

REFERENCES

Adams, M., Qian, Yi, Burtscheidt, J., Kaiser, E., Juhasz, C., "Conformance Testing of VMEbus and Multibus II Products," *IEEE Micro*, Feb. 1992, pp. 57-64.

Comer, D. E., and Stevens, D. L., *Introduction to Networking with TCP/IP*, two volumes, (Englewood Cliffs, N. J.: Prentice Hall, 1991).

Crossland, K. A. and Adams, S. J., "Bus Performance Simulation," in *Performance and Fault Modeling in VHDL*, J. M. Schoen, ed. (Englewood Cliffs, N. J.: Prentice Hall, 1992).

Dahbura, A., Sabnani, K., and Uyar, M., "Formal Methods for Generating Protocol Conformance Test Sequences," *Proc. IEEE* **78**, pp. 1317-1325, August 1990.

Fortier, P. J., and Desrochers, G. R., *Modeling and Analysis of Local Area Networks* (Boca Raton, FL: CRC Press, 1990).

Glass, M., "A Look at the SAE High-Speed Ring Bus," *Defense Electronics*, pp. 106-123, Sept. 1988.

Johnson, J. B., and Kassel, S., *The Multibus Design Book*, (N. Y.: McGraw-Hill, 1984).

Knudsen, H. K., lecture at University of New Mexico, April 2, 1992.

Limb, J. O., "Multiple-Access Protocols for High-Speed Networks," *Optics and Photonics News*, July 1992, pp. 17-22.

Lytle, J., "A Ride on the SBus," *BYTE*, pp. 283-287, May 1992.

Rickard, D., Anderson, G., McIver, G., *Very High Speed Integrated Circuits (VHSIC) Phase 2 Submicrometer Technology Development: Interoperability Standards*, AD-A203 629, Electrons Technology and Device Laboratory, U. S. Army Laboratory Command, Ft. Monmouth, N. J., November 1988.

Sha, L., Rajkumar, R., Lehoczky, J. P., "Real-Time Computing with IEEE Futurebus+," *IEEE Micro*, pp. 30-33, 95-100, June, 1991.

Stallings, W., *Data and Computer Communications*, 2nd ed. (N. Y.: Macmillan, 1988).

Appendix: Predefined Language Environment

Package STANDARD

Package STANDARD predefines a number of types, subtypes, and funtions. An implicit context clause naming this package is assumed to exist at the beginning of each design unit. Package STANDARD may not be modified by the user.

```
package STANDARD is

    -- predefined enumeration types:

    type BOOLEAN is (FALSE,TRUE);

    type BIT is ('0','1');

    type CHARACTER is (
            NUL, SOH,    STX,ETX,EOT,ENQ,  ACK,BEL,
            BS,  HT,  LF,VT,FF,CR,SO,SI,
            DLE, DC1, DC2,DC3,DC4,NAK,SYN,ETB,
            CAN, EM,  SUB,ESC,FSP,GSP,RSP,USP,

            ' ', '!', '"','#','$','%','&',''',
            '(', ')', '*','+',',','-','.','/',
```

```
' 0' , ' 1' , ' 2' ,' 3' ,' 4' ,' 5' ,' 6' ,' 7' ,
' 8' , ' 9' , ' :' ,' ;' ,' ' ,' =' ,' ' ,' ?' ,

' @' , ' A' , ' B' ,' C' ,' D' ,' E' ,' F' ,' G' ,
' H' , ' I' , ' J' ,' K' ,' L' ,' M' ,' N' ,' O' ,
' P' , ' Q' , ' R' ,' S' ,' T' ,' U' ,' V' ,' W' ,
' X' , ' Y' , ' Z' ,' [' ,' /' ,' ]' ,' ^' ,' _' ,

' `' , ' a' , ' b' ,' c' ,' d' ,' e' ,' f' ,' g' ,
' h' , ' i' , ' j' ,' k' ,' l' ,' m' ,' n' ,' o' ,
' p' , ' q' , ' r' ,' s' ,' t' ,' u' ,' v' ,' w' ,
' x' , ' y' , ' z' ,' {' ,' |' ,' }' ,' ~' ,DEL

' ' ,' ¡' ,' ¢' ,' £' ,' ¤' ,' ¥' ,' |' ,' §' ,
-- space above is no-break space
' ¨' ,' ©' ,' ª' ,' «' , ' ¬' , ' -' ,' ®' ,' ¯'
-- hyphen above is soft hyphen
' û' , ' °' ,' ±' ,' ²' ,' ³' ,' ' ,' µ' ,' ¶' ,' ·'
' ' ,' ¹' ,' º' ,' »' ,' 1/4' ,' 1/2' ,' 3/4' ,' ¿' ,


' À' ,' Á' ,' Â' ,' Ã' ,' Ä' , ' Å' ,' Æ' ,' Ç' ,
' È' ,' É' ,' Ê' ,' Ë' ,' Ì' ,' Í' ,' Î' ,' Ï' ,
' Ð' ,' Ñ' ,' Ò' ,' Ó' ,' Ô' ,' Õ' ,' Ö' ,' ×' ,
' Ø' ,' Ù' ,' Ú' ,' Û' ,' Ü' ,' Ý' ,' Þ' ,' ß' ,
' à' ,' á' ,' â' ,' ã' ,' è' ,' å' ,' æ' ,' ç' ,
' è' ,' é' ,' ê' ,' ë' ,' ¡' ,' ì' ,' í' ,' î' ,' ï'
' ð' ,' ñ' ,' ò' ,' ó' ,' ô' ,' õ' ,' ö' ,' ÷' ,
' ø' ,' ù' ,' ú' ,' û' ,' ü' ,' ý' ,' þ' ,' ÿ' );


type SEVERITY_LEVEL is (NOTE, WARNING,

  ERROR, FAILURE);

-- predefined numeric types:
```

```
--type universal integer is range
    implementation_defined;

--type universal real is range

    implementation_defined;

type INTEGER is range

    implementation_defined;

type REAL is range

    implementation_defined;

-- predefined type TIME:

type TIMEis range implementation_defined
  units
    fs;              -- femtosecond
    ps =  1000  fs;-- picosecond
    ns =  1000  ps;-- nanosecond
    us =  1000  ns;-- microsecond
    ms =  1000  us;-- millisecond
    sec  =  1000  ms;-- second
    min  =  60  sec;-- minute
    hr =  60  min; -- hour
  end units;

subtype DELAY_LENGTH is TIME range 0 fs

  to TIME' HIGH;

-- function that returns the current

  simulation time
```

```
impure function NOW return DELAY_LENGTH;

-- predefined numeric subtypes:

subtype NATURAL is INTEGER range 0 to
   INTEGER' HIGH;
subtype POSITIVE is INTEGER range 1 to

   INTEGER' HIGH;

-- predefined array types:

type STRING is array (POSITIVE range <>) of
   CHARACTER;

type BIT_VECTOR is array (NATURAL range <>)
   of BIT;

type FILE_OPEN_KIND is (

   READ_MODE,WRITE_MODE,APPEND_MODE);

type FILE_OPEN_STATUS is (

   OPEN_OK,STATUS_ERROR,

   NAME_ERROR,MODE_ERROR);

attribute FOREIGN:STRING;

end STANDARD;
```

Note:

The ASCII mnemonics for file separator (FS), group separator (GS), record separator (RS), and unit separator (US) are represented by FSP, GSP, RSP, and USP, respectively, in type CHARACTER in order to avoid conflict with the units of type TIME.

The no-break space prevents breaking surrounding words between lines. The soft hypen is omitted if it occurs at the end of a line.

Package TEXTIO

Package TEXTIO contains declarations of types and subprograms that support formatted ASCII I/O operations. We present this package as defined in IEEE-Std-1076-1987 and then list the enhancements contained in VHDL-92.

```
package TEXTIO is

    -- Type Definitions for Text I/O

    type LINE is private allow variable ;

-- a LINE is a pointer to a STRING value

    type TEXT is file of STRING;

-- a file of variable-length ASCII records

    type SIDE is (RIGHT, LEFT);

-- for justifying output data within fields

    subtype WIDTH is NATURAL;

-- for specifying widths of output fields

    -- Standard Text Files

    file INPUT: TEXT open READ_OPEN "STD_INPUT";

    file OUTPUT: TEXT open
```

```
WRITE_OPEN "STD_OUTPUT";

--  Input Routines for Standard Types

procedure READLINE (file F:inout TEXT;
   L:out LINE);

procedure READ (F:inout LINE; VALUE:

   out BIT;  GOOD:out BOOLEAN);
procedure READ (F:inout LINE; VALUE:out BIT);

procedure READ (F:inout LINE;
VALUE:out BIT_VECTOR;GOOD:out BOOLEAN);
procedure READ (F:inout LINE;
   VALUE:out BIT_VECTOR);


procedure READ (F:inout LINE;
   VALUE:out BOOLEAN;GOOD:out BOOLEAN);

procedure READ (F:inout LINE;
   VALUE:out BOOLEAN);

procedure READ (F:inout LINE;

   VALUE:out CHARACTER;GOOD:out BOOLEAN);
procedure READ (F:inout LINE;
   VALUE:out CHARACTER);

procedure READ (F:inout LINE;
   VALUE:out INTEGER;GOOD:out BOOLEAN);
procedure READ (F:inout LINE;
   VALUE:out INTEGER);

procedure READ (F:inout LINE;
```

```
          VALUE:out REAL;GOOD:out BOOLEAN);
  procedure READ (F:inout LINE;
     VALUE:out REAL);

  procedure READ (F:inout LINE;
     VALUE:out STRING;GOOD:out BOOLEAN);
  procedure READ (F:inout LINE;
     VALUE:out STRING);

  procedure READ (F:inout LINE;
     VALUE:out TIME;GOOD:out BOOLEAN);
  procedure READ (F:inout LINE;
     VALUE:out TIME);

  -- Output Routines for Standard Types

  procedure WRITELINE (F:out TEXT; L:in LINE);

  procedure WRITE(L:inout LINE; VALUE:in BIT;
     JUSTIFIED:in SIDE:=RIGHT;
     FIELD: in WIDTH :=0);

  procedure WRITE(L:inout LINE;
     VALUE:in BIT_VECTOR;
     JUSTIFIED:in SIDE:=RIGHT;
     FIELD: in WIDTH :=0);

  procedure WRITE(L:inout LINE;
     VALUE:in BOOLEAN;
     JUSTIFIED:in SIDE:=RIGHT;
     FIELD: in WIDTH :=0);

  procedure WRITE(L:inout LINE;
     VALUE:in CHARACTER;
     JUSTIFIED:in SIDE:=RIGHT;
     FIELD: in WIDTH :=0);
```

```
procedure WRITE(L:inout LINE;
   VALUE:in INTEGER;
   JUSTIFIED:in SIDE:=RIGHT;
   FIELD: in WIDTH :=0);

procedure WRITE(L:inout LINE; VALUE:in REAL;
   JUSTIFIED:in SIDE:=RIGHT;
   FIELD: in WIDTH :=0;
   DIGITS: in NATURAL:=0);


procedure WRITE(L:inout LINE;
   VALUE:in STRING;
   JUSTIFIED:in SIDE:=RIGHT;
   FIELD: in WIDTH :=0);

procedure WRITE(L:inout LINE; VALUE:in TIME;
   JUSTIFIED:in SIDE:=RIGHT;
   FIELD: in WIDTH :=0
   UNIT: in TIME:= ns);


-- File Position Predicates

   function ENDLINE(L: in LINE)
      return BOOLEAN;

-- function ENDFILE(file L: in TEXT)
        return BOOLEAN;
private

-- implementation defined


end TEXTIO;
```

Changes for VHDL-92

Files are now a fourth class of object, along with signals, variables, and constants. **file** is now a reserved word; files may be assigned attributes, e. g.,

> **attribute** Drive of Fle:**file is** 4;

The major change is that files may now be explicitly opened and closed, and may be opened for reading, writing, or appending. Thus VHDL-92 incorporates in package TEXTIO statements equivalent to (but not necessarily identical to) the following:

> **type** File_Mode **is**
>   (File_Open, File_Close, File_Append);
>
> **procedure** File_Open(F:**in** FILE;
>   FileName:**in** STRING; Mode:**in** File_Mode);
>
> **procedure** File_Close(F:**in** FILE);

Files may also be opened with a declaration such as:

file F: Text **open** Read_Open **is** "C:/vhdl/data.fil";

Predefined Attributes

For detailed discussion of the most significant attributes, see Chapter 6. Items within brackets [] are optional.

Defined for types and subtypes:

T' BASE T' LEFT T' RIGHT T' HIGH T' LOW T' POS (X)
T' VAL (X) T' SUCC (X) T' PRED (X) T' LEFTOF (X)
T' RIGHTOF (X)

BASE returns the base type of a type, and is only allowed as a prefix to another attribute, e. g., T'BASE'LEFT. The others are typically used with enumerated types, e. g.., in constructs which loop through the values of the type.

Defined for array objects:

```
A' LEFT[ (N)]  A' RIGHT(N)]  A' LEFT[ (N)]
A' HIGH[ (N)]  A' LOW[ (N)]  A' RANGE[ (N)]
A' REVERSE_RANGE[ (N)]  A' LENGTH[ (N)]
```

If (N) is omitted, it defaults to 1. These attributes return information about the Nth index of the associated array.

Defined for signals:

```
S' DELAYED[ (T)]  S' STABLE[ (T)]  S' QUIET(T)
S' TRANSACTION  S' EVENT  S' ACTIVE  S' LAST_EVENT
S' LAST_ACTIVE  S' LAST_VALUE
```

STABLE, QUIET, EVENT return BOOLEAN, TRANSACTION' returns type BIT, DELAYED and LAST_VALUE return a signal value for the associated signal, LAST_ACTIVE and LAST_EVENT return a result of type TIME.

Defined for block labels or architecture names:

```
B' BEHAVIOR  B' STRUCTURE
```

These return BOOLEAN values.

New for VHDL-92:

F′ FOREIGN

is used for specifying foreign functions

P′ PATH_NAME P′ SIMPLE_NAME

for obtaining the path name to precisely specify components,

A′ ASCENDING[(N)] T′ ASCENDING

for determing whether ranges are ascending or descending

T′ VALUE(X) T′ IMAGE(X)

for converting data to and from strings (the parameter, if present, gives the units). IMAGE is not defined for enumeration types!

S′ DRIVING S′ DRIVING_VALUE

The first determines if a driver is active. If it is, the second will return its non-null value. DRIVING_VALUE should not be called if the driver is inactive.

Index